The Bible speaks today
Series Editors: J. A. Motyer (OT)
John R. W. Stott (NT)

The Message of 1 Peter
The way of the cross

Titles in this series

The Message of
1 Peter

The way of the cross

Edmund P. Clowney
Professor of Practical Theology, Emeritus
Westminster Theological Seminary, Philadelphia

Inter-Varsity Press
Leicester, England
Downers Grove, Illinois, USA

InterVarsity Press
38 De Montfort Street, Leicester LE1 7GP, England
P.O. Box 1400, Downers Grove, Illinois 60515, U.S.A.

Unless otherwise stated, quotations from the Bible are from the Holy Bible, New International Version, copyright © 1973, 1978, 1984 by the International Bible Society, New York. Used in USA by permission of Zondervan Bible Publishers, Grand Rapids, Michigan, and published in Great Britain by Hodder and Stoughton, Ltd.

Inter-Varsity Press, England, is the book-publishing division of the Universities and Colleges Christian Fellowship (formerly the Inter-Varsity Fellowship), a student movement linking Christian Unions in universities and colleges throughout the United Kingdom and the Republic of Ireland, and a member movement of the International Fellowship of Evangelical Students. For information about local and national activities in Great Britain write to UCCF, 38 De Montfort Street, Leicester LE1 7GP.

InterVarsity Press, U.S.A., is the book-publishing division of InterVarsity Christian Fellowship, a student movement active on campus at hundreds of universities, colleges and schools of nursing. For information about local and regional activities, write Public Relations Dept., InterVarsity Christian Fellowship, 6400 Schroeder Rd., P.O. Box 7895, Madison, WI 53707-7895.

Cover photograph: Robert Cushman Hayes

First published 1988
Set in 11/12 pt Garamond
Typeset by Input Typesetting Ltd, London
Printed in the United States of America

UK ISBN 0-85110-789-3 (paperback)
USA ISBN 0-8308-1227-X (paperback)
USA ISBN 0-87784-925-0 (set of The Bible Speaks Today, paperback)

British Library Cataloguing in Publication Data
Clowney, Edmund P.
  The message of I Peter.
  1. Bible. N.T. Peter, 1st—Expositions
  I. Title II. Series
  227'.9206

Library of Congress Cataloging-in-Publication Data

Clowney, Edmund P.
    The message of 1 Peter: the way of the cross/Edmund P. Clowney.
    p. cm.—(The Bible speaks today)
    Includes bibliographical references.
    ISBN 0-8308-1227-X (U.S.)
    1. Bible. N.T. Peter, 1st—Commentaries. 2. Suffering—Biblical teaching. I. Title. II. Title: Message of First Peter.
III. Series.
BS2795.3.C57 1989
227'.9207—dc19.   *88-38860*
                                                                    CIP

20 19 18 17 16 15 14 13 12 11 10 9 8 7 6
12 11 10 09 08 07 06 05 04 03 02 01 00

General preface

The Bible Speaks Today describes a series of both Old Testament and New Testament expositions, which are characterized by a threefold ideal: to expound the biblical text with accuracy, to relate it to contemporary life, and to be readable.

These books are, therefore, not 'commentaries', for the commentary seeks rather to elucidate the text than to apply it, and tends to be a work rather of reference than of literature. Nor, on the other hand, do they contain the kind of 'sermons' which attempt to be contemporary and readable, without taking Scripture seriously enough.

The contributors to this series are all united in their convictions that God still speaks through what he has spoken, and that nothing is more necessary for the life, health and growth of Christians than that they should hear what the Spirit is saying to them through his ancient – yet ever modern – Word.

J. A. MOTYER
J. R. W. STOTT
Series Editors

Contents

Author's preface

This exposition has been written in the hope that it will be *read* and not just consulted. Writing it has brought new awe and joy before the miracle of God's word written and before the Lord of that word.

I have sought to bring five perspectives into relation:
1. Peter's testimony against the background of his own experience as Christ's disciple.
2. The Old Testament promises with which the letter is saturated.
3. The apostolic faith that Peter shared with Paul and other authors of the New Testament.
4. The Hellenistic world in which his hearers lived.
5. Our world and the significance of the letter for us.

Writing this exposition has deepened my admiration and gratitude for the devoted scholarship of Peter's interpreters through the years. There is surely no lack of excellent commentaries on 1 Peter, and some are eminently readable. The long commentary by Archbishop Robert Leighton, written in the seventeenth century, is a devotional classic. Wayne Grudem graciously provided me with a manuscript of his recent commentary; I regret that most of my work was finished before I had this scholarly (and readable!) study to consult. I would express particular appreciation to Samuel Bénétreau of the Free Faculty of Evangelical Theology at Vaux-sur-Seine, France. I trust that his commentary may yet appear in English translation.

My thanks are due to the Rev. John Stott for proposing this project and for his wise and patient guidance; to the Rev. Joseph F. Ryan and the elders and staff of Trinity Presbyterian Church, Charlottesville, Virginia, for their prayers and support; to Mrs Del Jones for typing the footnotes; and to our son-in-law and daughter, Jay and Deborah Weininger, whose generous gift first brought Trinity Church into the computer age.

My wife Jean has found many ways to bring loving assistance to this as to all the projects of our life together.

EDMUND P. CLOWNEY

Chief abbreviations

General

AF — *The Apostolic Fathers*, edited by J. B. Lightfoot (1869, 1885; Baker Book House, 1962).

ANET — *Ancient Near Eastern Texts Relating to the Old Testament*, edited by J. B. Pritchard (Princeton University Press, ²1955).

ASV — The American Standard Version of the Bible (1901).

AV — The Authorized (King James) Version of the Bible (1611).

BAGD — *A Greek-English Lexicon of the New Testament and Other Early Christian Literature*, translated and adapted by W. F. Arndt and F. W. Gingrich, second edition revised and augmented by F. W. Gingrich and F. W. Danker (University of Chicago Press, 1979).

BDF — *A Greek Grammar of the New Testament and Other Early Christian Literature*, by F. Blass and A. Debrunner, translated and edited by R. W. Funk (University of Chicago Press, 1961).

DSS — *The Dead Sea Scrolls in English*, edited by G. Vermes (Penguin, ²1970).

Eusebius — Eusebius of Caesarea, *Ecclesiastical History* (c. AD 325).

GNT — *The Greek New Testament*, edited by K. Aland, M. Black, *et al.* (United Bible Societies, ³1975).

KB — *Lexicon in Veteris Testamenti Libros*, edited by L. Koehler and W. Baumgartner (Brill, 1953).

LXX — The Septuagint (Greek Version of the Old Testament, 3rd century BC).

mg	margin.
NIV	The New International Version of the Bible (1973, 1978, 1984).
NTS	*New Testament Studies.*
ODCC	*The Oxford Dictionary of the Christian Church*, edited by F. L. Cross and E. A. Livingstone (Oxford University Press, ³1974).
OTS	*Oudtestamentische Studien*, Leiden.
RSV	The Revised Standard Version of the Bible (NT 1946, ²1971, OT 1952).
TDNT	*Theological Dictionary of the New Testament*, edited by G. Kittel and G. Friedrich, translated and edited by G. W. Bromiley, 10 vols. (Eerdmans, 1964–1976).
ThZ	*Theologische Zeitschrift.*
WTJ	*Westminster Theological Journal.*

Commentaries

Bénétreau	S. Bénétreau, *La Première épître de Pierre* (*Commentaire évangélique de la Bible* (Éditions de la Faculté Libre de Théologie Évangélique, 1984).
Beare	F. W. Beare, *The First Epistle of Peter* (Blackwell, ²1958).
Best	E. Best, *1 Peter* (*The New Century Bible*, Oliphants, 1971; Eerdmans and Marshall, Morgan & Scott, 1977).
Bigg	C. Bigg, *A Critical and Exegetical Commentary on the Epistles of St Peter and St Jude* (*The International Critical Commentary*, 1901; T. & T. Clark, 1978).
Calloud-Genuyt	J. Calloud and F. Genuyt, *La Première épître de Pierre* (*Lectio Divina* 109; Cerf, 1982).
Cranfield, *I and II Peter*	C. E. B. Cranfield, *I and II Peter and Jude* (*Torch Bible Commentaries*, SCM Press, 1960).
Goppelt	L. Goppelt, *Der erste Petrusbrief* (*Meyers Kritisch-Exegetischer Kommentar über*

	das Neue Testament; Vandenhoeck & Ruprecht, 1978).
Grudem	W. Grudem, *1 Peter* (*Tyndale New Testament Commentaries*, Inter-Varsity Press and Eerdmans, 1988).
Hiebert	D. E. Hiebert, *First Peter* (Moody Press, 1984).
Kelly	J. N. D. Kelly, *The Epistles of Peter and of Jude* (*Black's New Testament Commentaries*, A. & C. Black, 1969).
Leighton	R. Leighton, *Commentary on First Peter*, 2 vols. (1693, 1694; Kregel, 1972).
Luther	Martin Luther, *Commentary on the Epistles of Peter and Jude* (15??; Kregel, 1982).
Mounce	R. H. Mounce, *A Living Hope: A Commentary on 1 and 2 Peter* (Eerdmans, 1982).
Reicke, *Epistles*	B. Reicke, *The Epistles of James, Peter, and Jude* (*The Anchor Bible*, Doubleday, 1978).
Selwyn	E. G. Selwyn, *The First Epistle of St Peter* (*Thornapple Commentaries*, Macmillan, ²1947; Baker Book House, 1981).
Spicq, *Epîtres*	C. Spicq, *Les Epîtres de Saint Pierre* (*Sources bibliques*; Librairie Le Coffre, 1966).
Stibbs	A. M. Stibbs, *The First Epistle General of Peter* (*Tyndale New Testament Commentaries*, Tyndale Press and Eerdmans, 1959).

Special studies

Balch	D. L. Balch, *Let Wives Be Submissive: The Domestic Code in 1 Peter* (Society of Biblical Literature Monograph Series 26; Scholars Press, 1981).
Boismard	M.-E. Boismard, *Quatre hymnes baptismales dans la première épître de Pierre* (*Lectio Divina* 30; Paris, 1961).

13

Cranfield, 'Interpretation'	C. E. B. Cranfield, 'The Interpretation of I Peter iii. 19 and iv. 6', *Expository Times* 69 (September, 1958).
Dalton	W. J. Dalton, *Christ's Proclamation to the Spirits: A Study of 1 Peter 3:18 – 4:6* (Analecta Biblica 23; Pontifical Biblical Institute, 1965).
Elliott, *Elect*	J. H. Elliott, *The Elect and the Holy: an Exegetical Examination of 1 Peter 2:4–10 and the Phrase* basileion hierateuma (*Supplements to Novum Testamentum* 12; Brill, 1966).
Elliott, *Home*	J. H. Elliott, *A Home for the Homeless; A Sociological Exegesis of 1 Peter, Its Situation and Strategy* (Fortress Press, 1981; SCM Press, 1982).
Feinberg	J. S. Feinberg, '1 Peter 3:18–20, Ancient Mythology, and the Intermediate State', *Westminster Theological Journal* 48 (1986).
Reicke, *Spirits*	B. Reicke, *The Disobedient Spirits and Christian Baptism: A Study of 1 Pet. III 19 and Its Context* (*Acta Seminarii Neotestamentici Upsaliensis*, XIII; Munksgaard, 1946).
Spicq, *Vie*	C. Spicq, *Vie chrétienne et pérégrination selon le Nouveau Testament* (*Lectio Divina* 71; Cerf, 1972).
Traver	B. A. Traver, *Christ's Proclamation to the Spirits: The Interpretation of 1 Peter 3:18–22* (unpublished Master's thesis, Westminster Theological Seminary, 1980).

Introduction

'The First Epistle of Saint Peter – the most condensed New Testament résumé of the Christian faith and of the conduct that it inspires – is a model of a "pastoral letter".' Ceslas Spicq begins his rewarding commentary on 1 Peter with this apt description.[1]

Pastoral – Peter's letter is surely that. The apostle seeks to encourage and reassure Christian churches in Asia Minor as stormy seasons of persecution begin. Those storms rage on today – in India where a Hindu mob destroys a Christian church built at great sacrifice in the poorest slum of Bombay; in many Communist lands where to confess Christ brings the loss of educational privilege and job opportunities, and often results in imprisonment. In much of the English-speaking world such threats may seem distant; perhaps we fail to read the signs of the times. No Christian avoids suffering, however, and no true Christian escapes a measure of suffering for Christ's sake. Peter speaks to us all when he tells of suffering now and glory to come.

Peter's pastoral letter encourages us by instructing us. Our deepest needs drive us to our deepest beliefs. What hope do we have? Peter proclaims Jesus Christ, our sure hope now and for ever. Throughout his letter he grounds our hope in the reality of what God has done and will yet do for us through Christ. The apostle is a witness, not just to what Jesus did and said while he was in his fishing-boat or in his house, but to the meaning of Christ's life, death, resurrection, and ascension. Peter's testimony about the life of Jesus

[1] Spicq, *Epîtres*, p. 11.

is reflected in Mark's Gospel.[1] In this letter he shows us what that story means for us as Jesus calls us to take up our cross and follow him.

1. To whom is the letter written?

Pontus, Galatia, Cappadocia, Asia, and Bithynia are the provinces or areas where the Christians lived to whom the letter is addressed. If the terms are used to name Roman provinces, the area covers the whole of Asia Minor north of the Taurus mountain chain that skirts the southern coast. Most of modern Turkey would be included. It is possible, however, that the terms describe regions rather than official provinces.[2] If so, the area is smaller, since both Galatia and Asia, thought of as regions, were more restricted. The possible significance of the smaller area would be that some of the regions of Paul's intensive missionary work would not be included (e.g. Antioch of Pisidia, Iconium, Lystra, Derbe). Paul was restrained by the Spirit from entering Bithynia; was that region reserved for others? The early church historian Eusebius suggests that Peter himself may have had a part in the evangelization of the areas he names.[3] Obviously, Peter had some reason for addressing Christians in these provinces or regions and not in others. (He does not include Lycia and Pamphylia, or Cilicia, provinces south of the Taurus Mountains.) It is attractive to suppose that he has in view areas of Asia Minor that had been more directly related to his own ministry than to Paul's.

Pontus and Bithynia, on the shore of the Black Sea, are named separately although they had been joined into one Roman province. It has been suggested that Peter begins with Pontus and ends with Bithynia because he is thinking of the route that Silas or another messenger might take in delivering the letter; a traveller could start from Amisus at the eastern

[1] Eusebius, III:39, cites Papias (c. AD 60–130), bishop of Hierapolis in Asia Minor. Papias, in turn, quotes the elder John: 'Mark, having become the interpreter of Peter, wrote down accurately everything that he remembered, without however recording in order what was either said or done by Christ.' AF, p. 265.

[2] Kelly, p. 3; Elliott, Home, p. 60. Both scholars favour the broader geographical area of the Roman provinces.

[3] Acts 16:7; Eusebius, III:1:2–3. Eusebius seems to be inferring this from 1 Peter rather than from any independent tradition.

end of Pontus on the Black Sea and finish at Chalcedon in Bithynia. From there he could cross to Byzantium where ship passage could be found for Rome.[1]

The geographical areas addressed include a 'fantastic conglomeration of territories' – coastal regions, mountain ranges, plateaux, lakes and river systems. The inhabitants were even more diverse. They had 'different origins, ethnic roots, languages, customs, religions, and political histories'.[2] Galatia was so named after Gauls who had settled there; Gallic was still spoken there in the fourth century.[3] Luke refers to the language of Lycaonia spoken by the people of Lystra.[4] There was a substantial Jewish population in Asia Minor.[5] Jews from Cappadocia, Pontus, and Asia were present in Jerusalem at Pentecost, and heard Peter's sermon.[6] Converts returning to those provinces may well have planted the gospel there.

If the spread of the Christian faith in these regions followed the pattern of Paul's missionary strategy, we may suppose that churches were first established in urban centres, and that Jewish believers along with Gentile adherents to Judaism ('God-fearers') formed the original nucleus of many house churches and congregations. Much of the population was rural, however; the interior was dotted with tribal villages where Roman culture had made little impact.[7] The power of the Christian gospel among tribal peoples may first have become evident in Asia Minor. The experience of Paul and Barnabas at Lystra indicates the dramatic impact of the gospel in a region that was only partly Hellenized.[8]

While we do not know just what 'people-groups' or strata of society were included among the Christians of Asia Minor, we are struck by the unity that the gospel produces. Diverse as the backgrounds of these people were, they had become the new people of God, the brotherhood, the chosen people scattered in the world (2:9–10, 17; 5:9; 1:1).

---

[1] The most likely route of the bearer of the letter is traced by Colin Hemer, 'The Address of 1 Peter', *Expository Times* 89 (1978), pp. 239–243.

[2] Elliott, *Home*, p. 61; Selwyn, pp. 47–52.

[3] T. R. S. Broughton, 'Roman Asia Minor', in Tenney Frank, ed., *An Economic Survey of Ancient Rome* (Johns Hopkins Press, 1938), 4, p. 738, cited in Elliott, *Home*, p. 62.

[4] Acts 14:11.   [5] Elliott, *Home*, p. 66 n. 19.   [6] Acts 2:9.

[7] Elliott, *Home*, pp. 61–63.   [8] Acts 14:8–18.

The inclusive language in which this letter speaks of the church makes it clear that Peter is addressing the whole church, not just one segment of the Christian community. He writes not only to those who are 'alien residents' in the literal sense,[1] nor only to Jewish believers. This last issue has been long debated. If Peter were writing to Jewish converts, they certainly must have been lapsed Jews, for Peter speaks of 'the empty way of life handed down to you from your forefathers' (1:18). He describes that wicked lifestyle: 'doing what pagans choose to do – living in debauchery, lust, drunkenness, orgies, carousing and detestable idolatry' (4:3). Jews would be lapsed indeed who could be so described! But even if their lives were fully pagan, Peter would hardly say that such a way of life had been handed down from their fathers.[2] Neither could we understand pagan neighbours being surprised if such apostate Jews returned to the moral lifestyle of Judaism.[3] It seems clear, therefore, that Peter thinks of the churches to which he writes as predominantly Gentile. The extensive use that Peter makes of the Old Testament reveals his own Jewish training, but we need not assume the same background for his hearers. Paul's letters to predominantly Gentile churches are also steeped in the Old Testament.

2. Who wrote the letter?

The address of the letter claims the apostle Peter as the author, a claim that should not be discounted. It is not true that the church would regard such a claim as a 'harmless literary device'.[4] A number of other works claiming to be written by Peter were rejected as not apostolic. Since the apostles were rightly regarded as invested with Christ's authority for the establishment of the church, a false claim to that authority could not be taken lightly. We need only recall

[1] The 'elect transients of the Diaspora' should not be taken in the sociological sense, as though Peter were addressing only displaced persons or those without local citizenship. See Appendix A, 'Resident Aliens' – Literal or Figurative?'
[2] See Acts 15:10, where Peter alludes to the efforts of the fathers to bear the yoke of the law.
[3] Selwyn, pp. 42–44.
[4] The phrase is from Beare, p. 4. See Stibbs, p. 20; Bénétreau, p. 40, and the literature cited, n. 1.

18

Paul's defence of his apostolic office to see the importance that the church attached to apostolic authority.

The attestation of the letter in other writings is early and strong.[1] The earliest is the reference in 2 Peter 3:1. Clement of Rome (before the end of the first century) quotes from the letter, although he does not identify his quotation. Quotations continue to appear in other early Christian writers. Irenaeus, in the second century, expressly attributes his quotations to the epistle.

Those who hold that Peter was not the author of the letter advance four principal arguments.[2] First they maintain that the Greek style is too polished for a Galilean fishermen (a reference in Papias to John Mark as Peter's 'interpreter' is taken by some to mean that Peter needed an interpreter because he was not fluent in Greek).[3] Secondly, it is urged that the persecutions alluded to in the letter did not occur till after Peter's death. Thirdly, the letter is said to be too much like Paul's writings to have come from Peter. Fourthly, many who recognize significant differences from Paul's writings maintain, nevertheless, that 1 Peter contains traditional teaching materials from the early church and is not the kind of letter that one of the first disciples of Jesus would have written.

The last objection is met by recognizing the purpose of the letter. Peter's eye-witness to the words and deeds of Jesus had already been given. John Mark's 'interpreting' of Peter's message involved his recording of Peter's witness in the Gospel of Mark. In the epistle, knowledge of the story of Jesus is assumed, and Peter is concerned to instruct the church in the apostolic interpretation of the gospel. This apostolic teaching is found also in Paul's letters. The objection that 1 Peter is too Pauline is met by recognizing that Paul as well as Peter conformed his teaching to the apostolic 'pattern of sound teaching'.[4] On the other hand, Peter's

[1] See the summary in Selwyn, pp. 36–38.
[2] The arguments are presented in Best, pp. 49–63. They are summarized and answered in Grudem, p. 16
[3] Bigg, p. 5. Papias is quoted in Eusebius, III:39:15. See pp. 24–33. n. 2 above Grudem replies to the arguments of W. G. Kümmel, E. Best and others on the Greek style of 1 Peter.
[4] 2 Tim. 1:13; cf. 2:2 and 1 Cor. 15:1–11. For a summary of similarities between 1 Peter and Paul's letters, see Kelly, p. 11; Selwyn, pp. 20–21, 382–384, 459.

teaching has distinctive elements. For example, Paul does not employ the 'servant of the Lord' description of Christ's work as Peter does.[1]

It is true that the traditional date for the death of Peter under Nero precedes the major periods of Roman persecution. The letter, however, does not reflect a situation of official and general oppression. Rather, it is a time of local harassment and sporadic persecution, a time in which Christians are warned to prepare for greater suffering for Christ's sake in the future.[2]

The issue of Peter's proficiency in Greek has been made the key objection to his authorship. Some commentators who hold that the letter does come from Peter think that he must have had help, and that his mention of Silas (5:12) indicates who his helper was. This argument, too, has been challenged. For one thing, the Greek of 1 Peter is not as polished in style as has sometimes been suggested.[3] Further, the charge that Peter's Greek must have been minimal or lacking fails to take account of the bilingual culture of Bethsaida in Galilee. An imaginative grammarian of the Greek language has said that Galilee could be compared to a bilingual region like Wales and that Peter's Greek was probably as good as a Welshman's English.[4] Ceslas Spicq reminds us that Peter did, after all, receive the gift of tongues at Pentecost![5]

The greatest assurance of the authenticity of 1 Peter comes from the letter itself.[6] Its message is closely linked to the speeches of Peter reported in the book of Acts. Spicq points to 1 Peter 1:10–12, a section unique in the New Testament letters: it speaks of the searching inquiries of the Old Testament prophets as they looked forward to the day of Christ. This, he says, is only to be expected from the pen of the

[1] Spicq, *Epîtres*, pp. 23f.; Selwyn, p. 30.
[2] See Selwyn's comments on 1 Peter 1:6; 3:13–17; 4:12–19, pp. 53f.; also Bigg, pp. 24–33, and Kelly, pp. 5–11.
[3] Both Bigg and Kelly (p. 31) recognize this, while still convinced that the Greek is too good for Peter. The reference to Peter and John as 'unlearned' (Acts 4:13) does not mean illiterate; it seems that some critical commentators are as amazed as the Sanhedrin was at Peter's grasp of the Old Testament.
[4] J. H. Moulton, *Grammar of New Testament Greek*, I (³1906), pp. 6ff., cited in Stibbs, p. 24, n. 4.
[5] Spicq, *Epîtres*, p. 22.
[6] See summaries of the teaching of the letter in Selwyn, pp. 23–36; Spicq, *Epîtres*, pp. 23–25.

apostle 'who founded the first Christian apologetic in referring to their testimony (Acts 2:25–31; 3:18–25; 10:43)'.[1] So,
too, the references in the letter to the sufferings of Christ
reflect Peter's understanding of the calling of Jesus as the
Servant of the Lord: an understanding that was drawn from
Christ's own teaching and example. As Selwyn says, 'This
impression of eyewitness runs through the Epistle, and gives
it a distinctive character.'[2] Peter marvels at the love of those
who have never seen Christ (1:8); his message of the living
hope in Christ has its background in his despair at the cruci-
fixion, and his joy in fellowship with the risen Christ. His
emphasis on humility has poignant meaning after the boasting
that preceded his fall. The Lord had charged him to tend his
flock, and he passes that admonition on to other undershepherds.

On the role of Silas ('Silvanus' in some versions), see the
comments on 5:12. Silas was Paul's fellow-missionary in Asia
Minor and in Greece, and is associated with Paul in the
address of the letters to the Thessalonians. He was also a
representative of the apostles and elders in Jerusalem, and is
named as a prophet.[3] If he did serve as an editor or co-author
with Peter, he did so as an inspired man. Peter's phrase
describing the service of Silas is used of the bearer of a letter,
who was regarded as a representative of the sender. This was
the function of Silas in relation to the letter sent from Jerusalem as described in Acts 15. If Silas were the bearer in such
a role, he was much more than a letter-carrier. He had a
voice in the Jerusalem Council that prepared the letter he
carried for that body. So, too, he may have conferred with
Peter in the preparation of the letter, or may have drafted it
under Peter's direction.

3. What kind of letter is it?

In Peter's brief letter there is great variety in both form and
content. Quotations and allusions from the Old Testament
abound.[4] Psalm 34, for example, is directly cited twice (2:3;

---

[1] Spicq, *Epîtres*, p. 23.   [2] Selwyn, p. 28.   [3] Acts 15:32.
[4] No less than sixty verses or passages of the Old Testament have a reference
from 1 Peter set beside them in the 'Index of Quotations' found in *GNT*, pp.
897–918.

3:10–12), and its themes of hope for the persecuted exile echo through the letter.[1] While there is no direct quotation of the words of Jesus, 1 Peter, like James, continually reflects the sayings of the Master.[2]

Some would claim that 1 Peter is not a letter, but a sermon or catechetical instruction to accompany the sacrament of baptism.[3] It has even been represented as a liturgy for a baptismal service.[4] (The baptism is supposed to take place after 2:21.) As Wayne Grudem points out, however, the only explicit reference to baptism in the letter is in 3:21, and 'mention of the beginning of the Christian life does not in itself imply a reference to baptism'.[5] Another form that has been detected in the letter is that of early Christian hymns or credal statements.[6] The possibility cannot be excluded, but the rhythmic expression that suggests a hymn or creed may be simply the eloquence of preaching and teaching.

The best account of the form of 1 Peter remains the summary at the end of the letter: 'I have written to you briefly, encouraging you and testifying that this is the true grace of God. Stand fast in it' (or, 'in which you stand fast'; 5:12b). The letter is full of encouragement and witness common to the apostolic teaching; we may assume that this is not the first time that Peter has taught these things. But the letter is freely written; Peter does not piece together material drawn from others. He speaks with deep understanding and feeling out of his own knowledge as an apostle of Christ.

---

[1] Bénétreau (p. 50) calls attention to such expressions as approaching the Lord (Ps. 34:6, LXX; 1 Pet. 2:4); not being ashamed (Ps. 34:5; 1 Pet. 2:6); hoping (Ps. 34:8, 22); fearing (Ps. 34:9, 11); contrasting the good and the evil (Ps. 34:10, 11, 14, 15); blessed (Ps. 34:8); and the term for residing as an alien (Ps. 34:4, LXX; 1 Pet. 2:11).

[2] Robert H. Gundry lists the parallels in an article cited by Bénétreau and Grudem: 'Verba Christi in 1 Peter . . .' (NTS 13/4, 1966–67, pp. 336–351). Note the allusions to the Sermon on the Mount pointed out by Bénétreau, p. 47: the blessedness of the persecuted (Mt. 5:10; 1 Pet. 2:19ff.; 3:9, 14); good deeds (Mt. 5:16; 1 Pet. 2:12); calling on the Father (Mt. 6:9; 1 Pet. 1:17); the inheritance (Mt. 6:19–21; 1 Pet. 1:4).

[3] P. Carrington, The Primitive Christian Catechism (Cambridge University Press, 1940). See Selwyn, p. 18.

[4] F. L. Cross, 1 Peter: A Paschal Liturgy (Mowbray, 1954). See the treatment in the introduction to Grudem's commentary.

[5] Grudem, p. 41

[6] M. E. Boismard, Quatre hymnes baptismales dans la première épître de Pierre (Paris, 1961). See Bénétreau, pp. 16–20.

4. Where and when was it written?

The 'Babylon' from which Peter sends his greetings (5:13) can scarcely have been the desolate and ruined city in Mesopotamia. Rome is called 'Babylon' in the book of Revelation (16:19; 17:5; 18:2), and it is understandable that Peter would use the name in a symbolic way. He thinks of the Christian church as the people of God in exile and dispersion (1:1, 17; 2: 9–11). Babylon was the great city of world empire for the Old Testament prophets; it was also the city of exile, where Israel lived as resident aliens. Peter's use of the name 'Babylon' reminds his hearers that he, too, shares their status as a 'displaced person'.

Further, the early church fathers understood that both Peter and Paul had been martyred in Rome. Eusebius, the historian of the early church, quotes from both Papias and Origen to support this.[1] (Papias, the bishop of Hierapolis, died about AD 130.) John Mark, who is mentioned by Peter (5:13), is also mentioned by Paul, writing from Rome.[2]

Since Peter's letter mentions Mark but not Paul, it seems unlikely that Paul was in Rome at the time it was written. By the same token, Paul does not mention Peter in his letters, even when he seems to be naming the 'men of the circumcision' who remained his faithful comrades.[3] According to tradition, Peter was at Rome only at the end of his life.[4] It would seem, therefore, that Peter wrote from Rome after Paul had left, released from his first imprisonment in AD 62.[5]

It does seem unlikely that Nero's fierce assault on the Christians in Rome could have begun. One would suppose that Peter would have made some reference to it in describing the loyalty due to the king (2:13–17). The date AD 63, after Paul's departure and before Nero's persecution, has a high degree of probability.

5. What is its message?

Facing impending assaults on the gospel, Peter witnesses to the grace of God, the overwhelming reality of what God has

[1] Eusebius, II:15:2; III:1:2–3. [2] 2 Tim. 4:11; Phm. 24.
[3] Phil. 2:20–21; Col. 4:10–11. [4] Eusebius, III:1:2.
[5] Grudem, pp. 35–37.

done in Jesus Christ. The apostle knows that Jesus rose from the dead; he saw him ascend to heaven. He knows, too, why Jesus died, and what his death accomplished: 'He himself bore our sins in his body on the tree, so that we might die to sins and live for righteousness; by his wounds you have been healed' (2:24). The reality of what Christ has done makes sure the hope of the Christian 'brotherhood'. Christians can not only endure suffering for Christ's sake; they can rejoice, for in their agony they are joined to Jesus who suffered for them. Their very sufferings become a sign of hope, for, as Christ suffered and entered into his glory, so will they. The Spirit of glory and of God rests on them (4:14).

Whether their neighbours attack or respect them, they can bear witness to the grace of God by their Christian lifestyle. Quietly and humbly they can live holy lives, not seeking to claim their own rights, but honouring others. Such humble living is in no way servile or demeaning, for Christians know themselves to be the royal people of God's own possession, the chosen heirs of the new creation. They need not avenge themselves, nor need they claim for themselves what is their due; their trust is in the judgment of God. Christians are 'resident aliens' in Babylon, but they are members of God's own household.

The gift of God's love, the blood of Jesus Christ, has redeemed Christians from the corrupt and empty lifestyle of their pagan past; that grace now unites them in fervent love for one another. They serve and help one another, using the rich spiritual gifts with which God's grace equips them. Jesus Christ, the great Shepherd of the flock of God, watches over his people. He calls undershepherds to serve him in guarding his sheep. The victory of Jesus Christ over all the powers of darkness frees his people from the power of Satan. They can repulse the roaring lion; in the fires of trial their faith will not be destroyed but purified like gold in the furnace. They may cast all their cares on God, knowing that he cares for them.

The grace that already fills Christians with joy will be brought to them fully at the appearing of Jesus Christ. The Lord, whom they love but have not seen, they will see and adore. Knowing well the doom and darkness from which they were delivered, the new people of God sing forth his praises. Their hallelujahs ring from their assemblies, their homes, even from the prison cells where their fear of God has set them free from the fear of man. Their witness is a witness of praise. Nourished by the unfailing Word of God, they taste already the goodness of their Saviour. The true grace of God has called them to his glory: everything, even their sufferings, will serve his purpose who redeemed them at such a price.

Some may scorn the comfort and triumph of Peter's letter as unpractical theology. His answers are answers of faith. But Peter knows that his witness is true, that Jesus Christ is real. He has tasted that the Lord is good, and that his goodness will not fail. 'This is the true grace of God. Stand fast in it' (5:12).

Armando Valladares closes his account of twenty-two years in Castro's prisons in Cuba with these words, recalling his thoughts as he was released:

And in the midst of that apocalyptic vision of the most dreadful and horrifying moments of my life, in the midst of the gray, ashy dust and the orgy of beatings and blood, prisoners beaten to the ground, a man emerged, the skeletal figure of a man wasted by hunger, with white hair, blazing blue eyes, and a heart overflowing with love, raising his arms to the invisible heaven and pleading for mercy for his executioners.

'Forgive them, Father, for they know not what they do.' And a burst of machine-gun fire ripping open his breast.[1]

---

[1] *Against All Hope: the Prison Memoirs of Armando Valladares*, translated by Andrew Hurley (Hamish Hamilton, 1986), p. 380.

1. The apostle to the Jews blesses God's true people

Peter, an apostle of Jesus Christ,
  To God's elect, strangers in the world, scattered throughout Pontus, Galatia, Cappadocia, Asia and Bithynia, ²who have been chosen according to the foreknowledge of God the Father, through the sanctifying work of the Spirit, for obedience to Jesus Christ and sprinkling by his blood:
  Grace and peace be yours in abundance.

1. He greets them with blessing

Greetings cards are big business in the United States and Britain. Misty photographs of lovers, paintings of little gamins, grotesque cartoons: they crowd long display racks. But for all their variety, the cards still repeat standard formulas of greeting. There are only a limited number of ways to say 'Get well soon' or 'Happy birthday'.

But Christians, and especially Christian apostles, may think of greetings as more than formalities. Early Christians did use the common greeting 'Wish you joy!'[1] But Peter, Paul and John salute the church with greetings that become blessings; a wish for joy becomes an apostolic pronouncement of grace.[2] The Old Testament form of this blessing is on the lips of David: 'May the Lord now show you kindness and faithfulness.'[3] The New Testament heightens the meaning of God's mercy and grace. Grace 'signifies God's love in

---

[1] *Chairein*, NIV 'Greetings', Jas. 1:1; Acts 15:23; *cf.* 23:26.
[2] *Charis* appears in the salutation of Paul's letters from 1 Corinthians on; John uses it also (2 Jn. 3; Rev. 1:4).
[3] 2 Sa. 2:6; 15:20.

action in Jesus Christ on behalf of sinners.'[1]

What makes a greeting a blessing? Peter gives the answer in the words that precede his blessing. It is the work of the Spirit. When a minister of God's word pronounces a blessing at the end of a service of worship, it is the action of God's Spirit that gives power to his words. *Grace* is a gift; God is the giver. Our words of blessing are not magic; they do not communicate grace by their own power, or because we speak them. But when they are spoken in faith to the people of God, God honours them. They are much more than wishes; more, even, than prayers. They declare God's own favour toward those who are in Christ.

Coupled with grace in apostolic greetings is *peace*. *Grace* transforms the greeting of the Greeks; *peace* gives new meaning to *shalom*, the salutation of the Hebrews. The priests of the Old Testament pronounced God's blessing of peace upon the people: 'The Lord turn his face toward you and give you peace.'[2] Sinful Israel forfeited that blessing and brought upon itself the judgment of captivity. But the prophets foresaw a day when God would deliver his people, not only from their oppressors, but from their sins.[3] God himself would be their Saviour: 'O Lord, thou wilt ordain peace for us, thou hast wrought for us all our works.'[4]

Simon Peter, the Galilean fisherman, knew the Prince of Peace of whom Isaiah spoke. In the upper room at the last supper, and again after the resurrection, Jesus had blessed the disciples with his peace.[5] That peace was not the political peace that the people expected the Messiah to bring. The world, Jesus said, could not give it or take it away. The Messiah's peace was given in the shadow of the cross. Jesus gave his peace not only in spite of the cross, but because of the cross. By his death he bore the judgment of God's just wrath and made peace not only between Jew and Gentile, but between God and man.

Peter's brief greeting, *Grace and peace be yours in abundance,* gives in miniature the whole message of his letter. He writes to those who already feel the scorn and malice of an unbelieving world. Writing from Rome under the emperor Nero, Peter knows that they will experience much worse.

[1] Cranfield, *I and II Peter*, p. 18.　[2] Nu. 6:26.　[3] Mi. 7:14–20.
[4] Is. 26:12, RSV; *cf.* Is. 9:6.　[5] Jn. 14:27; 16:33; 20:19.

Can he really pronounce peace in abundance to those who are only beginning to discover the suffering to which Christians are called? Peter writes for that very purpose. Once he had fought to defend the *shalom* of the Messiah. Under the olive trees of Gethsemane, he drew his sword to resist those who came to arrest Jesus. But Jesus had made him sheath his weapon after one misdirected stroke. Peter wanted to fight because he feared that the death of Jesus would end all hope of victory, all hope of the Messiah's peace. But the death of Jesus had done the opposite. It had accomplished the salvation of God's Anointed. Now Peter, the apostle of the risen Lord, can pronounce peace; the peace that comes, not by the sword, but by the cross. His letter expands on the blessing that is distilled in his greeting.

Peter prepares for his letter by identifying himself and his readers. We are struck by a contrast; he says so much about them and so little about himself. Peter is simply *an apostle of Jesus Christ*. He makes no claim to be a prince among the apostles, but neither does he feel any need to justify or defend his apostolic office, as Paul had occasion to do. Peter's calling as an apostle would be well known wherever the gospel had been preached. Peter was one of the twelve chosen by Jesus to be with him.[1] He was the first to confess, in the name of all, that Jesus is the Christ, the Son the living God. To him Jesus replied, 'You are Peter, and on this rock I will build my church, and the gates of Hades will not overcome it.'[2]

To be sure, Peter is not the foundation rock apart from his confession. Christ's words are addressed to the Peter who has received revelation from the Father in heaven.[3] When Peter a little later rebukes Jesus for speaking of the cross, Jesus does not call him Peter, but rather Satan. He has become the rock in a different sense; not the rock of foundation, but a rock to stumble over.[4]

Neither may Peter be isolated from the eleven. Jesus grants to them all the power of the keys of the kingdom that he gave to Peter. The church is not built on Peter as an isolated stone, but upon the foundation of the apostles and prophets,

---

[1] Mk. 3:14–19.   [2] Mt. 16:16, 18.   [3] Mt. 16:17.
[4] Mt. 16:23; in Aramaic the phrase for 'stumbling-block' would include the same word that appears in Peter's name 'Cephas'.

those who like Peter have received the revelation of
Christ.[1]

At the same time, neither may we separate Peter's
confession from Peter. Jesus does not build his church on a
confession in the abstract, but on the confessing apostle. To
Peter's word 'You are the Christ,' Jesus replies, 'You are
Peter.' Peter had recognized Jesus, the Christ; Jesus will
recognize Peter, the rock. To Peter is given the calling to
open the gates of the kingdom to Jewish and Gentile
believers. He does so at Jerusalem in the midst of the eleven,
and at Caesarea as one of the eye-witnesses of the resurrection.[2] Peter has a prominent role to fulfil as an apostle and
an eye-witness, but he is not given a higher authority than
that of other apostles. It is enough for Peter, in this letter,
to identify himself as an apostle; he bears witness not to
himself, but to Christ as the chief cornerstone of God's
spiritual temple (2:5–8).

Peter's witness is strong. He knows what he has seen and
heard; he knows, too, his appointment by Jesus, and the
revelation from the Father that has equipped him to serve.
Simon Peter the fisherman can put the rabbis to shame; he
can stand before rulers to give a reason for the hope that he
has.[3] He does so as Christ's apostle, rejoicing in the faith of
those who have not seen and yet have believed (1:8).

Peter is Christ's apostle, too, in giving inspired and authoritative teaching to the church. When we think of Peter as
the author of this letter, we may at first be disappointed.
Why did not Peter report to us more of the words of Jesus,
more of his miracles? What scenes from the life of Jesus Peter
could have painted! Every Bible student notices how similar
Peter's first letter is to the letters of Paul. But Paul was never
with Jesus in the synagogue of Capernaum, or in a fishing-
boat on the lake, or in the upper room at Jerusalem. How
can Peter fail to draw on his days with Jesus as he writes to
people who have never seen the Lord?

As we saw in the Introduction, the absence of such
personal references has led some scholars to conclude that
Peter could not have written the letter.[4] Yet it is presumptuous, to say the least, for us to imagine that we know what

[1] Mt. 18:18; Eph. 2:20; 3:5.   [2] Acts 2:14–41; 10:34–42.
[3] 1 Pet. 3:15; Acts 4:13.   [4] See the arguments of Best, pp. 49–53.

the apostle must have written. More than that, it shows a misunderstanding of Peter's witness as an apostle and of his particular purpose in writing.

As an apostle, Peter shared with others in teaching the faith.[1] He did not desire to attract a personal following of those who would relish his distinctive insights or experiences. He was one of a company charged by the risen Christ to testify that 'he is the one whom God appointed as judge of the living and the dead.'[2] The teaching of Jesus during his ministry, and especially in the forty days between his resurrection and ascension, moulded the apostolic tradition. The gospel that Paul received[3] was the apostolic deposit, the pattern of sound teaching that proclaimed the fulfilment of the Old Testament promises in Christ. The apostolic message was not a *melange* of individual testimonies prepared as the twelve spoke for five minutes each on 'what the resurrection means to me'. Rather, it was the Lord's interpretation of his own work in the light of his own word; he must 'suffer these things and enter into his glory.'[4] Peter preached the apostolic message at Pentecost; the church was established in the tradition of apostolic teaching.[5] Peter continues to teach this in his letter. It is a message saturated with the Old Testament, a message that proclaims the fulfilment in Christ of all that the prophets promised.[6]

Peter's purpose in writing this letter is not to give a first announcement about the words and works of Jesus. Peter's preaching on that subject is reflected in the Gospel of Mark.[7] Neither does Peter address one local church in order to deal with its particular problems (as Paul often does). Rather, his purpose is to deepen the understanding of the whole Christian church in Asia Minor so that believers may face the testings that await them with strong hope in Christ. His letter may reflect the teaching he and others would give to prepare new converts for baptism. Some passages may echo hymns or credal statements from the apostolic period. What is clear throughout is that Peter teaches the common doctrine of the apostolic testimony.

We do well to remember the authority of Peter as an

---

[1] Acts 2:42.   [2] Acts 10:42.   [3] 1 Cor. 15:3.   [4] Lk. 24:26; 1 Pet. 1:11.
[5] Acts 17:2–3.   [6] Acts 3:18–26; 10:43; 1 Pet. 1:10–12.
[7] See Introduction, p. 16. n. 1.

apostle. Jesus taught with unique authority as the Son of God, but he also commissioned his apostles to teach in his name. He promised his Spirit to bring his words to their memory and to teach them other things after his resurrection.[1] The church is built upon the foundation of the apostles and prophets because they received the revelation of Christ.[2] The office of the apostle does not and cannot continue, for the apostles were eye-witnesses of Christ's resurrection.[3] Peter, as an apostle, together with Silas, a prophet, laboured with other apostles and prophets to lay the foundation of the church. Together they taught the doctrine that Jesus committed to them in the Spirit. The church is apostolic today to the extent that it remains upon the doctrinal foundation established by the apostles. No-one today can claim the authority of an apostle, either by virtue of ecclesiastical office or charismatic enduement. The work and calling of the apostle are finished in witnessing to the final revelation of God in Jesus Christ. He is the final Prophet, just as he is the final Priest, and Peter writes to bear authoritative witness to him.

Why are we drawn to Peter's letter? Certainly it is fascinating to read a genuine document written by one who knew Jesus so well. Today, as in Peter's time, there are storms of persecution rising against the church. Never was it more important to understand how the church is to be related to the world. But we are drawn to Peter's letter by a more fundamental reason. Peter is an inspired apostle, and what he writes is the word of God. We come to a letter that is addressed to the Christians of Asia by Peter, but to the church of all ages by the Spirit of Christ.

2. He greets them as the true people of God

After briefly identifying himself, Peter addresses those to whom he writes as the people of God. They are the new Diaspora, *scattered* in the world, but *chosen* by *the Father*, sanctified by *the Spirit* and cleansed by the *sprinkling* of Christ's *blood*.

Feel the drama in that description. Peter is writing primarily to Gentiles, to those who had no part in the people

[1] Jn. 14:26; 15:26–27; 16:13–14.   [2] Eph. 2:20; 3:4–5; Heb. 1:1–2; 2:3–4.
[3] Acts 1:21–22.

of God, but who followed the 'empty way of life handed down to you from your forefathers' (1:18). They had lived to the full the Gentile life of 'debauchery, lust, drunkenness, orgies, carousing and detestable idolatry' (4:3). Peter, a pious Jew, would regard pagan Gentiles with scorn and loathing. Indeed, even as an apostle, Peter had been called to minister particularly to Jewish Christians. He was sent to the 'circumcision.'[1] Peter was shocked when God, in a vision, commanded him to eat food that was not kosher.[2] Only after God's rooftop session of reorientation was Peter ready to go to the house of Cornelius, a Gentile army officer. There he explained that God's revelation had overcome his conviction 'that it is against our law for a Jew to associate with a Gentile or visit him.'[3]

This is the apostle who writes to Gentiles living in Asia Minor (now Turkey) and greets them as God's chosen and holy people! What could cause such an about-face on the part of this very Jewish fisherman? The answer, of course, is Jesus. Peter came to a new understanding of what it meant to belong to the people of God: it meant to belong to the Messiah, the Son of God.

Nothing is more astonishing than that he should call these Gentiles the *chosen* of *God the Father* (1:2). Israel was God's chosen people. Theirs was 'the adoption as sons; theirs the divine glory, the covenants . . .'.[4] God 'set up boundaries for the peoples according to the number of the sons of Israel. For the Lord's portion is his people.'[5] How could Gentiles be called God's chosen, his elect?

Think of the answer Peter might have given. He could not deny that Cornelius and his family had been added to the people of God. They had received the same Holy Spirit who had come upon the Jewish believers at Pentecost. But Peter might have felt that these Gentiles were second-class citizens. They had been added, he might have suspected, as a divine afterthought. When many of the Jews did not believe, the Lord decided to admit a few Gentiles on a provisional basis.[6]

---

[1] Gal. 2:7–8.   [2] Acts 10:14.   [3] Acts 10:28.   [4] Rom. 9:4.   [5] Dt. 32:8–9.

[6] Paul might seem to say something close to this when he warns Gentiles against pride (Rom. 11:17–24). But Paul stresses precisely the divine purpose in breaking off the natural branches in judgment so that the wild branches might be grafted in by grace.

Peter's answer is entirely different. These Christian Gentiles are God's chosen people because he has known them from all eternity. Jesus Christ was foreknown by the Father before the world was created.[1] The chosen people of Christ are also foreknown by the Father. Their inclusion in the people of God is no accident, no afterthought, but God's purpose from the beginning. Those who are foreknown by God are foreknown in and with Christ. The expression *foreknowledge* does not mean that God had information in advance about Christ, or about his elect. Rather it means that both Christ and his people were the objects of God's loving concern from all eternity.

Paul speaks of God's foreknowledge in the same way. As a Pharisee he could not conceive that Israel might reject the Messiah and be themselves rejected. After Jesus met him on the road to Damascus he preached the message he had sought to silence. Yet, in a new form, the problem remained. His former friends now rejected *his* message. 'Did God reject his people?' Paul asks.[2] It might seem so. But Paul answers, 'By no means! I am an Israelite myself . . . God did not reject his people, *whom he foreknew.*'[3]

God's foreknowledge is of crucial importance for Paul, as for Peter. Paul has reflected on the Old Testament teaching about the 'remnant'. God has not cast off *all* Israel. A remainder is left. Paul is a case in point. What then distinguishes at last those who were cast off from those who remained? Certainly nothing in them. Paul was not wiser, more responsive, less stubborn or less self-righteous than his Pharisaical colleagues who continued to hate the name of Jesus. No, Paul is distinguished from them only by God's choosing, God's electing grace. Christ met Saul the persecutor; the Spirit of God gave him new birth. He was chosen by God in Christ before the foundation of the world.[4] God does not cast off those, like Paul, whom he foreknew. There is therefore a choosing within the choosing of Israel, 'a remnant according to the election of grace'.[5] They are not all

[1] 1 Pet. 1:20. The NIV translates 'foreknown' as *chosen* in this passage. The translation conveys the meaning well, but obscures the parallel between God's foreknowledge of Christ and of Christians, since 'foreknowledge' appears in the translation of 1:2 but not in the translation of 1:20.
[2] Rom. 11:1. [3] Rom. 11:1b–2a (italics added).
[4] Eph. 1:4; Gal. 1:15–16. [5] Rom. 11:5, AV.

Israel that are of Israel, nor are all of Abraham's descendants true children of God.[1]

Since it is God's choosing, not physical descent, that establishes the true people of God, God is surely free to choose others outside of Israel. Paul makes this clear: if in royal grace God determines to call a renewed Israel 'Ammi', 'my people', when they had been 'Lo-ammi', 'no people', then he may say the same to Gentiles.[2] This, indeed, has been promised by the prophets. God will gather a remnant from the nations along with the remnant of Israel to assemble his new people.[3]

What mighty assurance Peter gives to these Gentiles! As Christians they are the people of God, not just as Israel was, but in the ultimate spiritual sense. Chosen in Christ, those who were no people are now the objects of God's free grace and choosing love. God is their Father, not simply as God was a Father to Israel his beloved son,[4] but as God is the Father of Jesus Christ, the eternal Beloved (1:3).

Whether we are descended from Abraham as Peter was, or are Gentiles, as were most of those addressed by Peter, we share together the wonder of God's amazing grace in Christ. The mystery of God's choosing will always offend those who stand before God in pride. Forgetting their rebellion and guilt before God, they are ready to accuse him of favouritism. But those whom God's love has drawn to Christ will always confess the wonder of his initiative in grace:

> I find, I walk, I love, but, O
> The whole of love is but my answer, Lord, to thee;
> For thou wert long beforehand with my soul,
> Always thou lovedst me.[5]

God's choosing is the final reason that polluted Gentiles can be called his people. But God's choosing also means that he will act to make these Gentiles his own. To belong to God they must be redeemed from their sin and washed from its stain. They must be made holy as God is holy (1:16).

To describe what God has done to bring about his great

---

[1] Rom. 9:6–8.   [2] *Cf.* Ho. 1:9; 2:23; Rom. 9:23–26.
[3] Is. 45:20; 49:22f.; 66:19–21; Je. 48:47; 49:6, 39; Zc. 9:7; *cf.* Is. 19:24–25.
[4] Ex. 4:22–23; Ho. 11:1.   [5] Anonymous.

design, Peter refers to the Holy *Spirit* and to *Jesus Christ*. God's choosing of his people is applied to them *through the sanctifying work of the Spirit, for obedience to Jesus Christ and sprinkling by his blood* (1:2). It is by the Spirit that God 'has given us new birth' (1:3), and it is by Christ's blood that we are cleansed and redeemed (1:18–19). The triune God, Father, Son, and Holy Spirit, accomplishes our salvation.

The obedience of which Peter speaks seems to refer, not to our whole life of obedience, but to our initial submission to Christ as Lord. He again speaks of this obedience as obedience to the truth in verse 22. Paul, too, speaks of the obedience of faith in this sense.[1] Of course, the Holy Spirit who makes us holy initially through the blood of Jesus Christ continues to work in us as 'obedient children', making us holy in our new lifestyle (1:14–16). Peter may have in view this ongoing work of the Spirit. On the other hand, he is emphasizing the new position of Gentiles as those given a new birth by God into a living hope (1:3). That suggests that *the sanctifying work of the Spirit* refers to our initial cleansing (symbolized in baptism) rather than to the continuing work of the Spirit.

The cleansing of God's chosen people requires not only washing by the water of the Spirit, but also *sprinkling by* the *blood* of Christ. In this phrase Peter takes us back to the dramatic scene at Mount Sinai after the exodus from Egypt. While the mountain shook at the presence of the Lord, the people were assembled to enter into covenant with God. At an altar with twelve pillars, sacrifice was offered. Half of the blood was sprinkled on the altar. Moses read again the words of God's covenant, and the people vowed their obedience. Moses then sprinkled the people with the rest of the sacrificial blood, saying, 'This is the blood of the covenant that the Lord has made with you in accordance with all these words.'[2]

At Sinai Israel was made the people of God; they were joined to him in his covenant. Now Peter speaks of Gentiles becoming obedient to Christ through the new covenant in his blood. We are sprinkled, not with the blood of oxen, but with the blood of Christ. The altar that is sprinkled with his

[1] Rom 1:5; *cf.* 6:7; 10:3; 16:26; Acts 6:7; 2 Cor. 9:13.   [2] Ex. 24:8.

blood does not stand before Sinai, but in heaven; it is the very throne of God.[1] The symbolism powerfully declares that Christ's death satisfies God's justice and makes atonement for our sins. The blood of Christ sprinkled on us marks God's acceptance of us because the penalty of sin has been paid. It also symbolizes God's claim on us. As Peter says, we were bought, not with silver or gold, but 'with the precious blood of Christ' (2:18–19).

Peter had once urged Jesus not to go to his death on the cross: 'Never Lord! This shall never happen to you!'[2] But now Peter understands the necessity of the death of Christ, and the meaning of his resurrection. Jesus himself 'bore our sins in his body on the tree, so that we might die to sins and live for righteousness' (2:24).

In Christ Peter found the reality foreshadowed at Sinai. Israel miserably failed to keep their covenant oath. The yoke of the law, Peter himself said, was one that 'neither we nor our fathers have been able to bear'.[3] But now Peter can rejoice in the new covenant. God cleanses the hearts of Jew and Gentile by faith in the sacrifice of Christ.[4] The reality to which the prophets testified, and to which all the ceremonies pointed, had come at last.

3. He greets them as the people of God in the world

What difference does it make that Gentiles can be called the people of God, chosen of the Father, made holy in the Spirit, sprinkled with the blood of the new covenant? To mark the difference, Peter uses two words that turn the world upside down for those inhabitants of Asia Minor, and for us. He calls them the *scattered* people, and says that they are *strangers*, aliens who are transients, temporary residents, travellers headed for their native land.

These terms give us the key to Peter's whole letter. Peter is writing a travellers' guide for Christian pilgrims. He reminds them that their hope is anchored in their homeland. They are called to endure alienation as strangers, but they have a heavenly citizenship and destiny.

John Bunyan's *Pilgrim's Progress* gave classical expression

[1] Heb. 12:24; 9:11–12, 23–24.   [2] Mt. 16:22b.   [3] Acts 15:10.
[4] Acts 15:9, 11.

to the theme of following Christ as a journey. Today, however, Bunyan's traveller, Christian, seems to have more critics than followers. In his earnest haste to reach the Celestial City, Christian did not take much account of the world he was passing through. He tried to speak a good word to his companions, but he did not set up an evangelistic booth at Vanity Fair, nor did he seek funding for a project to drain the Slough of Despond. In Bunyan's defence, it might be said that his own life was better than his allegory. But how are we to understand the Christian pilgrimage? Does the Christian flee from the world, fight it, conform to it, change it – or is there a deeper meaning to the call to pilgrimage?

Certainly the questions are not new. Those who received Peter's letter faced them, too. What does it mean that they – and we – are the scattered people, transient aliens in a land that is not our homeland?

The 'Diaspora' (the dispersed) was the common term for the Jews scattered through the world after the exile of 587 BC.[1] Although the scattering of the Jews began with their forced deportation by the Assyrians and Babylonians, it was greatly increased by voluntary emigration. The Gentiles to whom Peter wrote may have been familiar with the term as it described dispersed Jews. Indeed, they may have resented the Jewish Diaspora among them. Anti-Semitism was strong in the Roman empire. But Peter includes *Gentile* readers in the Diaspora. In what sense are they the 'dispersed'? To be sure, many of their forefathers had come from other regions, but they were now settled residents, living where they had always lived, in their own lands, cities and home towns.[2]

They must not take offence, however, but rather rejoice in a title of honour. They are the Diaspora, because they are the people of God, scattered in the world. Jesus had looked with compassion on 'the lost sheep of the house of Israel', because they were 'harassed and helpless, like sheep without a shepherd'.[3] He had come to gather his 'little flock', including other sheep that were not of the sheepfold of

---

[1] *Cf.* Jn. 7:35; Psalms of Solomon 9:2, 'The diaspora . . . according to the word of God'. *Cf.* Spicq, *Vie*, p. 63, n. 15.
[2] Selwyn, p. 47. See Appendix A.   [3] Mt. 10:6; 9:36.

Israel.[1] Peter writes in the joyful assurance that the Gentiles in Asia Minor are part of the Lord's flock. Once they were without God and without hope in the world, following the 'empty way of life' handed down from their fathers, but now they are 'returned to the Shepherd and Overseer' of their souls (1:18; 2:25).

The fact that these Gentiles are included in God's Diaspora accounts for the other term that Peter uses. Since they are citizens of heaven, and have another country to which they are going, they are *strangers*, transients in the world in which they live.[2] In relation to their homeland, they are the Diaspora; in relation to their place of residence, they are aliens. They carry another passport; they are on pilgrimage to the city of God.

God's people must be aliens in a world of rebels against God. That point is often made in the Old Testament. God called Abraham out of the city of Ur to a life of pilgrimage. He wandered in Canaan, the land of promise, as a stranger: 'I am an alien and a stranger among you,' he told the Hittite residents.[3] Jacob, brought to Egypt by Joseph, confessed to Pharaoh that 'the years of my pilgrimage' were 'few and difficult'.[4]

In Egypt the Pharaohs exploited Israel as a workforce of undesirable aliens, despised and feared. After God delivered them in the exodus, Israel became a pilgrim people, journeying through the wilderness to the land of promise. That wilderness experience became the model for understanding the life of God's people as a pilgrimage. God met with his people, taught and tested them, led them by day and night, fed them with bread from heaven and water from the rock, and placed his tent among them.[5] His care watched over their journey till they reached their home, the place where God would dwell with them. The path through the wilderness is therefore the way of the Lord, the way that leads to life.

After the sin of Israel brought God's judgment, the

[1] Lk. 12:32; Jn. 10:16.
[2] See Phil. 3:20; Heb. 11:13–16. *Parepidēmos, transient*, appears also in 1 Pet. 2:11 and Heb. 11:13. It designates the stranger who is not a resident, but a traveller passing through. Spicq, *Vie*, p. 69.
[3] Gn. 23:4.   [4] Gn. 47:9.
[5] Ex. 19:4; 29:45; Nu. 10:35; 9:15–23: Dt. 8:3; Ps. 78:14–29; Dt. 29:5.

prophets took up the exodus theme anew. In exile, God's people were again aliens in a strange land. The prophets promised that a remnant of the people would be spared and restored. God would deliver them from the graves of their captivity as he had delivered them from the graves of Egyptian bondage.[1] The Lord would again march through the desert, leading his people out of exile and wandering. 'In the desert prepare the way for the Lord; make straight in the wilderness a highway for our God.'[2]

The Qumran community on the shore of the Dead Sea looked out across the water to the wilderness where God had marched with Israel. The community regulated its life to make ready in the wilderness for the coming of the Lord.[3] John the Baptist went into the desert to preach the preparation of the way of the Lord, and announced Jesus as the One who was to come.[4] Jesus led his disciples in the way and told them, 'I am the way and the truth and the life. No-one comes to the Father except through me.'[5]

The words of Jesus in John 14:1–6 reflect Moses' words in Deuteronomy 1:29–33. Jesus, like Moses, tells his disciples not to be afraid, but to believe. Moses says that God will go before them, overcome the enemy, lead them, and prepare a place for them. That promise Jesus will fulfil. He is the Way; he has overcome the world, and goes to prepare a place in his Father's house. Christians are people of 'the Way', following Jesus in the pilgrimage of their lives.[6]

Peter recognizes that the Christians to whom he writes are not just transients, spending the night in the place of their sojourn. Like the exiles addressed by Jeremiah, they must be ready to live among the Gentiles for months and years.[7] Peter is therefore concerned about their lifestyle as resident aliens, and about their witness to those among whom they live (2:11–12; 3:14–15). Peter does not call us as Christians to flee from the world. Neither does he write to isolated pilgrims pursuing a lonely way through the desert. Rather

---

[1] Je. 23:7–8; Ezk. 37:11–14.

[2] Is. 40:3–5, 9–11; cf. Je. 23:7–8; Is. 41:17–18; 42:16; 43:16–21; 48:21; 49:10–13; 52:12.

[3] *The Manual of Discipline* (IQS) 8:15; 9:19, in *DSS*. See J. T. Milik, *Ten Years of Discovery in the Wilderness of Judea* (Allenson, 1959), p. 116.

[4] Lk. 1:80; Jn. 1:23–27.   [5] Jn. 14:6.

[6] Acts 9:2; 24:14; cf. Heb. 11:8–10.   [7] Je. 29:4–7.

Peter writes to the scattered Christians as a community; they are the people of God in the world. Like the Diaspora of Israel, they, the true Israel, may be recognized in the world by a different lifestyle. Indeed, through the power of the Spirit, their lives are to be more radically different. Peter dedicates most of his letter to showing the motivation and pattern of the new lifestyle of the pilgrim people.

Christians, indeed, are not the real aliens in God's world. Ironically, these wandering pilgrims will inherit the earth, while those who think they can claim the world as their own will lose it in God's judgment. God makes Cain a wanderer, bearing the mark of his crime.[1] The city that Cain builds cannot have enduring foundations.

Jean Brun has written vividly about 'the vagabonds of the West',[2] picturing man as a wanderer, seeking escape from the prison of himself. He finds a picture of Western man in the myth of Tantalus, condemned to suffer eternal thirst under the boughs of ripe fruit that are for ever just beyond his reach. Frustrated by his desire, man in Western civilization vainly seeks to overcome the limits of space and time, devising technologies to extend his reach or to improve his grasp.

The pilgrimage of the East is differently conceived. Brun sees it in the figure of the Buddha, not reaching out, but with his hands folded. He would find escape by quenching his desires. The Eastern mystic does not grasp tools to build a tower to the heavens; he uses his hands in the stylized gestures of meditation and dance, the *mudra* motions that picture the changing forms of the world's illusion.[3]

We may look back along the road of man's endless quest: Alexander the Great seeking new worlds to conquer; medieval pilgrims; Crusaders; Columbus seeking the lost earthly paradise with missionary vision; American pioneers; space-age cosmonauts. The object of the quest may be a religious symbol; the Holy Grail was sought as the cup of the Last Supper and the container for the blood of the Son of God. Legend, myth, and Christian tradition may be blended: Ponce de Leon was not the last to search for the fountain of youth in Florida!

[1] Gn. 4:15.   [2] Jean Brun, *Les Vagabonds de l'occident* (Desclee, 1976).
[3] *Ibid.*, p. 13.

40

Nor has the wandering quest ended. Modern mythology holds before a technological age the hope of extra-terrestrial intelligence to be contacted. 'There must be someone out there!' Or evolution, aided by genetic engineering, will produce superman, a new race of beings in tune with the cosmic 'Force'.[1] Science fiction cheerfully imagines possibilities that gradually become the assumptions of young people raised on *Star Wars* and computerized space games.

Whatever wars man may imagine in the stars, fierce and bloody conflicts are being fought on earth in the quest for a secularized earthly paradise. Deep in our Western worldview is a humanistic version of the coming of the city of God. Communism demands religious commitment, for it seeks not simply to transform social and economic situations, but to metamorphose humanity.[2] For that reason Jean-Paul Sartre, the French existentialist and atheistic apostle of liberty, did not hesitate to demand the death penalty for political dissent. Since a revolutionary regime must rid itself of those who threaten it, state execution is the only safe policy. The problem with the French revolution was not that it sent too many to the guillotine, but that it sent too few.[3]

The theme of Christian pilgrimage stands over against the wandering of an unbelieving world. Christians are transients here, but they have an eternal home. They are aliens by faith, because by faith they are citizens of the city of God. Peter's letter eloquently presents the sure hope of the Christian pilgrim; hope in a salvation already sealed in Christ, a present as well as a future possession.

'For we have not here an abiding city, but we seek after the city which is to come.'[4] Peter writes from 'Babylon' (5:13), the city of human pride, where mad emperors raised monuments to their own deity in the Roman forum, and where frenzied mobs would scream for Christian blood in the spectacles of the Colosseum. But the Roman Babylon lies under the judgment of God's prophets.[5] Babylon is not a city that will endure, for at last every wall shall fall.[6] As the centre of man's pride, the city is also the centre of his

---

[1] See Jeremy Rifkin, *Algeny* (Penguin, 1984).
[2] *Cf.* Brun, *op. cit.*, p. 77.   [3] *Ibid.*, p. 71, n. 52.
[4] Heb. 13:14, ASV *cf.* 11:14–16; Phil. 3:20.   [5] Is. 13; Je. 50; Rev. 18.
[6] Ezk. 38:19–23. See the comments on 5:13 for Babylon as a term for Rome.

41

sin. The Bible tells of the perversions of Sodom, the blood-lust of Nineveh, and the oppression of Babylon. We find all the pagan sins still flourishing in the cities of our civilization: the flagrant licentiousness of Times Square in New York, the atheistic idolatry of Red Square in Moscow, the cynical secularism of London or Paris.

Babylon is not holy, but neither is Babylon as yet judged. Jesus would not bid the fire that consumed Sodom to fall on the village of Samaria that refused him.[1] God withholds his final judgment for a purpose. He sent his Son not to judge the world, but that the world might be saved. His restraint of judgment calls people to repentance.[2]

Peter is concerned, therefore, about the *witness* of the Christian church to the pagans of their cities and towns (2:11–12; 3:15–16). They are transients and aliens, but they are also ambassadors. They reject conformity to the city, but they accept responsibility, living as law-abiding citizens and honouring their rulers and their fellow residents (2:9–10, 13–17; 3:1).

Babylon is not an enduring city, but neither is Jerusalem. By becoming the people of God, these Gentiles are not called to the earthly Jerusalem. They join those who, like Peter, have gone forth 'to him outside the camp, bearing the disgrace he bore'.[3]

There is no enduring city here; we must not live as though there were. Rather, we come to the heavenly Jerusalem in our worship.[4] To yield the religious devotion demanded by the political gospels of our day is to be guilty of idolatry. The elect pilgrims of the Diaspora are children of the holy Father, purchased by the precious blood of Christ, washed by the Spirit. They must keep themselves from idols.[5]

Peter will describe the political and social duties of the Christian pilgrim. But first the pilgrim must know his calling. It is not to pursue the mirage of humanistic hope. Neither is it to bow down to worship the imperial images of totalitarian power. It is to obey Jesus Christ until the day of his appearing.

---

[1] Lk. 9:52f. [2] Jn. 3:17; Rom. 2:4–5. [3] Heb. 13:13.
[4] Heb. 12:22–24. [5] 1 Jn. 5:21.

2. Bless God for our hope in Christ

1. God establishes our hope in Christ (1:3)

Praise be to the God and Father of our Lord Jesus Christ! In his great mercy he has given us new birth into a living hope through the resurrection of Jesus Christ from the dead . . .

In his play *No Exit*, Jean-Paul Sartre gives his own vision of hell. Two women and a man, doomed to perdition, enter a room that seems to threaten no torment. But they are sentenced to remain together in that same room for ever – without sleep and without eyelids. All three enter with pretensions about their past. The man pretends that he was a hero of the revolution. In reality, he was killed in a train wreck when he tried to escape after betraying his comrades. The women have even more sordid lives. In the forced intimacy of the room their guilty secrets are all wrung out. Nothing can be hidden, and nothing can be changed. Sartre's imagination has well prepared us for his famous line, 'Hell is other people.' But the moral of the play is the line of doom to which the drama moves: 'You are – your life, and nothing else.'[1]

Sartre rejected Christianity, but his play invites heart-searching. Who wants to say that he is what he has been rather than what he meant to be, or what he hopes to be? Sartre implies that hell begins when hope ends. Sartre's image falls far short of the reality of hell, for God's judgment exposes sinners not simply to the lidless eyes of other sinners,

[1] Jean-Paul Sartre, *No Exit and Three Other Plays*, tr. S. Gilbert (Vintage, 1946), p. 45

but to the all-seeing gaze of God himself. Yet Sartre reminds us of how desperately we need hope. While there is life, there is hope, we say. But if hope dies, what life can remain?

Peter writes a letter of *hope*. The hope he proclaims is not what we call a 'fond hope'. We cherish fond hopes because they are so fragile. We 'hope against hope' because we do not really expect what we hope for. But Peter writes of a sure hope, a hope that holds the future in the present because it is anchored in the past. Peter hopes for God's salvation, God's deliverance from sin and death. His hope is sure, because God has already accomplished his salvation in *the resurrection of Jesus Christ from the dead.*

The resurrection of Jesus was a life-changing reality for Peter. When Jesus died on the cross, it was the end of all Peter's hopes. He knew only bitter sorrow for his own denials. The dawn could not bring hope; with the crowing of the cock he heard the echo of his curses.

But Jesus did not stay dead. On that Easter morning Peter learned from the women of the empty tomb and the message of the angels. He went running to the tomb and saw its evidence. He left in wonder, but Jesus remembered Peter and appeared to him even before he came to eat with the disciples in the upper room. Hope was reborn in Peter's heart with the sight of his living Lord. Now Peter writes to praise God for that *living hope*. The resurrection did much more than restore his Master to him. The resurrection crowned the victory of Christ, his victory for Peter, and for those to whom he writes. The resurrection shows that God has made the Crucified both Lord and Christ.[1] At the right hand of the Father Jesus rules until the day that he will come to restore and renew all things.[2] With the resurrection of Jesus and his entrance into glory, a new age has begun.[3] Peter now waits for the day when Jesus will be revealed from heaven (1:7, 13). Peter's living hope is Jesus.

Praise be to the God and Father of our Lord Jesus Christ! Peter blesses God, rejoicing in what he has done. He uses a form of praise to God that was an important part of worship

---

[1] Acts 2:36.
[2] Acts 2:33–35; 3:21.
[3] The 'new age' of Christ's heavenly authority is the antithesis of the occult 'New Age' movement that would substitute theosophy and paganism for the gospel.

in the Old Testament.[1] The eighteen 'blessings' that we know from the later synagogue service go back to early times, perhaps in some form even to Peter's day. Those blessings look forward to the fulfilment of the promises of God, yearning for the time of realization:

> Speedily cause the offspring of David, Thy servant, to flourish, and let his horn be exalted by thy salvation, because we wait for Thy salvation all the day. Blessed art Thou, O Lord, who causest the horn of salvation to flourish.[2]

How different from the plaintive longing of that benediction is the astonished joy of the apostle Peter! Peter can bless the God and Father of his Lord, Jesus Christ. He can exult in the Offspring of David, raised up in salvation to the throne. God's promises have all come true in Christ. There is more to come, for Christ is to come, but our living hope is real in our living Lord.

Christ's resurrection spells hope for us not just because he lives, but because, by God's mercy, we live. *In his great mercy he has given us new birth into a living hope through the resurrection of Jesus Christ from the dead.* By the resurrection of Christ, God has given life, not only to him, but to us. We are given new birth by God; he fathers us by the resurrection of his Son. In Christ's triumph God makes all things new, beginning with us.

The resurrection carried Christ not only out of the grave but to his Father's throne. The great day of the renewal of all things had already begun. Yet Peter preached that heaven must receive Christ until the time of renewal, a time still to come.[3] The time of new birth for the universe will come when Christ comes again. But for those united to Christ in his death and resurrection, that new day has already dawned.

When we speak of the *new birth*, we think of the change

[1] Gn. 9:26; 14:20; 24:27; Ex. 18:10; 1 Ki. 8:15, 56; Ps. 18:46; 28:6; 31:21; 41:13; 66:20; *etc.*; Dn. 3:28; *cf.* Lk. 1:68. God's blessing of man declares his favour towards the one who is blessed. Man's blessing of God cannot grant favour to God, but seeks God's favour towards himself. 'Hallowed be your name' is a blessing in this sense. We ask God to lift up his own name, to be what he is.
[2] *Prayer Book, Abridged for Jews in the Armed Forces of the United States* (National Jewish Welfare Board, 1943), Morning Service, p. 158. See the citation and comment in Bénétreau, p. 83.
[3] Acts 3:21. Note Mt. 19:27f.

that God's grace works in us. We are brought from death to life. Peter speaks of our being born of imperishable seed through the living word of God that was preached to us (1:23–25). But if we think only of what happens to us, we may be puzzled by the statement that we are given *new birth* by the *resurrection of Jesus Christ*. The means of our new birth is not first the *message* of the resurrection; it is the *fact* of the resurrection. When Christ rose he secured our salvation. He entered that new day of which the prophets spoke, and he brought us with him. Peter is saying what Paul also declared: when Christ rose, we rose. In giving life to Christ, God gave life to all those who are united to Christ.[1] God's elect have a hope that is as sure as Christ's resurrection. Christ has not just made their salvation possible; he has made it sure.

Like Paul, Peter also speaks of baptism as the sign of our union with Christ in his death and resurrection (3:21).[2] Some commentators would see this passage, or indeed the whole letter, as instruction given in a service for baptism. But Peter does not in the least focus on the sign, but on the spiritual reality of our new life in Christ. His teaching is beautifully appropriate for baptismal instruction, but gives no real evidence of being designed for this specific purpose, far less limited to it.[3]

The Father, who gives new birth to his children through the resurrection of Christ, also through Christ brings them to a living faith (1:5; 3:21). Our faith and hope are in God; his living word, the good news of the gospel, has brought life to us (1:23). The things to which believers in Old Testament times looked forward have now happened (1:12).

Yet we, too, look to the future. The salvation that was sealed by Christ's resurrection and planted in our hearts by the seed of the Word will be revealed completely when Christ comes again in glory. Our hope is anchored in the past: Jesus rose! Our hope remains in the present: Jesus lives! Our hope is completed in the future: Jesus is coming! (1:5, 7, 13).

[1] Col. 3:1–4; Rom. 6:1–11; Eph. 2:4f.; Tit. 3:5.
[2] Rom. 6:3–5; Gal. 3:27.
[3] For relating 1 Peter to baptism see the commentaries of Grudem, Kelly, Carrington, and Selwyn. Bénétreau gives a brief summary in his commentary, pp. 16–17. Kelly shows the distinctiveness of the NT doctrine of the new birth and the decisive role of the teaching of Jesus in shaping it (pp. 48–50).

The apostle leads us to praise God that our salvation is his work. We could not even begin to accomplish it, and we do not in any sense deserve it. Yet, as trophies of God's grace, we have the privilege of adoring the Father of our Lord Jesus as *our* Father. Peter's praise is not a mere formula; praise is the goal of God's gracious work, as Peter later reminds us (2:9).

2. God maintains our hope: our inheritance (1:4–5)

... and into an inheritance that can never perish, spoil or fade – kept in heaven for you, 5who through faith are shielded by God's power until the coming of the salvation that is ready to be revealed in the last time.

As those given birth by God, we also receive our *inheritance* from him. That inheritance is *kept* for us, and we are kept for it. We may sometimes envy those whose financial future seems secure because of their birth. Sons or daughters of a wealthy family, they are heirs of a fortune. Peter had heard Jesus teach about a better treasure stored in heaven; no moths are there to eat the robes of glory, no rust can corrode the crowns of gold, and no thieves can break into the city of God.[1]

Peter, however, is speaking not simply of our treasure, but of our *inheritance*. God gave the land to Israel as an inheritance, and in the land he gave every tribe and family an inheritance, with the lasting right of ownership.[2] While they wandered in the wilderness, they were sustained by the promise of their inheritance. Like Israel in the wilderness, the New Testament people of God are aliens and pilgrims. They make their way through a world that is becoming more hostile. Yet they are not wandering beggars, cast off from their possessions. They hold a sure title to the inheritance God has given them.

Our hope is sure, for nothing can happen to our inheritance. The words that Peter uses to describe our unchangeable inheritance all relate to the land that was the inheritance of Israel. First, our inheritance *can never perish (aphtharton).*

[1] Mt. 6:19.
[2] Gn. 17:8; 28:4; Dt. 1:8; 30:3–5; Ps. 79:1. See Beare, pp. 56f.

The land of Israel was at times ravaged and destroyed by invading armies. The prophet Isaiah describes the utter destruction of the whole world in God's judgment:

> The earth will be completely laid waste
> and totally plundered.
> The Lord has spoken this word.
> The earth dries up and withers,
> the world languishes and withers . . .[1]

In the Septuagint version of Isaiah, the word-stem for 'laid waste' and 'wither' is the same that Peter uses. But Peter uses the word in a negative form. The world will be destroyed, but our inheritance is indestructible.[2]

Secondly, Peter says that our inheritance *can never... spoil* (or is 'undefiled', RSV). Isaiah, just quoted, goes on to tell how people have defiled the earth by breaking God's law. In the prophecy of Jeremiah, too, God declares that he gave Israel a fertile land, 'But you came and defiled my land and made my inheritance detestable.'[3] The land of Canaan, Israel's inheritance, was defiled first by heathen inhabitants, then by Israel's idolatry. In total contrast, the inheritance we have is undefiled and undefilable.

Thirdly, our inheritance is perennial. It will not *fade*, wither or dry up. Canaan was not only destroyed by invaders and polluted by its inhabitants; it was also parched with drought in God's judgment.[4] Isaiah reflects on the judgments of God that cause the land and its inhabitants to wither like grass or flowers: 'The grass withers and the flowers fall, but the word of our God stands for ever.'[5] Peter quotes that passage at the end of this chapter, and in that context again uses *aphtharton*, the first word of this series (1:23).

Canaan as the inheritance of Israel is contrasted with our inheritance. Israel received the earthly foreshadowing; we

---

[1] Is. 24:3–4, *cf.* v. 1. See Selwyn, p. 124.

[2] Peter reverses the term by using it with the negative prefix *a-*. The word is *aphtharton*.

[3] Je. 2:7. Again the word for *defile* is reversed by Peter in the term *amianton*. Israel defiled the land by idolatry and sexual vices (Je. 3:2; Ezk. 20:43; Hg. 2:14).

[4] Je. 23:10; Joel 1:12, 10. The verb form of the word that Peter uses (without its privative *a-*) is found in the LXX of Jb. 15:30; 24:24 to describe the withering of flowers and herbs.

[5] Is. 40:8.

receive the heavenly fulfilment. Because our inheritance is in heaven, nothing on earth can alter or destroy it. Peter must use negative terms to describe it ('imperishable', 'undefiled', 'unfading'; 1:4, RSV) because its reality surpasses our present comprehension. In John's vision it can be seen as the city of God, but the language is still symbolic. Our inheritance is not simply a land, a city, or even a new earth. It is all that God will give us; his *salvation.*

God has prepared his salvation for us (1:5). The term *ready* suggests that there need be no delay. Our inheritance will be revealed at the last day, but God has it ready for us now. It is finished. Nothing need be added to God's preparation. The salvation that God has got ready does not need a few final touches from us, nor are we called to serve as consultants in designing God's plan. God's salvation, finished, perfect, and unchangeable, is kept for us by God himself. Unlike our utopian dreams, or the fantasies of science fiction, God's plan for the future is already a reality. As pilgrims we travel to the city of God, but we know that the city to come is the city that comes to us with Jesus Christ. Indeed, our final inheritance is not merely kept by God; it actually is the Lord himself. God said to Aaron, 'You will have no inheritance in their land, nor will you have any share among them; I am your share and your inheritance among the Israelites.'[1] God claims his people as his inheritance and gives himself as their inheritance.[2]

Not only is our inheritance kept for us; we are kept for our inheritance. It would be small comfort to know that nothing could destroy our heavenly inheritance if we could lose it at last. The wonder of our hope is that the same *power* of God that keeps our inheritance also keeps us. We *are shielded* until the great day when our salvation will be revealed. The word *shielded* means 'kept under guard'. It is used of protective custody. God has put us under arrest, as it were, to keep us safe for his day.[3] Pilgrims we may be, but the cloud of God's power that leads us in the way

[1] Nu. 18:20; *cf.* Ps. 16:5.

[2] Dt. 32:9; Je. 10:16; 51:19; Ps. 73:26; 16:5. As the Old Testament unfolds, the distinctive inheritance of Aaron and Levi becomes the inheritance of all the true Israel.

[3] *Phroureō* is used in this sense in Gal. 3:23. The gates of Damascus were guarded to keep Paul in (2 Cor. 11:32). See BAGD, p. 867.

becomes a wall of fire about us.

Salvation is God's work. He and he alone is the Saviour.[1] He delivered Israel from Egypt in the Old Testament model of salvation. Hemmed in by the armies of Pharaoh at the Red Sea, the freed Israelites were told to stand firm and see the salvation of God.[2] God's salvation was more than his mighty acts of deliverance; he brought Israel out of Egypt to bring them to himself. Salvation meant that he would be their God and they his people. That promise became the ground of the prophetic message. Israel had sinned, but God would do a yet greater work of salvation in the future. He would deliver his people not only from their enemies, but from their sins.[3] God their Saviour would come and lead them as of old through the desert.[4] He would come with the coming of the Messiah.[5]

Peter preaches the fulfilment of that promise. The salvation that the prophets anticipated is the grace that Christians have now received (1:10–11). Yet Christians still await the salvation to come. Complete as salvation is, ready as it is, even experienced as it is, it still has a glorious future. *In the last time* it will be *revealed* when Jesus Christ is revealed. Our salvation is our inheritance, the full glory of being with the Lord for ever.

We are kept, however, *through faith*. Peter has described God's saving work for us. God keeps his finished salvation for us, and us for his salvation. But he does not keep us in a cage, or against our will. God who works for us also works in us. Our faith is his way of keeping us; it is his gift. Why does God use faith as the instrument of his keeping power? Because faith is not our achievement, but trust in God's achievement; 'your faith and hope are in God' (1:21). Peter writes to those who have not seen the Lord, but who rejoice with him in what the Lord has done. They already begin to receive what will be theirs when Christ comes, the goal of their faith, the salvation of their souls (1:9).

---

[1] Ho. 13:4; Is. 43:11; 45:21.   [2] Ex. 14:13.   [3] Mi. 7:17–19.
[4] Is. 40:3–5; 43:14–16; 48:20f.; 51:9f.
[5] Is. 9:6; 49:1–6; Zc. 12:8; Mal. 3:1–2.

3. Joy through trials in Christ our hope (1:6–9)

In this you greatly rejoice, though now for a little while you may have had to suffer grief in all kinds of trials. ⁷These have come so that your faith – of greater worth than gold, which perishes even though refined by fire – may be proved genuine and may result in praise, glory and honour when Jesus Christ is revealed. ⁸Though you have not seen him, you love him; and even though you do not see him now, you believe in him and are filled with inexpressible and glorious joy, ⁹for you are receiving the goal of your faith, the salvation of your souls.

Reflection on what God has done for us fills us with exultant joy. *In this you greatly rejoice.* The text could also be translated, '. . . in *whom* you greatly rejoice'. Since Peter uses the same verb in verse 8 to describe our joy in Christ, it is possible that he is thinking, not just of all the blessings we have in Christ, but of Christ in whom we have the blessings.[1]

Dramatically, Peter moves from ecstasy to agony. We who *rejoice* in Christ *suffer grief in all kinds of trials.* No doubt Peter thinks not only of suffering Christians, but of Christ himself. Peter well knew how Jesus had been put to grief (2:21–22). Yet because of his grief we have joy, even in suffering.

Peter is now dealing with the heart of his concern in writing this letter. He wants to assure Christians of their hope as they face trials. He now gives four reasons why we can not only endure trials, but rejoice in hope in the midst of trials. The first reason is that our hope in Christ points us beyond the trials. Our troubles last only for a little while; our hope in Christ is for ever. Peter returns to this theme when he writes the conclusion of the letter (5:10). Jesus himself endured the cross and despised the shame because of the joy that was set before him.[2]

Not only does our joy point beyond grief. In the second

---

[1] Some commentators link the phrase 'in this' (1:6) to 'the last time' (1:5) and understand the rejoicing that Peter describes to be the joy of the last day. Most understand the rejoicing to be in the blessings described in vv. 3–5. The verb 'rejoice' could be translated as an imperative, but the indicative fits the form of the passage and the theme of Peter – our future joy is already present. See Bénétreau, pp. 88–89. For the thought of inexpressible joy, see Rom. 8:26; Is. 44:4; 1 Cor. 2:9.
[2] Heb. 12:2.

place, it is actually strengthened through the very sufferings that we endure. Peter has declared that God keeps us for glory by faith. Our faith, then, must continue to the end of our life-long pilgrimage. If our faith is to endure, it must be purified and stress-tested. Like *gold* it must pass through the furnace (verse 7). Trials should not surprise us, or cause us to doubt God's faithfulness. Rather, we should actually be glad for them. God sends trials to strengthen our trust in him so that our faith will not fail. Our trials keep us trusting; they burn away our self-confidence and drive us to our Saviour. The fires of affliction or persecution will not reduce our faith to ashes. *Fire* does not destroy gold: it only removes combustible impurities. Yet even gold will at last vanish with the whole of this created order. Faith is infinitely more precious and more enduring. Like a jeweller putting his most precious metal in the crucible, so God proves us in the furnace of trial and affliction. The genuineness of our faith shines from the fire to his praise.[1]

A third reason joins joy to suffering. We know that when Jesus comes, he will bring far more than an end to suffering; he will bring his reward of blessing. Our trials are never forgotten by the Lord; he keeps our tears in his bottle.[2] Paul says that 'our light and momentary troubles are achieving for us an eternal glory that far outweighs them all'.[3] Our present sufferings cannot be compared to the glory that will be revealed in us.[4] Peter, too, speaks of the crown of glory that does not fade away, that we will receive when Christ comes (5:4). Our faith will then be found to be precious, for by it we (and he) will receive *praise, glory and honour* (1:7).[5] Peter

[1] The NIV gives the sense of verse 7 well: *that your faith ... may be proved genuine and may result in praise. Dokimion* means 'genuineness' rather that 'proof'. It is the genuineness of our faith that will be found to praise and glory. See BAGD, p. 203:, Selwyn, p. 129.

[2] Ps. 56:8.   [3] 2 Cor. 4:17.   [4] Rom. 8:18.

[5] Praise, glory and honour are normally ascribed to God in Scripture (1 Tim. 1:17). Peter affirms the glory of God as the final goal of all our service (4:11). He says that we have been made a nation of priests to show forth his excellencies (2:9). Jesus will be revealed in glory (4:13; Heb. 2:9). But we will share in the revealed glory of Christ (5:1), and will receive an unfading crown of glory (5:4). It would seem, therefore, that we are to understand the *praise, glory and honour* as the grace that we receive at Christ's revelation (1:13; Rom 2:7). Since this is a sharing in Christ's glory, however, the thought of all praise being directed to God is essential to the passage. See Selwyn, p. 130; Bénétreau, p. 90 and Excursus, 'Joie et souffrances pour Dieu', pp. 259–263.

saw the glory of the Lord when he was transfigured on the mountain; he heard the promise of his return as he ascended in the clouds.[1] He knows that the end of all things is near; judgment is already beginning for the people of God. The day of God when the universe will be remade is the day of the Lord Jesus, the day when he will be *revealed*.[2] That day brings terror to those who do not know the Lord, but joy beyond expression to those who love him.

In the fourth place, the supreme reason for joining joy to suffering comes into view. That reason goes beyond even the glory that we will receive from the hand of the Lord. For, of course, our tested faith does not *earn* the glory that will be given to us. We receive glory as we share in Christ's glory. Indeed, it is not even certain that Peter is speaking of the *praise, glory and honour* that we receive. He may be referring to the praise *God* receives from our proven faith.[3] We seek in all things that God may be glorified (4:11). If we receive crowns of glory, it will be our joy to cast them at the feet of the Saviour.[4]

When Jesus Christ is revealed, the gold of our faith will shine to his praise. The whole nature of suffering is changed for the Christian when he realizes that his anguish brings honour to Christ. The Museum of the Desert in the Cevennes mountains of southern France commemorates the sufferings of the Huguenot martyrs. When Louis XIV revoked the Edict of Nantes in 1685, Protestant public worship was made a crime. Men caught at secret worship services in the fields were sent to the galleys. Chained to a rowing bench, they slaved at the oars until they died. A replica of one of the great galley oars hangs in the museum today. Underneath is a model of a galley. Beside it are inscribed the words of a Reformed Christian galley slave: 'My chains are the chains of Christ's love.'

Peter reflects on the love that his readers have for Christ, love that makes them ready to suffer so that their proven faith can be his tribute. *Though you have not seen him, you love him*. Peter, of course, had seen the Lord. His love for Jesus could bring pictures to mind: Jesus in Capernaum, being served supper by Peter's mother-in-law, cured of her

---

[1] Mk. 9:2–8; Acts 1:11.   [2] 1 Pet. 4:7,17; 2 Pet. 3:10, 12.
[3] 2 Thes. 1:10.   [4] Rev. 4:10.

fever; Jesus on the sea, lifting Peter from the water – 'You of little faith, why are you so afraid?'; Jesus in the hall of the high priest, looking at Peter after his denials; Jesus on the cross; Jesus, alive again, sitting by the coals of a fire on the shore of the Lake of Galilee – 'Simon son of John, do you truly love me more than these?'

Peter had seen Jesus, and loved him. Does it amaze him that distant and scattered Gentiles who have never seen Jesus also know and love him? Peter well knows that it is not his physical association with Jesus that joins him to his Saviour. He knows Jesus as the Son of God by the gift of the Father in heaven. He realizes that Gentiles, too, have received the Spirit.[1] By faith we Gentiles who have never seen Jesus may share with Peter in loving him. It is not necessary for us to have been in Galilee with Jesus. Through the witness of Peter and the other apostles we learn about what Jesus said and did. They bear witness through the Holy Spirit, and by the witness of the Spirit we are brought to know and love the living Lord.

We did not see Jesus; we do not now see Jesus; but we shall see Jesus. Peter contrasts the past and the present with the future (1:8). The day is coming when Jesus will be revealed. In that day the goal of our faith will be realized. Our eyes will behold the One we have trusted and loved.

Peter's expressions march forward: *You have not seen* Jesus, but *you love him*; *you do not see* Jesus, but *you believe in him*; you will see Jesus and rejoice in him. But notice the change that Peter makes. He says that *you . . . are* (present tense) *filled with an inexpressible and glorious joy.*[2] Not only do we have faith in Jesus and love for Jesus now; we also know already the joy that we will experience when we see him. Such is the faith and hope of those who know Jesus. The salvation of our souls in the last day is the goal of our faith. We wait for the salvation that Christ will bring with him at his appearing. Yet we are already experiencing that salvation. This apparent paradox forms the warp and woof of New Testament hope. Because Jesus has already come, in the flesh and in the Holy Spirit, the kingdom of God has already come. Our hope is realized: we know Jesus. But

[1] Acts 15:8.
[2] Literally, 'You rejoice with joy inexpressible and glorified.'

because Jesus is coming again, the kingdom of God is yet to come, and the goal of our faith is still future. Christians live in a future that is already present, not just in imagination or expectation, but in realization: the reality of Christ's presence in the Spirit.

4. God's promises of hope are fulfilled in Christ (1:10–12)

Concerning this salvation, the prophets, who spoke of the grace that was to come to you, searched intently and with the greatest care, 11 trying to find out the time and circumstances to which the Spirit of Christ in them was pointing when he predicted the sufferings of Christ and the glories that would follow. 12It was revealed to them that they were not serving themselves but you, when they spoke of the things that have now been told you by those who preached the gospel to you by the Holy Spirit sent from heaven. Even angels long to look into these things.

Sufferings now, *glories* to follow. Peter wants to encourage Christians who face the first to look for the second. He has pointed our hope to the glory of Christ, and to his return. Now he would have us remember that the Christ of glory is the Christ of the cross. The sequence of our lives follows the sequence of Christ's life. He suffered first, then entered into his glory. So must we. Jesus understood that order well. It was the pattern predicted for the Messiah in the Old Testament.[1] After Peter's confession, Jesus had plainly predicted his betrayal, sufferings and death. Peter had protested violently, 'Never, Lord! This shall never happen to you!'[2] Jesus

[1] This exposition assumes that the sufferings and glory of Christ are spoken of in v. 11 as the subject of prophecy. Selwyn argues that the prophets are NT prophets, and that they predicted sufferings *for* Christ, the woes to precede the glory at the end (pp. 262ff.). The phrase *eis Christon* can readily be translated 'for Christ,' but may mean 'of Christ' (BAGD, pp. 229–30). The same prepositional construction is used earlier in v. 10. The prophets told of 'the grace *unto you*'. This seems to explain the repeated phrase. Grace is prophesied for us (meant for us); sufferings are prophesied for Christ (meant for him). In the whole passage the vision of the prophets is identified with the gospel preached by the apostles (v. 12). The prediction of sufferings and glory for Christians cannot support this identification. The mystery that angels desire to look into is not the fate of Christians, but the mystery of Christ, foreknown from the foundation of the world (1:20).
[2] Mt. 16:22.

told Peter that his response was from Satan, but Peter had continued to resist the thought that Jesus must suffer. Peter could rejoice in the glory of Christ on the mount of transfiguration, but he had failed to understand why Moses and Elijah had there talked with Jesus about his death – the death he must accomplish before he entered the glory that was his. In the night arrest in Gethsemane, Peter had drawn his sword to rescue Jesus from suffering.

Peter's misunderstanding was shared by the other disciples. On the very day of Christ's resurrection, two disciples were returning to Emmaus confused and dismayed because Jesus had been crucified. On the road Jesus joined them; before he made himself known to them, he taught them from the whole Old Testament that the Messiah must first suffer and then enter his glory.[1] It was from the risen Lord himself that the apostles learned how Christ's suffering and glory fulfilled the Scripture. They proclaimed that message in the apostolic gospel.[2]

Glory is the goal of the Old Testament promises. From the first oracle in the garden of Eden, God promised victory over the serpent through the Son of the woman.[3] Peter, preaching after Pentecost, declared that Christ would remain in heaven until his coming again when 'the time comes for God to restore everything, as he promised long ago through his holy prophets'.[4]

Even a casual reading of the Old Testament prophets reminds us of their vision of glory. That vision stands out against the history of Israel. God promised Abraham that his descendants would be blessed, and would be a blessing to the nations. God did redeem and bless Israel. Solomon could say, when the temple was dedicated, that all God's promises of blessing had been kept. He looked for the nations to be drawn to pray at God's temple, and asked God to hear those prayers.[5] But the glory that filled Solomon's temple did not remain. Solomon himself turned his back on the house of God to dedicate a shrine to Chemosh on the Mount of Olives. Idolatry brought God's judgment: the glory departed from the house of the Lord. Where the glory cloud had rested, the smoke of destruction pillared upward.

---

[1] Lk. 24:25–27. [2] Acts 17:3. [3] Gn. 3:15.
[4] Acts 3:21. [5] 1 Ki. 8:56, 41–43.

Israel in the north, then Judah in the south, went into captivity.

The message of the prophets pronounces God's judgment on the sin of his people, but it does not stop with judgment. The final vision of the Old Testament is not of dry bones in death valley.[1] Rather, it is renewal beyond conceiving. The prophets picture the restoration of all that had been lost: the land, the temple, the sacrifices, the priesthood.[2] But the restoration does not look back to recover the past; it looks forward to God's final renewal. God's fulfilment will transform everything. Not only will the remnant of Judah and Israel be gathered, but the remnant of the Gentiles will be gathered with them.[3] Not just Israel, but Egypt and Assyria will be called the people of God.[4] Eden will be restored, and more: God will make a new creation where peace will be universal and darkness will be gone.[5]

This incredible glory can come only because the God of glory will come. The Lord God will appear in order to save his people and renew creation.[6] The coming of the Lord is joined to the coming of the Angel of the Lord, and to the coming of the Messiah, the Servant of the Lord.[7] On the mount of transfiguration Peter saw the glory of the Lord shine from the face of Jesus, the Son and Servant of God. Now Peter looks for the return of Christ in glory to finish his fulfilment of the promise of the prophets.

The Old Testament also describes the sufferings of the Messiah, the Servant of the Lord. In the Psalms we hear the cry of the righteous servant as the reproaches directed against God fall on him.[8] David's wanderings to escape Saul's jealous fury become a symbol of the innocent suffering of the Lord's anointed. The prophets themselves suffer for their faithful proclamation of the word of the Lord.[9] The prophets show, too, that the animal sacrifices of the ceremonial law cannot

[1] Ezk. 37. [2] Is. 2:2–4; 56:7; Ezk. 40:2; 44:9–31; Je. 33:18.
[3] Is. 2:2–4; 56:6–8; Mi. 4:1–3. [4] Is. 19:19–25; 66:21; Zc. 14:16–20.
[5] Is. 11:6–9; 30:26; 35:9; 60:20; 65:17; 66:22.
[6] Is. 35:1–10; 40:3, 10, 30; 60:1, 20; Zc. 14:16.
[7] Is. 9:6; Zc. 13:8; Mal. 3:1–2; Is. 40 – 42; Ezk. 34:11, 23. *Cf.* Pss. 2; 45; 72; 110.
[8] Pss. 69:9; 22:1–21; 57:4, 6; 59:3–4.
[9] Elijah, himself a resident alien, suffers for the word (1 Ki. 17:1; 18:17; 19:2); so does Jeremiah (15:10), and most of the prophets (Mt. 21:35–36; 23:31, 37; Acts 7:52).

make final atonement for sin. There must be a better sacrifice, a sacrifice God will provide; not the ram caught by its horns on Mount Moriah, but the willing offering of the Servant of the Lord, whose soul will be an offering for sin.[1] Suffering precedes glory because the precious blood of the Lamb of God opens glory for believers.[2]

The pattern of sufferings and glory has profound meaning for the church. Job's anguished accusations from the ashes have an astonishing answer. Our suffering is not a sign that Christ has betrayed us, or that he is no longer Lord; rather it is a sign of our fellowship with the risen Lord who first suffered for us. Suffering, indeed, becomes a sign of the glory that is to follow. But Peter is not announcing a general principle that those who look for reward must be prepared to pay in suffering. The prophets did not enunciate a principle: they predicted the sufferings and glory of the one who is himself the Lord. Christ is the end of prophecy, the goal of history. He is not one example of sufferings and glory among many; his is the suffering that brought salvation, his is the glory that brings the new creation. Jesus is therefore not simply the one of whom the prophets speak; he is the one who speaks through the prophets. The prophets spoke as they were moved by the Holy Spirit.[3] The Spirit of God who inspired them is the Spirit of Christ. 'The testimony of Jesus is the spirit of prophecy.'[4] Not only does prophecy bear witness to Jesus, but Jesus bears witness through prophecy. The incarnate Lord is the true witness; the eternal Logos is the source of the prophetic testimony.

Peter knows that his Lord is the Son of the living God; he understands that the Spirit that filled him at Pentecost was sent from the throne of glory. That Spirit of Christ illumined him, fisherman that he was, to preach what the rabbis had missed: the Old Testament witness to Christ's resurrection. Now his understanding sweeps back to the prophecies that the Spirit interpreted for him. They were prophecies given by the same Spirit, the Spirit of the Son of God. Peter opens our eyes to see Christ in the Old Testament not only as the promised Messiah, but as the Lord. The Spirit that was fire in the bones of the prophets was the Spirit of Christ, driving

[1] Ho. 6:6; Is. 1:11–17; Gn. 22:13–14; Is. 52:13 – 53:12.
[2] 1 Pet. 1:2, 19; 2:24.   [3] 2 Pet. 1:21.   [4] Rev. 19:10.

forward to the salvation he must bring. 'The lion has roared – who will not fear? The Sovereign Lord has spoken – who can but prophesy? ' The Lion of the tribe of Judah who opens the seals of the book of God's decrees is the Lion who thunders in the voice of the prophets.[1]

The same Spirit of Christ, sent from his ascended glory, now fills the apostles who preach the prophecies come true.[2] One Lord through the ages, one great plan of salvation, one revealed message, heralded by the prophets of old and now announced by the apostles of Christ – all is focused on the lordship of Jesus Christ. Peter's thrilling witness to one Lord and one scriptural gospel was attacked by Marcion in the second century. For Marcion the God of the Old Testament was a tyrant to be replaced by the God of love. Many since Marcion have missed what Peter teaches: both Testaments bear witness *to* Christ; both are the witness *of* Christ.

Peter presents one community of the people of God as well as one gospel. The Spirit of Christ did not inspire the prophets apart from their own involvement in the message. Their prophecies excited their own hopes; they yearned for fuller and clearer revelation. They sought to interpret the oracles they received, inquiring into the time when God's great salvation would come.[3] But the full meaning of their prophecies could not appear until Christ appeared. Peter could well remember the marvelling conversation of Moses and Elijah with Jesus when they stood with him on the mountain.[4] God's plan was amazing beyond comprehension. The prophets ministered mysteries still hidden from them and their own generation; they ministered those marvels to us, as they spoke of the things of Christ.

Peter is not saying that the prophets had no ministry to their own time, or that they spoke in inspired riddles that made no sense to them or to their hearers. The very diligence of their search for better understanding shows how the prophecies challenged and intrigued them. What Peter is eager to point out is that his hearers are the heirs of the full message of the prophets. The least disciple of Christ is in a better position to understand Old Testament revelation than

[1] Am. 3:8; Rev. 5:5.
[2] 1 Pet. 1:12; Jn. 15:26; 16:14; Acts 2:33.
[3] Dn. 9:2; 12:4.   [4] Lk. 9:30–31.

the greatest prophet before Christ came.[1]

Indeed, suffering Christians have the advantage not only over the prophets. The very angels of heaven peer into the mysteries of salvation that are revealed by the Spirit to those who are redeemed by Jesus Christ. The verb Peter uses well describes the action of straining to see: angels peering, as it were, over the battlements of heaven to behold what God has done in Jesus Christ. Paul reminds us that the apostles were set forth as a spectacle to angels as well as to humans.[2] The cosmic sweep of God's redemption is all centred in Christ, whom we know and love. The petty dreams of earth's little tyrants shrivel before the majesty of the kingdom of God, ministered by prophets and apostles, but now realized for those who know Jesus Christ.

[1] Mt. 11:11.   [2] 1 Cor. 4:9.

3. Live obediently in hope

1. Hope is ready (1:13)

Therefore, prepare your minds for action; be self-controlled; set your hope fully on the grace to be given you when Jesus Christ is revealed.

The imperatives of Christian living always begin with 'therefore.' Peter does not begin to exhort Christian pilgrims until he has celebrated the wonders of God's salvation in Jesus Christ. The indicative of what God had done for us (and in us) precedes the imperative of what we are called to do for him. 'Without the indicative of what God does, the imperative is addressed to a helpless sinner, the victim of his illusions; it becomes a commandment that crushes or that drives to vain and presumptuous efforts.'[1] Our hope is God's gift, an inheritance created for us by Christ's resurrection (1:3). Because we have been given hope, we are called to live in it.

Peter's exhortations continue through his letter. Yet he also continues to remind us of the reality of redemption that underlies his call to obedience. In the rest of this chapter he summons us to the obedience of hope, hope that is marked by readiness and holiness.

Set your hope fully, he says. The form of this imperative suggests a clear-cut, decisive action.[2] The force of the command is heightened by the adverb *fully* or 'firmly.' Since

[1] Bénétreau, p. 99.
[2] An aorist imperative describes a specific action or the beginning of an action in distinction from the ongoing action of the present imperative. The present is therefore more usual in general ethical commands (BDF, p. 337).

61

our hope is sure, we can bank on it. It is not so much an attitude to be cultivated as a reality to be recognized. To set our hope is to believe the gospel. Our faith and hope are in God (1:21). We cannot first improve our skill in hoping and then direct our more hopeful attitude toward God. Hope moves the other way. It is our response to God's work. We look to God, hear his word of promise, see his salvation in Christ, and fix our hope on him. Peter makes this clear by defining again the object of our hope. It is the grace that is being brought to us at the revelation of Jesus Christ. To fix our hope is to fix our gaze on the coming glory of Christ's appearing (4:13). The blessing (grace) of that day is future, but it is already arriving, for we already have a foretaste of what God will give us when Christ appears.[1]

The certainty of our hope has a remarkable effect on our lives. Hoping Christians cannot live carelessly, seeking self-indulgence and pleasure. *Prepare your minds for action:* literally, 'Gird up the loins of your mind.' The figure describes what a man wearing a long robe had to do if he were to go into action – gather the garment up between his legs and tuck it into his belt. Like Israel in Egypt, we have been called out of our slavery to begin a journey to the promised land. The Israelites were commanded to eat the passover, their last meal in Egypt, 'girded' for travel.[2] God calls his servants to be girded for mission; Elijah to run and Jeremiah to prophesy.[3] Peter may have been thinking especially of the words of Jesus, 'Let your loins be girded about, and your lamps burning; and be ye yourselves like men looking for their lord, when he shall return from the marriage feast; that, when he cometh and knocketh, they may straightway open unto him.'[4]

Jesus contrasted the watchful expectancy of the faithful servant with drunken indifference to the return of the Lord.[5] Peter makes the same contrast; we are to be sober, 'self-controlled', disciplined in mind. Sobriety, both literal and figurative, marks the Christian lifestyle (4:7; 5:8). Drunken stupor is the refuge of those who have no hope. But Christians who look for the coming of the Lord live in hope. They

[1] For 'grace' as 'blessing' in this expression, see Selwyn, p. 140.
[2] Ex. 12:11.   [3] 1 Ki. 18:46; Je. 1:17.   [4] Lk. 12:35–36, ASV.
[5] Lk. 12:45.

will not seek escape in the bottle, for they have tasted already of the Spirit of glory. Alive and alert, they look for the Lord.

To be sober is to be realistic. Drunkenness brings delusions before stupor sets in. The hallucinations of spiritual drunkenness are not amusing pink elephants, but devouring monsters; the ideologies of political oppression, the fantasies of sexual lust, the jealous hatreds of personal spite. The world seeks orgies of perversion before it sinks into the drunken stupor of hopelessness. Sober reflection is the opposite of the carousings of the old life in lustful inebriation (1:14). Sober watchfulness grows with the practice of prayer (4:7), and is alert to the assaults of the devil (5:8). Christian realism knows the actuality of sin and the folly of utopian dreams. Yet Christian sobriety is not joyless gloom, but glad hope in the new order to come with Christ. Peter had seen the Gadarene demoniac wild and naked on the shore. Jesus had cast out the demons, clothed him with his right mind and girded him to proclaim salvation in his own village.[1] Christian living needs order as well as ardour. Our joyful hope is expressed, not in mindless ecstasy, but in alert wisdom that seizes opportunities to serve the Lord.[2]

2. Hope is holy (1:14 – 2:3)

a. The holiness of children of the Father (1:14–17)

As obedient children, do not conform to the evil desires you had when you lived in ignorance. [15]*But just as he who called you is holy, so be holy in all you do;* [16]*for it is written: 'Be holy, because I am holy.'*

[17]*Since you call on a Father who judges each man's work impartially, live your lives as strangers here in reverent fear.*

The alert and disciplined mind of the Christian is fixed not simply on the coming event, but on him who will come, Jesus Christ, and on our Father God who calls us to himself. Because God calls us to stand before him, our hope brings accountability as well as triumph. Does not that accountability change our hope to dread? Can any sinner hope for

[1] Mk. 5:15.   [2] Eph. 5:15–18.

the day of judgment? Knowing that God will judge each person's work must surely inspire reverent fear, but does it not inspire much more – consuming terror? Who can stand before the throne of God?

The apostolic teaching about God's judgment has been misunderstood. On the one hand, some have considered that God's justifying grace must remove accountability to God in the day of judgment. They have therefore denied that the Christian will stand before God's judgment seat. On the other hand, many have affirmed accountability in the day of judgment, but have interpreted God's final verdict as justification by works added to an initial salvation by grace. No Christian could then be sure of heaven until the last judgment.[1]

The New Testament writers do not share the confusion of either error. The reality and finality of God's judgment are often affirmed; we are taught that Christ will be the Judge in that day.[2] At the same time we are told that God's verdict on us has already been pronounced; in Christ we are justified; we have passed from death to life. The Judge in the last day is our Saviour.[3] God's final judgment will glorify his justice; he will pronounce for all the redeemed the satisfaction of Christ's atoning death and the merit of his perfect obedience. Yet the faithfulness of the Lord's people will also be displayed, not as the basis of their acceptance, but to show the reality of their faith in the Saviour. To those who have been unfaithful, the Lord himself will declare the folly of their hypocritical confession: 'Then I will tell them plainly, "I never knew you. Away from me, you evildoers!" '[4] God's examination of his saints will also make evident the worthlessness of shoddy ministry. Heavenly reward will be proportionate to the faithfulness of the Lord's redeemed stewards.[5]

---

[1] This was at issue in the Protestant Reformation. The Roman Catholic teaching, defined at the Council of Trent, was that justifying grace could not be obtained by faith alone, could be lost, and was preserved or increased by good works. (The Council of Trent, 'On Justification', propositions anathematized, 9–24, in Henry Bettenson, *Documents of the Christian Church*, Oxford University Press, 1943, p. 368.)

[2] Mt. 16:27; Acts 10:42; Rom. 2:16; 14:10, 12; 2 Cor. 5:10; Eph. 6:8.

[3] Jn. 3:18, 36; 5:24; Rom. 8:33–34; 1 Pet. 1:3–5.

[4] Mt. 7:23; 25:41.   [5] 1 Cor. 3:13–15; Mt. 25:14–30.

Peter, therefore, does not call us to soul-destroying dread. The Judge is our Father, who has begotten us to be his children and given us a sure hope as heirs of his blessing. Yet Peter does call us to reverent fear. Our Father is the living God. He is holy: holy in the high mystery of his deity, holy in the perfection of his righteousness. Because he is holy, we too must be holy, for we are his people. Peter quotes a central passage from the old covenant.[1] Israel as the people of God were to be holy; they were separated from the nations by the presence of God in their midst. The purity that God's presence demanded was symbolized by elaborate ceremonies of washing and cleansing. Israel's soldiers, for example, were required to carry a shovel with their weapons. Hygiene in the camp honoured in symbol the presence of the Lord in their camp.[2]

Soiled flesh or clothing, however, served only to picture spiritual defilement. Israel was to be clean from idolatry and from the immoral practices of the Gentile nations.[3] Peter, on a housetop in Joppa, was shown that God's laws for ceremonial cleanness had been fulfilled in Christ. No longer were certain foods unclean, nor would Peter be defiled by eating with Gentiles.[4] Rather, the holiness of the true Israel was now to be seen in the fruits of an obedient life. Israel had been summoned to Sinai to enter into covenant with the Lord. They had vowed to obey him, to be his true and devoted people. Now Peter writes to those who have heard and heeded the call of the gospel. They are, literally, 'children of obedience'. This Hebrew form of expression is not the same as *obedient children*. It is an idiom describing those who are characterized by obedience, as though obedience were their parent.[5] The term for 'obedience' derives from the word for 'hearing'. Christians are those who have 'hearkened' to the gospel.[6] They have turned from sin to submit themselves to Christ as Lord and Saviour. Reverent submission to God furnishes the key to Peter's exhortations in this letter.

Coming to God as our holy Father means leaving the

---

[1] Lv. 19:2.   [2] Dt. 23:12–14.   [3] Lv. 18:1–5, 24–30; 19:3–4; 20:22–26.
[4] Acts 10:9–16.

[5] The word 'children' does not have any separate force in the idiom. See Selwyn, pp. 140f.

[6] Rom. 6:17; 10:16; 2 Thes. 1:8. The holiness of the people of God was shown by God's judgment on Ananias and Sapphira (Acts 5:1–11).

lifestyle handed down from our fathers (1:18). We cannot continue to follow the lusts that controlled us when we lived in ignorance of our Father in heaven (1:14). Peter with Paul describes the Gentiles as not knowing God, without hope and without God in the world.[1] When God is not acknowledged, a void is opened at the heart of life and culture (1:18). Into that void rush desires for power and sexual exploitation. Again Peter reflects the charge given to the Old Testament Israel: they were not to pattern their lives on the customs of the land of Egypt that they had left behind, nor on the customs of the land of Canaan that they were to enter.[2] Rather, they were to pattern their lives on God's commandments.

The murals of Pompeii reflect the decadence of the Gentile world of Peter's day. Hollywood still titillates viewers with images of Nero's saturnalian orgies. Contemporary Western culture seems to be overtaking the Roman world in moral decay. Pornographic magazines and video films, licentious music and dance forms, and sex-ridden advertising, have fed the 'flood of dissipation' that Peter describes (4:4). Perhaps more threatening is the 'power' philosophy of popular 'success' literature; a cynical appeal to selfish exploitation. Ruthlessness in climbing over others can be seen in arbitrageurs as well as in the blitzing tackles of American football. A dictators's grasp on power through torture and assassination only shows the mania openly.

Charles Colson describes an interview on American television. Mike Wallace was speaking with Yehiel Dinur, a concentration-camp survivor who testified against Adolf Eichmann at the Nuremberg trials. Wallace showed a film clip from the 1961 trial of this Nazi architect of the Holocaust. Colson describes the scene as Dinur walked into the courtroom to come face to face with the man who had sent him to Auschwitz eighteen years earlier.

> Dinur began to sob uncontrollably, then fainted, collapsing in a heap on the floor as the presiding judicial officer pounded his gavel for order in the crowded courtroom.

[1] Acts 17:23; Rom. 1:28; Eph. 2:12; Gal. 4:8; 1 Cor. 1:21; 1 Thes. 4:5; 2 Thes. 1:8.

[2] Lv. 18:1–5; Dt. 12:30–32.

Was Dinur overcome by hatred? Fear? Horrid memories?

No; it was none of these. Rather, as Dinur explained to Wallace, all at once he realized Eichmann was not the godlike army officer who had sent so many to their deaths. This Eichmann was an ordinary man. 'I was afraid about myself,' said Dinur. '. . . I saw that I am capable to do this. I am . . . exactly like him.'[1]

It is the reality of sin in the heart of everyone that patterns the evil and oppression in the world. Holiness means that the pattern is broken, that the sinner is transformed.

God himself becomes the model for the repatterning of our lives. We are to be imitators of God as beloved children; holy as he is holy, perfect as our Father in heaven is perfect.[2] *Be holy in all you do* (1:15). The pattern of holy living cannot be reduced to a limited number of 'holy' actions. God's righteous deeds flow from his holy nature; holiness patterned on his must express transformed hearts. On the one hand, this seems to set an impossible standard: how can we be like the holy God? On the other hand, there is a marvellous simplicity in a holiness patterned on God himself; it does not require encyclopedic grasp of endless directives and prohibitions. It flows from the heart; its key is love. To be holy is to love the Lord our God with heart, soul, strength and mind, and to love our neighbour as ourselves.[3] We imitate the love of grace that saved us, the love of God's compassion poured out in our hearts by the Holy Spirit.[4]

Peter had encountered the holiness of God in his fishing-boat. After a night of fruitless labour, he had cast his nets again at the word of Jesus. The catch had been miraculous; Peter had fallen down at the feet of Jesus: 'Go away from me, Lord; I am a sinful man!'[5] Kneeling amid the fish, Peter had recognized the Lord of creation, the Holy One. The holiness of the *lamb without blemish* (1:19) is the holiness of the Father revealed in the Son. To be holy is to sanctify Christ in our hearts as Lord.[6]

God's holy people are no longer at home in this world.

[1] Charles Colson, *Who Speaks for God?* (Crossway, 1985), p. 137.
[2] Eph. 5:1; Mt. 5:48; 1 Thes. 2:12.   [3] Lk. 10:27–28; Mt. 22:36–40.
[4] Mt. 5:44–48; Lk. 10:27, 33, 37; Rom 5:5; 1 Pet. 1:22–23.
[5] Lk. 5:8.   [6] 1 Pet. 3:15; 1:15.

They are *strangers*, residing in a land that is not their own.[1]
Their citizenship is in heaven.[2] Like Israel in exile, they pray
for the peace of the city where they live,[3] but their hearts are
in Jerusalem – the heavenly city of God.[4] In spite of their
humanness, Christians are 'extra-terrestrials' at heart. Or,
better, they are 'neo-terrestrials', representatives of the new
humanity in Jesus Christ.

The new Israel in exile has not been banished from the
house of God. They *live ... in reverent fear* of the Father.
Their lifestyle as a holy people is a witness to the nations.
Christians are therefore called to set about living as strangers
with a mission.[5] They are ambassadors on earth, revering
their Father in heaven.

Awe for the Father does not drive us away from him, but
draws us to his care and compassion. The role of the father
is so trivialized in our society that the thought of reverence
toward a father has become a novelty. As E. G. Selwyn
points out, however, 'in the hierarchy of Jewish society, the
father ranked higher, and was a more "numinous" figure,
than the judge; for it was the father's function *par excellence*
to command and teach, which was held to be a more august
function than the judge's giving rewards and punishment'.[6]

The One whom we call 'Abba, Father' is not only our
creator and judge; he is also our redeemer. He has given his
Son for us, as a lamb for the sacrifice (1:19). We may with
confidence call him Father, not only because the whole family
in heaven and on earth is named from him, but because he
has revealed the infinite reach of his compassion in the price

---

[1] The term for 'stranger' here differs from that in 1:1. It denotes those who live
in a place without holding citizenship (BAGD, '*paroikeō*,' pp. 628–629). It may be
contrasted with *parepidēmos*, a stranger passing through. The two may be joined,
however (Gn. 23:4, LXX; 1 Pet. 2:11). See Spicq, *Vie*, pp. 61–71.

[2] Heb. 11:9; Acts 13:17; Phil. 3:20; *cf.* Eph. 2:19. Abraham was a resident alien
in Canaan; Israel had that status in Egypt. The biblical pattern of Christian *paroikia*,
however, is that of the captivity in Babylon.

[3] Je. 29:5–7. Spicq, *Vie*, p. 66, n. 24, quotes a passage from Diodorus of Sicily
in which the resident aliens took part in the defence of a city.

[4] Ps. 137:5–6.

[5] The verb for *live your lives* has a form that implies setting about it. Peter later
makes explicit the witness that Christian living provides (2:9, 12).

[6] Selwyn, p. 142. He notes that in the 'Law of Holiness' (Lv. 19:3, quoted in
1 Pet. 1:16), the command to be holy is followed by, 'Ye shall fear every man his
mother, and his father.'

of our redemption.[1] The word that Peter uses for 'calling' is regularly used for formal appeals, and for calling by name.[2] Peter is clearly referring to our use of the name 'Father' as we appeal to him in prayer.

b. The holiness of redeemed believers (1:18–21)

For you know that it was not with perishable things such as silver or gold that you were redeemed from the empty way of life handed down to you from your forefathers, ⁴but with the precious blood of Christ, a lamb without blemish or defect. ⁵He was chosen before the creation of the world, but was revealed in these last times for your sake. ⁶Through him you believe in God, who raised him from the dead and glorified him, and so your faith and hope are in God.

Peter has encouraged us to holy living by pointing us to the Lord. Christ's coming spurs us on (1:13); the holiness of God gives us his pattern and his demand (1:14–16); the judgment of our Father fills us with fear, but a fear that calls on his name (1:17).

Now Peter comes to the heart of our salvation: how can we as sinners be drawn to the holiness of God? The answer is redemption. Unless God had made us his, we could not gain his holiness or want it. But God has claimed us as his own, claimed us at a cost that sears our minds with the flame of his love. Peter appeals to the two most profound emotions our hearts can know. One is love, love that sees the price God paid to redeem us. The other is fear, the fear of despising God's love. What judgment would we merit if we were to trample upon the blood of Christ, and treat God's precious ransom with contempt, the contempt that mere gold and silver would deserve in comparison? Remember Peter's response to the magician Simon who offered him money for the Holy Spirit: 'May your money perish with you, because you thought you could buy the gift of God with money!'[3]

The way in which Peter speaks of our redemption here shows how central it was to the apostolic gospel. Some have

---

[1] Eph. 3:14–19.
[2] Acts 25:11–12, 21, 25; 26:32; 28:19. *Cf.* 2 Cor. 1:23; Acts 22:16.
[3] Acts 8:20.

suggested that Peter is using credal or liturgical formulas in this passage. More probably any fixed form is rooted in apostolic preaching.[1]

In the Hellenistic world a slave might be redeemed by a payment made to his master, sometimes through a temple treasury.[2] The Old Testament law provided for the redemption of slaves, and noted the special privilege of a *gō'ēl*, a close relative who could redeem family members or possessions.[3] In the prophecy of Isaiah, God takes the role of the *gō'ēl* of his people. He makes himself 'next of kin' by the ties of his love. He assures his people that the Creator, the Holy One, is also their *gō'ēl*, and will exercise his right of redemption.[4] Peter makes this same connection. God, the Holy One, has bought back his people as his inheritance.

The price paid is not always in view when the Old Testament speaks of redemption. God's redeeming of Israel from Egypt refers to the bondage from which they were delivered and the liberty into which they were brought, rather than to the payment of a price.[5] Yet the need of a ransom, a price to be paid, is not forgotten.[6] God asserts his power to ransom when he declares, 'You were sold for nothing, and without money you will be redeemed.'[7] No-one can pay the price to redeem his soul from death; only God can redeem his people.[8]

Peter stresses the costliness of the ransom that is paid; he

[1] See Bénétreau, pp. 15–20; Kelly, p. 72; Selwyn, pp. 17–24; The treatment of this question is excellent in Stibbs, pp. 42–48.

[2] See the articles on *lyō* and derivatives in *TDNT* IV, pp. 328–356.

[3] Lv. 25:25, 48f.; Ru. 2:20; 3:9; 4:3ff.

[4] Is. 41:14; 43:14; 44:24; 47:4; 48:17; 49:7, 26; 54:5, 8; 60:16.

[5] Ex. 6:6; 15:13; Pss. 74:2; 77:15; Dt. 7:8; 9:26; 2 Sa. 7:23.

[6] The law provides for redemption money so that a person's life should not be forfeit, but no redemption can apply to murder. Ex. 21:30; Nu. 35:31–32. Every firstborn Israelite boy had to be redeemed by the payment of a ransom: a sign that all Israel was guilty before God and spared by his grace (Nu. 18:15; Ex. 30:12).

[7] Is. 52:3.

[8] Herman Ridderbos, in *Paul: An Outline of his Theology* (Eerdmans, 1975), points out that in Paul our ransom is paid by Christ, and that the price that is paid is the penalty of God's curse against sin. 'The price is not thus paid by God, but rather to God' (p. 193). As the Judge, God receives the price that redeems us from the curse of his holy law (Gal. 3:13). But since God is also the Redeemer, he does pay the price, the gift of his love (Rom. 5:8; 8:32). Christ is therefore both the Lamb of God by whose blood God redeems us, and the Redeemer who gave himself as a ransom (1 Tim. 2:6; 1 Cor. 6:19–20; Acts 20:28; Gal. 3:13; Tit. 2:14; Ps. 49:7–9, 15; Je. 31:11; *cf.* Ho. 13:14; 1 Cor. 15:55).

also makes it clear that it is God who pays it. Psalm 34 was much in Peter's thoughts as this letter was written; the psalm closes with the exultant affirmation: 'The Lord redeems his servants; no-one will be condemned who takes refuge in him.'[1] Peter makes it plain that we cannot redeem ourselves. At best, we could offer only corruptible *silver or gold*. Not money, but a life must be given to ransom our lives. God has paid that price in the life of Christ offered up for us. He is God's lamb of sacrifice; the chosen Servant of the Lord, who bore our sins on the tree (2:24). Peter preached what he had heard his Lord say, 'For even the Son of Man did not come to be served, but to serve, and to give his life a ransom for many.'[2]

Again, as in the salutation of his letter, Peter links the blood of Christ's sacrifice with the saving purpose of God (1:2). As Peter had heard John the Baptist declare, Jesus is 'the Lamb of God, who takes away the sin of the world'.[3] God's lamb is perfect, without spot or blemish. This was required of all animals for sacrifice, and specifically for the passover lamb.[4] Peter may also have had in view the meek lamb of Isaiah 53:7.

The price of Christ's blood has been paid to redeem us from death. His blood is given for our blood. God's redemption breaks not only the chain that binds us to future doom; it breaks also the chain of the dead past. We are redeemed from the meaninglessness of pagan life. 'Vanity' is a synonym for 'idols' in the Old Testament. Jeremiah describes the Gentile nations as coming to confess, 'Our fathers have inherited lies, even vanity and things wherein there is no profit.'[5]

Peter contrasts the traditions that Gentile Christians had received from their fathers with the gospel they have received from the Father. Human culture preserves the past to structure the present. Every society reveres its fathers, whether

[1] For the allusions to Psalm 34 in 1 Peter, see the table in Selwyn, pp. 408–410, and his discussions, pp. 157, 190. Compare the following references from 1 Peter with the verses from Psalm 34 (in parentheses): 1:15–17; 2:4 (v. 11); 2:3 (v. 8); 3:10–12 (vv. 13–17); 3:14 (v. 19); 1:18 (v. 22).
[2] Mk. 10:45.   [3] Jn. 1:29.   [4] Lv. 22:17–25; Ex. 12:5.
[5] Je 16:19b, ASV. Interpreting the meaning of 'lies' and 'vanity', the NIV translates, 'Our fathers possessed nothing but false gods, worthless idols that did them no good.' See Dt. 32:21; Je. 8:19.

71

they be Confucius or Marx, Jefferson, Darwin or Freud. Peter describes the liberation of Christians from the traditions of the fathers; not simply from a few mistaken ideas that have been hallowed by time, but from the deepest meaning (or lack of meaning) of cultural tradition. Not just a few customs, but a whole lifestyle has been swept away by God's redemption. To be sure, Peter is thinking of the immorality and vice of idolatrous paganism, but modern paganisms have produced lifestyles no less corrupt.

In contrast with the empty life of 'hollow men', Christians are given faith and hope in God. Meaninglessness evaporates in the glory of ultimate meaning: the eternal plan and purpose of God. The awesome cost of God's redemption fulfills his infinite design. God has revealed Christ now, at the end of time, to accomplish the purpose that was his before creation. God's sovereign purpose centres on Jesus Christ; all history culminates in him. The Father knows the Son in the eternal fellowship of the Trinity.[1] But here Peter speaks of God's *fore*knowledge to describe his choosing and appointment of Christ the redeemer. God's purpose, even before creation, was that Christ would come to die and rise again for the salvation of all who are chosen in him.[2] The astonishing truth is that God's eternal purpose in Christ is *for your sake* (1:20)![3] Aliens and transients Christians may be in this age, but their hope is sure. They are foreknown with Christ before the world was made (1:2), beloved of God the Father who made the worlds and gave his Son for them.[4]

Historians may mark off the ages according to developments in politics or technology (the iron age, the colonial period, the computer age), but in God's book the last age of human history is ushered in by the coming of Jesus Christ; it will last until Christ comes again.[5] It is the age of Christ's

---

[1] Jn. 1:18.   [2] 1 Pet. 1:2; Eph. 1:3–11.

[3] The usual translation *but was revealed . . . for your sake* puts too much weight on the Greek particle *de* by translating it 'but'. God's foreknowing and revealing of Christ are expressed in parallel participles connected by *de*. While *de* may express contrast, it often connects phrases where contrast is scarcely discernible. Since Peter speaks of God's elect as being foreknown (1:2) as well as Christ, it would seem better to apply the *for your sake* to the choosing as well as the manifesting of Christ.

[4] Peter's teaching runs parallel to that of Paul in 2 Timothy 1:9–10 and Rom. 16:25–26. *Cf.* Jn. 17:24.

[5] Heb. 1:2; 9:26; 1 Jn. 2:18; *cf.* Rom. 16:25. Peter preaches the fulfilment of God's promises in the last days in Acts 1:17.

resurrection and glory, a time when the light of eternity shines on the pilgrim people of God, illumining the life of the humblest believer.

The marvellous salvation that God has planned for us and accomplished for us is also given to us. Christ has paid the price of our redemption, and Christ seals his redemption to our hearts. We believe on him, but, as Peter says, we also believe *through* him. Paul speaks of the way God used the witness of the apostles to bring people to faith in Christ. Paul and Apollos were 'servants, through whom you came to believe'.[1] But Paul and Apollos were servants of Christ; it is the Lord Jesus himself who, by his Spirit, is the agent of our salvation. Peter knew that at first hand. The risen Lord himself, who had prayed that Peter's faith should not fail, had appeared to him personally on Easter morning to restore his faith. Peter rejoiced in the fact that the Lord who had brought faith to his heart was the same Lord who granted repentance to the Gentiles.[2]

All that Peter says centres on God's revelation in Jesus Christ. When he says that Christ *was revealed in these last times*, he implies not only that Christ is the goal of God's eternal plan; he indicates as well the divine pre-existence of Christ.[3] Our salvation is all of God. He planned it, he accomplished it through the sacrificial death and triumphant resurrection of Jesus Christ, he brought it to us through Christ. Our *faith and hope are* therefore *in God*.[4] Human traditions, idolatrous religions offer empty illusion. Hope can be found only with faith, faith in the God who raised Christ from the dead. This was Peter's own experience as he saw first the empty tomb, and then the living Lord.

c. Holiness through the word of truth (1:22 – 2:3)

Now that you have purified yourselves by obeying the truth

---

[1] 1 Cor. 3:5; *cf.* Jn. 1:7.   [2] Acts 11:18; *cf.* Rom. 11:36.

[3] While the fact that Christ is foreknown does not necessarily imply his pre-existence (we, too, are foreknown, 1:2), Peter's use of 'made manifest' does. See Kelly, p. 76.

[4] The clause *and so your faith and hope are in God* (NIV) might also be translated 'that your faith and hope might be in God' (AV). The NIV translation seems closer to Greek usage and fits the affirmative emphasis of the passage. See Kelly, pp. 77f., and Selwyn, pp. 147f.

so that you have sincere love for your brothers, love one another deeply, from the heart. ²³*For you have been born again, not of perishable seed, but of imperishable, through the living and enduring word of God.* ²⁴*For,*

> *'All men are like grass,*
> *and all their glory is like flowers of the field;*
> *the grass withers and the flowers fall,*
> *but the word of the Lord stands for ever.'*

And this is the word that was preached to you.
^{2:1}*Therefore, rid yourselves of all malice and all deceit, hypocrisy, envy, and slander of every kind.* ²*Like newborn babies, crave pure spiritual milk, so that by it you may grow up in your salvation,* ³*now that you have tasted that the Lord is good.*

Believers in God are redeemed from their empty and guilty past; they are bound to their Lord and also to one another. Holiness flames in devotion to God and in love of the brethren. Peter therefore exhorts Christians to love one another. His earlier exhortation to holiness (1:13) was at once supported by a strong affirmation of redeeming grace (1:18–21). Now again, as he urges Christians to *love one another*, he shows that what we are to do is grounded in what God has done. God's word renews, cleanses, and matures us for a life of love.

Love and truth, so often set at odds in contemporary Christianity, are bound together by Peter. Clearly, Peter requires love for fellow-Christians as the great mark of true holiness. He is not satisfied with tolerance or acceptance, far less with formalized distance. He will have love, sincere love, without pretence or hypocrisy. (In the New Testament, 'unhypocritical' always describes love.) But even sincerity is not enough: our love must be 'deep' and intense. Peter uses a word that means 'stretched' or 'strained'. The same term describes the earnestness of Christ's prayer in Gethsemane.[1]

The deep, heartfelt love that Peter urges is in no way artificial. It is the brotherly love that unites the family of God. Paul says to the church of Thessalonica, 'Now

[1] Lk. 22:44.

about brotherly love we do not need to write to you, for you yourselves have been taught by God to love each other.'[1]

How can such love be commanded? Peter writes to people divided by the jealousies and hatreds of their past; some were Jews, some Gentiles. To bind them in family love Peter directs them to the one source. The love that binds the redeemed flows from the love of the Redeemer. Christian love is the love of grace, the love of compassion. For such love to appear, the pride and selfishness of our alienation from God must be swept away. They must be replaced by a heart made new with the motives of grace. Peter shows how both needs are to be met. It is the *word of God*, the good news of the gospel, that is the means both of our new birth and of our nurture in holiness.

Because God's love is the source of ours, the message of his love is what kindles ours. Christian love may be demonstrated by a hug, a holy kiss, or a helping hand, but Christian love cannot be transmitted that way. Christian love is born as Christians are born: through the truth of the gospel. That which clears away the *malice . . . deceit, hypocrisy, envy, and slander* of the old lifestyle is the cleansing of our souls through obedience to God's truth. Peter addresses those who already know that cleansing; they experience true brotherly love because they *have purified* themselves *by obeying the truth*' (1:22). He exhorts them to deepen and strengthen a love they already have. In the same way, Paul urges the Thessalonians to love 'more and more' as God has taught them.[2]

The obedience to the truth of which Peter speaks is the initial submission to the claims of the gospel. In saving faith the truth of God is heard and heeded.[3] If these words reflect the catechetical teaching that accompanied Christian baptism, as some scholars think, it is striking that God's *word* rather than the water is described as the cleansing agent. Christian baptism carries a deeper symbolism than the ceremonial

---

[1] 1 Thes. 4:9; *cf.* Rom. 12:9–10; Heb. 13:1; 2 Pet. 1:7.

[2] 1 Thes. 4:10. Calloud-Genuyt point out that 1 Peter is written, not to bring about restoration from a bad situation, but to develop a positive situation by encouraging appropriate behaviour (p. 29).

[3] See the comment on 1:14.

washing of the old covenant.[1] It symbolizes not only the removal of all defilement, but also the renewing of the Holy Spirit and the beginning of new life. Not only are we purified by the word; we are also given new birth by *the living and enduring word of God.*

Peter compares the life-giving power of the word of God to human procreation. It is the *seed* of life, sown in our hearts to create new life. God's word is creative: he speaks, and it is done; he commands and it stands fast. 'By the word of the Lord were the heavens made, their starry host by the breath of his mouth.'[2] Since God's word is his vocalized breath, it goes forth with the power of his Spirit. The word of the gospel is God's call; it communicates and converts. Both Abraham and Sarah had laughed at God's impossible word of promise: 'Will Sarah bear a child at the age of ninety?'[3] God had replied, 'Is any word too difficult for God?'[4] When the angel promised to Mary an even more miraculous birth, she did not laugh, but she did marvel. Gabriel repeated to her the word that had been spoken to Sarah, 'For no word is impossible with God.'[5] God's word of promise is self-fulfilling. By the word of God Jesus was born of the virgin Mary; by the word of God we are born anew. The people of God respond to the gospel call with the words of Mary's faith, 'May it be to me as you have said.'

The word of God that has given us life is *enduring*; it is not subject to decay or change. God's eternal word creates eternal life. The physical life of human procreation is no more permanent than the grass of the field. But the life that God gives is more than physical; it is the life of the Spirit. Peter cites the prophecy of Isaiah to contrast our mortality with the eternity of God's word.[6] That same passage goes on to promise good tidings to Zion: 'Here is your God!' Recalling this, Peter adds, *And this is the word that was*

---

[1] Stibbs, p. 93. Baptism also deepens the symbolism of proselyte baptism in Judaism, since it replaces circumcision as well.

[2] Ps. 33:6, 9.   [3] Gn. 17:17.

[4] Gn. 18:14, my more literal translation. *Dābār* may mean either 'word' or 'thing'. Since the issue is God's word of promise, the translation should be 'any word' rather than 'anything.'

[5] Lk. 1:37, my translation. The Greek word *rhēma* that translates *dābār* has the same double meaning.

[6] Is. 40:6–8.

preached as good tidings *to you* (1:25).[1]

In the power of his gospel, God has indeed come to cleanse and renew his people. The Lord Jesus Christ 'loved the church and gave himself up for her to make her holy, cleansing her by the washing with water through the word, and to present her to himself as a radiant church, without stain or wrinkle or any other blemish, but holy and blameless'.[2] Peter describes the cleansing of the church as already accomplished. With Paul, he would say of their former wicked life: 'And that is what some of you were. But you were washed, you were sanctified, you were justified in the name of the Lord Jesus Christ and by the Spirit of our God.'[3]

Even when Peter lists the evils from which they have been cleansed (2:1), he is describing what has already happened to them as God's gospel has changed their hearts; 'Having therefore put off all wickedness, all deceit, pretences and jealousies, and all recriminations . . .'[4] Of course, by reminding Christians of what their conversion means, Peter is indirectly warning them against the sins from which they have been delivered. Yet he states what is already the case. The filthy garments of their past have been removed; they have put them off in receiving the gospel of Christ.[5] In later liturgies, perhaps in reference to his scriptural language, candidates for baptism removed their clothing before entering the water and donned a new set after the ceremony.[6]

The evils from which Christians have been converted are the very opposite of the strenuous love that Peter has pressed upon them. They are contrasted with the fruits of the Spirit and the outworking of sound teaching. Similar lists are found in other letters.[7] Peter first mentions evil in a general sense, then deceit, hypocrisy, jealousy, and defamation. Pagan moralists, too, recognized and sometimes listed such vices.[8]

[1] This more literal translation brings out the force of the verb for 'preach' here. It means 'bring good news' and is used in Is. 40:9, LXX.
[2] Eph. 5:25–27.
[3] 1 Cor. 6:11.
[4] Kelly's translation, p. 81. See his defence of it, p. 84.
[5] *Cf.* Zc. 3:2.
[6] See the passages cited in Kelly, who thinks that at least the 'putting off' of clothing before baptism was seen to be symbolical as early as the apostolic age (p. 84).
[7] Rom. 1:29–31; 2 Cor. 12:20; Eph. 4:31; Col. 3:8; 1 Tim. 1:9–11.
[8] See the references in Selwyn, p. 153.

LIVE OBEDIENTLY IN HOPE

They are easily identified as poisons in social life; they are not so easily set aside! Yet Christians have been delivered from them by the power of the gospel; they have cast them away.

Christians who have been given new birth by the word must also grow. They are cleansed by the converting power of the gospel, but they must mature in their new life. What will advance their growth? What will deepen their love? The same truth of God that gave them birth also nourishes them. If the word of God is water to wash us, it is also *milk* to build better bodies in Christ. Christians must be addicted to the Bible.

Like newborn babies, crave the pure milk of the word. The wonder of a mother at the birth of a child becomes delight at the readiness of her infant to feed. Any delay at feeding-time brings a powerful reaction from the tiny person. For an infant, milk is not a fringe benefit. Peter writes to young churches; he has in view many who have only recently confessed their faith in Christ and been baptized. Some were no doubt senior citizens; they are nevertheless newborn in Christ. They must have an infant's desperate desire for basic nourishment.

Peter is not the first to compare the receiving of truth to feeding. In the hymns of the Dead Sea community the Teacher of Righteousness likens his disciples to suckling babies with open mouths.[1] Both Paul and the author of Hebrews use the figure of milk to describe the initial teaching of those who are babies in Christ.[2] Peter, however, is not thinking of milk as infant diet to be replaced by meat. In Peter's figure the milk of the abiding word is simply the Christian's necessary food.

The word *logikon*, translated *spiritual* in the NIV, may mean simply 'metaphorical' in contrast to 'literal'. It may also mean 'reasonable' or that which is related to the word (*logos*). Since Peter has just been describing the living *logos* by which Christians are given new birth, it would seem that

[1] 1QH 7:21, in *DSS*. As Kelly and Bénétreau point out, it is unlikely that Peter borrowed the figure from the mystery religions, in some of which initiates were given milk (Kelly, pp. 85f.; Bénétreau, p. 115). The milk and honey given to the baptized in third-century Christianity (continued in the Coptic church) appear to refer to the abundance of Canaan (Ex. 3:8).

[2] 1 Cor. 3:2; Heb. 5:12.

he is using *logikon* in that sense: 'the milk of the word', as the AV has it.

Peter commends a milk product that is free from additives. The word of God abides without preservatives. Consumers in the ancient world were well aware that milk or wine could be watered down; when Paul says that he was not a huckster of the word of God, he alludes to the common practice of selling diluted wine.[1] Peter uses a word that was employed by merchants to describe *pure*, unadulterated products.[2] The term contrasts with the 'deceit' that Christians have renounced (2:1). While this letter does not contain the warnings against false teaching that we find in 2 Peter, it is clear that the growth of new Christians must be in the truth of the apostolic word.[3] Peter's letter sets forth the truth that new Christians must earnestly desire. *The word of the Lord ... that was preached* (1:25) is more than an abbreviated formula describing the way of salvation. It is the full gospel message that we find in this letter, grounded in the revelation of the Old Testament and expanded in the sweep of apostolic teaching. Simple formulas of gospel truth are to be prized, and Peter presents us with some of the most memorable in the New Testament.[4] But the gospel is unique in richness as well as simplicity. The milk that Peter recommends is 'the whole will of God'.[5]

How does growth take place through the word of God? The appeals and exhortations of the gospel are grounded in the proclamation and instruction of the gospel. Growth is always growth in faith. The word of the Lord constantly presents the Lord of the word. Coming to the word is coming to the Lord. This central truth cuts both ways. We cannot detach the word from the Lord and, like the scribes and the Pharisees, profess to cling to the Scriptures while refusing the Lord. On the other hand, neither can we profess obedience to the Lord while rejecting his word. To separate a living Lord from a 'dead' book or a divine Lord from a merely human

[1] 2 Cor. 2:17; *cf.* Is. 1:22, LXX; 2 Pet. 2:3.
[2] Kelly cites papyrus inscriptions where the word has this technical meaning (p. 85).
[3] 2 Pet. 1:16; 2:1. Paul also calls for teaching the 'sound words, even the words of our Lord Jesus Christ', 1 Tim. 6:3, ASV; 1 Tim. 1:10; 2 Tim. 1:13.
[4] For example: 2:24; 1:19–21.
[5] Acts 20:27.

book is to reject the apostolic gospel. For Peter, God's word is living as well as enduring (1:23). When Paul describes how the church is built up in faith, he begins with the ministry of the word. By the word the Lord's servant is equipped for the upbuilding of the saints.[1]

The goal of our growth is salvation, the full salvation in Christ that the gospel proclaims, and for which we are kept (1:5).[2] Again we see the alpha and omega of our hope. Peter writes to those who have already been given new birth by the word, who have already come to the Lord and tasted that he is good.[3] Theirs is a sure hope, for their inheritance is kept for them and they are kept for it. Yet their hope is also future; they do not merely wait for it, they grow toward it, like flowers toward the sun. Faith is purified, love is intensified, grace is tasted as we are tested.

Peter again shows that the Lord who gave us new birth by the word also gives us growth by the word. The word for 'grow up' is in the passive: we grow only as we are 'grown' by the milk of God's word. Peter and Paul may plant and water, but it is God who gives the growth.[4]

What quickens our desire for the life-giving word of God? Peter answers that we know the taste. Our culture makes the image clear; advertisers spend millions to promote the taste of a cola. Reading the Bible is addictive when we begin to get the taste. What we taste in Scripture is not simply the variety and power of the language. What we taste is the Lord. Peter refers to Psalm 34:8, 'Taste and see that the Lord is good; blessed is the man who takes refuge in him.'[5] Peter omits 'and see' in his reference. Perhaps he would keep just the tasting in view; he knows that those to whom he writes have not seen the Lord as he has. Yet, not having seen him, they love him in the same personal way. They have found the Lord in the word of the gospel, or, better, he has found them by his living word.

Those who read the word of God, and surely those who teach it, must never forget why the word is given and whom

[1] Eph. 4:11–12; 2 Tim. 3:15–17.
[2] 'Unto salvation' (RSV) is a more accurate translation than *in your salvation* (NIV).
[3] The Greek reads 'if you have tasted', but the NIV translates the sense well. See the 'if' in 1:17 and Eph. 4:20. See Heb. 6:4–6.
[4] 1 Cor. 3:5–7.
[5] See above, p. 22 n. 1, for allusions to Psalm 34 in this letter.

it reveals. The word shows us that *the Lord is good*; his words are sweeter than honey to our taste because in them the Lord gives himself to us.[1]

---

[1] Ps. 119:103, Spicq, *Epîtres:* 'The accent is on the verb "to taste" which signified at the same time "to savour" (Heb. 6:4–5) and "to swallow, to assimilate" with a nuance of certitude and personal possession (Lk. 9:27)' (p. 81). See Ezk. 3:3.

4. Live as the people of God
I: The life of the spiritual temple

As you come to him, the living Stone – rejected by men but chosen by God and precious to him – 5you also, like living stones, are being built into a spiritual house to be a holy priesthood, offering spiritual sacrifices acceptable to God through Jesus Christ. 6For in Scripture it says:

> *'See, I lay a stone in Zion,*
> *a chosen and precious cornerstone,*
> *and the one who trusts in him*
> *will never be put to shame.'*

7Now to you who believe, this stone is precious. But to those who do not believe,

> *'The stone the builders rejected*
> *has become the capstone,'*

8and,

> *'A stone that causes men to stumble*
> *and a rock that makes them fall.'*

They stumble because they disobey the message – which is also what they were destined for.
9But you are a chosen people, a royal priesthood, a holy nation, a people belonging to God, that you may declare the praises of him who called you out of darkness into his wonderful light. 10Once you were not a people, but now you are the people of God; once you had not received mercy, but now you have received mercy.

1. The building of the temple in Christ

In the first chapter Peter showed the wonder of God's salvation through Jesus Christ. Now he wants to show the status that Christians have as the true people of God, so that he may encourage us to live before the world with that awareness.

He intends to emphasize the humility and submission to which Christians are called. That humility, however, is not slavish subjection to others. Rather, it is modelled on the humility of the Lord. It is the free and willing service of a royal people. Jesus willingly endured humiliation, but God has exalted him. God indeed calls us to humility, but he has already joined us to Christ's exaltation. In Christ we are God's people, God's temple, his kingdom and priesthood.

As you come to him, the living Stone – rejected by men but chosen by God and precious to him . . . . As always, Peter begins with the Lord. The status of Christians depends upon the status of Christ, for they are joined to him. How striking it is that Peter names Christ the *Stone*! Peter's given name was Simon. It was Jesus who named him Cephas (in Greek, Peter), the 'rock'.[1] Peter gratefully used the name Jesus gave him as an apostle (1:1). But Peter points us, not to himself, but to Christ as our Rock.

Peter draws this name for Christ from Isaiah 28:16, a passage that he proceeds to quote. Isaiah's prophecy alludes to one of the master figures of the Old Testament, the temple as the house of God.[2] Isaiah speaks the word of the Lord against the princes of Jerusalem who foolishly suppose that their city is secure against the threat of invasion. They speak as though they had a treaty with death and hell so that the lethal waters of the abyss could never sweep over them. God declares that their pride is no refuge, their covenant with death no security. Only one edifice can stand against the storm of destruction: God's building, established upon one sure foundation stone.

It is this figure that Jesus used when he said to Peter that

[1] Jn. 1:42; Mt. 16:18.
[2] See E. P. Clowney, 'The Final Temple' in *WTJ* 35:2, pp. 156–189.

83

the gates of hell could not prevail against his church.[1] In the word of Jesus, he was himself the builder and Peter an apostolic rock of foundation; in the figure that Peter takes from Isaiah, Christ is the *precious* and tested *cornerstone*.

In the building technique from which the figure is drawn, the cornerstone of the foundation would be the first stone to be put in place. Since both the angle of the walls and the level of the stone courses would be extended from it, the cornerstone must be square and true. Large and precious stones were cut for the foundation of Solomon's temple.[2]

The passage Peter quotes had already been seen to be messianic: some Greek versions of Isaiah had translated, 'He that believeth on him shall by no means be ashamed' (adding the words 'on him').[3] Peter identifies the cornerstone with Christ. He calls him a *living Stone*; he would not have us think of his Lord as inert marble! Christ is the living Stone, however, not just because he is a living person, but because he is alive from the dead as the risen Lord. God set his cornerstone in place by the resurrection.[4]

Christ, the foundation stone, fulfils the image of the temple as God's house. God sets him in place in spite of his rejection by the builders. Peter knew well the passage from Psalm 118:22 that he quotes in verse 7. He had been troubled to hear Jesus cite that scripture after his parable about the wicked tenants.[5] What could Jesus mean? He spoke of the leaders of Israel killing the Son sent by God to receive from them his due. 'Therefore I tell you that the kingdom of God will be taken away from you and given to a people who will

[1] Psalm 18 sets 'the cords of Sheol' in parallel with 'the floods of Belial' and 'the waves of death' (vv. 5–6). David praises God his Rock for drawing him from the waters. See Jonah 2:2, 6. The Qumran psalmist uses this Old Testament figure. As a drowning man in a storm sinking down into the gates of death, he is delivered by God and set on a rock (1QH 3:17; 6:24, in *DSS*).

[2] 1 Ki. 5:17. A foundation stone is precious because it is labour-intensive in selection and preparation. The foundational cornerstone is to be distinguished from an ornamental topstone on the coping of a building or surmounting columns (Zc. 4:7).

[3] The Massoretic Hebrew text lacks the 'on him'. The Targum of Isaiah 28:16 and of Ps. 118:22ff. refer the stone to the king as Messiah. See Elliott, *Elect*, pp. 27f.

[4] See Elliott, *Elect*, p. 37, n. 6. Perhaps Peter thinks also of Christ the Rock as the source of living water. See Appendix B below, and Spicq, *Epîtres*, pp. 81f.

[5] Mt. 21:33–42.

produce its fruit.'[1] As for *the builders* who *rejected* God's cornerstone, Jesus had said, 'He who falls on this stone will be broken to pieces, but he on whom it falls will be crushed.'[2]

After the resurrection and the coming of the Holy Spirit, Peter understood the words of Jesus. He confronted those very 'builders' and boldly challenged them with the words of the Psalm, adding, 'Salvation is found in no-one else, for there is no other name under heaven given to men by which we must be saved.'[3] Now, in his letter, Peter refers to the same Old Testament passages he had heard from the lips of Jesus. Peter had learned that the death of Christ was not an unthinkable defeat for the Son of God and the kingdom of God. Rather, by the cross and the resurrection God's eternal purpose of salvation had been fulfilled. Those who had crucified Jesus had accomplished what God's 'power and will had decided beforehand should happen'.[4] In their rejection of Christ, the builders, in spite of themselves, served to put God's Stone in place.

Salvation is in no other; there is no other Son of God, no other atoning cross, no other resurrection life. Peter's message begins and ends in the purpose of God; God has set in place his chosen cornerstone; God has determined, too, the rejection and doom of the builders.[5]

It is not merely the leaders of Israel that have rejected Christ. The living Stone has been *rejected by men* (2:4). 'Indeed Herod and Pontius Pilate met together with the Gentiles and the people of Israel in this city to conspire against your holy servant Jesus, whom you anointed.'[6] The severity of God's judgment falls not only on the builders who had rejected God's chosen Stone, but on all unbelievers. Peter repeats the solemn warning of Jesus.[7] Those who stumble at the word of the gospel are broken in their unbelief. The translation in 1:7, *capstone*, is misleading; the phrase, literally rendered 'the head of the corner', refers to the same foundational cornerstone.[8] This is the stone over which

[1] Mt. 21:43.   [2] Mt. 21:44.   [3] Acts 4:11–12.   [4] Acts 4:28.
[5] The verb for the 'setting' of the cornerstone in v. 6 is the same as the verb for the 'appointing' of God's reprobation in v. 8.
[6] Acts 4:27.   [7] Lk. 20:18.
[8] R. J. McKelvey, *The New Temple* (Oxford University Press, 1969), pp. 198ff. The 'head' here means the first stone in the course, from which the other foundation stones proceed.

people trip when they refuse to hear the word of God.

The Stone that people have rejected is the Stone that God has *chosen*. Peter stresses God's choosing and honouring of Christ as the precious cornerstone of his holy temple. He does so not only to rejoice in the person and work of Christ, but also to show the holy and honoured place that Christians have, united to their Lord. In 2:4–5 Peter summarizes this argument. Then, in 2:6–10 he gives the basis in Scripture for his affirmations. Verses 6–8 are quotations from the Old Testament; verses 9–10 are a series of descriptive epithets drawn from the Old Testament.

Peter makes the same contrast that we find in Isaiah 28, the contrast between the foolish pride of man and the sure work of the Lord. God's choice of his precious cornerstone rebukes human arrogance. The term *precious*, used in Isaiah, can be applied to gemstones as well as to the value of a great cornerstone.[1] Peter has just said that the Lord is good.[2] How good he is, the Father has shown; he has chosen him as precious beyond describing. Peter could bear witness to the voice from heaven, 'You are my Son, whom I love; with you I am well pleased.'[3] The Father's words concerning his Son reflect his prophetic words concerning his Servant: 'Here is my servant, whom I uphold, my chosen one in whom I delight; I will put my Spirit on him.'[4] Consider the intensity of the Father's love for his only Son as he took the role of a servant, accepted the Father's will in Gethsemane and accomplished his task on Calvary.[5] The delight of the Father in the finished work of his Son is seen in 'the resurrection of Jesus Christ, who had gone into heaven and is at God's right hand – with angels, authorities and powers in submission to

---

[1] *E.g.* 2 Sa. 12:30; 1 Ki. 10:2, 10–11. KB gives the translation 'meeting' for *yiqᵉrah* (Is. 28:16), yielding the meaning 'the corner where the foundation walls meet'. However, under *'eben*, 'stone', KB also cites Is. 28:16 with the translation 'costly stones'. In view of 1 Ki 5:17 (5:31 in Hebrew), this translation is to be preferred. For *bohan* ('chosen') KB gives 'schist-gneiss', a kind of granite, assuming that it is a loan-word from Egyptian. E. J. Young points to a difficulty with the transcription from Egyptian to Hebrew on this assumption (*The Book of Isaiah; The New International Commentary on the Old Testament*, 2; Eerdmans, 1969, p. 287, n. 30). It is better to translate 'tested' as the Septuagint does, from the frequently used Hebrew verb *bāhan*.

[2] Verse 3. In Greek the phrase is *chrestos ho kyrios*, suggesting *christos ho kyrios*, 'Christ the Lord'.

[3] Mk. 1:11.   [4] Is. 42:1.   [5] Is. 53:10–22; Jn. 10:17.

him.' (3:21–22).

Peter now spells out the wonder of God's salvation: the delight that the Father has in his Son is given to *us*. As Christ is precious to the Father, so are we made precious (2:7).[1] As Christ is the cornerstone of God's temple, so are we stones in that house of God. He is the living Stone; we, too, are *living stones* (2:5), born again by his resurrection life (1:3). Peter does not explicitly call Christ the Priest of the house of God, but it is through Christ's priestly work that we, his people, may offer up *spiritual sacrifices acceptable to God* (2:5).

These blessings are ours through faith. By faith we *come to him* (2:4, 7). Peter uses a word from the Greek Old Testament that describes the approach of the worshipper to God. Once far off in the darkness, we now have access by faith to God's house; indeed, we are built into that living temple, the true people of God. Many medieval churches in Europe have crypts where kings, queens and nobles are entombed. Effigies of the dead may be seen in the dim light, silent figures carved in stone on the lids of coffins. Not so are Christians made part of God's temple. They are *living stones*, and they are part of a growing house. God's architecture is biological. His house grows as new stones are added, but also as the stones in place are perfected. The living stones, as Paul says, grow into a holy temple of the Lord.[2]

To speak of a growing temple of living stones stretches an Old Testament figure to convey New Testament reality. The figure of the tabernacle/temple pictured the presence of God among his people. God's tent was pitched in the centre of Israel's wilderness camp; in the land of promise God made the temple at Jerusalem his dwelling. God was there, among his people; they belonged to him, and he to them.

When the Word became flesh and 'tented' among us, the symbol became reality. The God of glory came to dwell with us: 'We have seen his glory, the glory of the One and Only,'

---

[1] Literally, 'To you that believe is the honour.' The word is *timē*, related to *entimon* in v. 6. The use of the article emphasizes a particular honour or value. If the reference is to Christ's honour, the NIV translation is good. But if the contrast is with the shame mentioned at the end of v. 6, the honour is like that of 1:7. This fits the purpose of the whole passage, to show the new status of believers. See Spicq, *Epîtres*, p. 88.
[2] Eph. 2:21.

John testifies.[1] The true temple is Christ's body.[2] We are united to Christ; the living stones are joined to the cornerstone. In that way the church becomes the true house of God. Peter's language is corporate. He thinks of the spiritual temple, not as the body of an individual believer, but as the body of believers, the company of those who are joined to Christ. Yet, as the instructions of the letter show, Peter is concerned about the holiness of God's temple not only when Christians are assembled for worship, but in their daily lives as well. The reality of union with Christ is seen in the life of each living stone. Our mutual union with Christ removes the tension between the claims of the individual and of society. In Christ we find the meaning of our personal lives; in Christ we find the joy of belonging to one another. We rejoice in the honour and the ministry of being built together.

The word *house* that Peter uses may mean not only a dwelling, but also the family that lives in it. The living temple that Peter describes is also the 'household' of God, made up of those who are brought near to God as his sons and daughters.[3]

2. The ministry of a priestly people

In this section of his letter, as we have seen, Peter presents the high calling of the people of God to prepare us for his instructions about our lifestyle. The people of God are a holy temple, united to Jesus Christ, the chief cornerstone. Two main emphases shape this section. As God's dwelling-place, the church has both a status and a ministry. In verse 5 Peter summarizes these two points, then proceeds to support and expand them with quotations from Scripture. First, he describes our standing before God. We are *a spiritual house* and *a holy priesthood*. He validates that from the Old Testament: *a chosen people, a royal priesthood, a holy nation, a people belonging to God*, the recipients of mercy (2:9–10). Then, after saying who we are, Peter tells us what we do. We offer *spiritual sacrifices* that God accepts. He supports that statement by saying that we *declare the praises of him who called* us *out of darkness into his wonderful light* (2:9).

[1] Jn. 1:14.   [2] Jn. 2:21.   [3] Spicq, *Epîtres*, p. 84 Elliott, *Home*, pp. 23f.

What Peter says about our standing is set in the framework of the grace of God. God's claim upon us makes our position secure, and places us in the closest fellowship with him. This is the teaching of the beautiful language that Peter marshals from the Old Testament. In fellowship with God we are *a royal priesthood, a holy nation.* Peter cites a key passage from the book of Exodus.[1] In making this covenant with Israel, God declares that he has redeemed them from Egypt; he has brought them on eagles' wings to himself at Mount Sinai. Now he claims them as his people, distinct from all the peoples of the earth, to be a holy nation and a kingdom of priests. The point of the passage is not to appoint Israel a priesthood for the nations; neither does it exclude a special priestly office within Israel. The point is that Israel has been brought into such close fellowship with God that their access to him is priestly.[2] God dwells among them. They are holy because he is holy.[3] God's calling comes as a command as well as a promise. Israel is called to be what it is, *a holy nation.*[4]

The people of Israel broke God's covenant and defiled themselves with immorality and idolatry. God delivered his judgment through the prophets: they had become Lo-Ammi, 'no people', no longer the holy people of God.[5] Yet God also promised a marvellous restoration. Israel would again be made holy. Instead of shame they would be given glory. 'And you will be called priests of the Lord, you will be named ministers of our God.'[6] The prophets describe the marvel of God's restoration in the latter days. Not only will the remnant of Israel be gathered to worship the Lord; the remnant of the nations, even the enemy nations, will be

---

[1] Ex. 19:6. Although *basileion hierateuma* (2:9) may fairly be translated 'royal priesthood,' the phrase is taken directly from the Septuagint translation of Exodus 19:6, where the word order follows the Hebrew. The closest translation may be 'a kingdom, a body of priests'. See Elliott, *Elect*, pp. 63–76. In this case the corporate identity of the true Israel as God's holy people is reflected in both nouns.

[2] This is well argued by R. B. Y. Scott, 'A Kingdom of Priests (Ex. 19:6)', *OTS* 8 (1950), pp. 213–219, and by Elliott, *Elect*, pp. 53–59.

[3] The holiness of Israel is the demand as well as the promise of God's covenant. It can never become a matter of presumption; to claim that 'the whole congregation is holy' in revolt against God's anointed leaders is to invite the judgment of the Lord (Nu. 16:3).

[4] 1 Pet. 1:15–16; Lv. 11:44–45; 19:2; 20:7.

[5] 1 Pet. 2:10; Ho. 1:10; 2:23; Rom. 9:25.   [6] Is. 61:6.

gathered, too. In an amazing passage, Isaiah describes the Egyptians worshipping in Assyria, and the Assyrians in Egypt, both passing by Jerusalem to do so. 'In that day Israel will be the third, along with Egypt and Assyria, a blessing on the earth. The Lord Almighty will bless them, saying, "Blessed be Egypt my people, Assyria my handiwork, and Israel my inheritance." '[1] In the day of God's salvation, the covenant blessing will shared by the enemy nations.

It is this fulfilment that Peter proclaims. The temple of the new covenant is a spiritual temple; those who are made a nation of priests are not simply the restored of Israel, but believers whom Christ gathers from the nations. If Israel through sin had become no people, and had lost the right to the covenant promise, then the grace that can restore Israelites to their forfeited inheritance can equally bring polluted Gentiles into the intimacy of fellowship with God (2:10).

The change of the new covenant is intensive as well as extensive. Not only are Gentiles included in God's nation of priests; their priestly access is *spiritual*, not merely ceremonial (2:5). Uncircumcised Gentiles were prohibited by the law from entering the temple. They were barred, of course, from the sanctuary, where only priests could minister. Neither could they come with the people of God into the courts of the Lord. They were kept outside, on pain of death. But now Gentiles are no longer aliens; they are 'fellow-citizens with God's people and members of God's household, built on the foundation of the apostles and prophets, with Christ Jesus himself as the chief cornerstone. . . . And in him you too are being built together to become a dwelling in which God lives by his Spirit.'[2]

How can Gentiles gain this priestly privilege? The book of Leviticus cannot be amended to admit uncircumised Gentiles into God's courts. That is what Paul's enemies accused him of doing; bringing Gentiles into the sanctuary of the Lord. They tried to tear him limb from limb.[3] They were right in thinking that the law could not be altered. Their mistake was in refusing to see that it had been fulfilled. The breadth of the gospel flows from its depth. Outward washing, the cutting away the flesh, the offering of bulls and

[1] Is. 19:24–25; *cf.* 56:6–8; 66:19–21.   [2] Eph. 2:19b–20, 22.
[3] Acts 21:27–36.

goats, could never remove sin or qualify any sinner to stand
in the presence of the Holy One of Israel. Those elaborate
preparations and safeguards bore witness to the reality of
God's holiness, and to the need of cleansing and atonement.
But only God could provide the true and spiritual sacrifice.
Only One who had clean hands and a pure heart could
ascend at last the hill of the Lord. Jesus Christ came; the one
righteous, covenant-keeping Servant of the Lord. His atoning
death fulfilled the temple sacrifices. His blood provided the
cleansing that the old ceremonies could only picture.

Our approach to God in worship is now our coming to
the living Stone of God's appointment. It is not a physical
approach into an earthly edifice: it is the spiritual approach
of faith in Christ. By the same token, the holiness of the
believer cannot be achieved by outward washing with water;
it must be the cleansing of the heart by God's Spirit. Spiritual
holiness is required of the Gentiles as new members of the
people of God.[1] Peter describes the spiritual reality of our
position in order to remind us of the spiritual depth of the
holiness God requires.

The church of the new covenant is not only a holy temple
and priesthood enjoying the presence of God; it is also an
elect race, the *people* of God's own possession (2:9). God
dwells among his people because he has chosen them. The
heart of the covenant is God's electing love. The scriptural
teaching of God's choosing is sometimes questioned because
it is not understood, and sometimes hated because it *is* understood. It can be received only by faith, for to receive it one
must confess that God is God. The wonder is not that God
chooses some and not others (Abel, not Cain; Isaac, not
Ishmael; Jacob, not Esau).[2] The wonder is that God chooses
any. Certainly God does not choose an élite. Israel is a *chosen*
people, but not a choice people.[3] God's elect have no ground
for pride. On the contrary, God chooses not the wise, the
mighty, or the noble, but the foolish, the weak, the despised

[1] 2 Cor. 6:16 – 7:1.
[2] 'The whole story of the patriarchs has this motif', Norman H. Snaith, *'Choose'*,
in Alan Richardson, ed., *A Theological Word Book of the Bible* (SCM Press, 1950),
p. 43. See Rom. 9:10–13.
[3] *Bāḥûr*, the passive participle of *bāḥar*, is not used of Israel, for it means 'chosen'
in the sense of 'choice' – soldiers in their prime, for example. The form *bāḥîr* is
used to describe the chosen as the elect (Ps. 106:4; Is. 43:20–21).

(Paul says, indeed, the 'zeroes'). No-one may boast before him.[1]

If God does not choose his people for their worth or their serviceability, why does he choose them? The answer is clear. 'The Lord did not set his affection on you and choose you because you were more numerous than other peoples, for you were the fewest of all peoples. But it was because the Lord loved you and kept the oath he swore to your fore-fathers.'[2] The Lord loves . . . because he loves! Nothing can explain the love of God for sinners. God's 'good pleasure' is the movement of his own will, springing from his own nature.[3] How the language of love is lavished upon God's people in the Old Testament! They are God's inheritance, his personal and prized possession, his treasure.[4] God bears them on his shoulders, carries them in his arms, holds them in his hand, seats them at his feet.[5] He loves them with a jealous love; they are to be his alone to the exclusion of all other gods; they bear his name.[6] The love of a father for a son, of a husband for a wife, is used to describe God's love for his people.[7]

The claim of love that God makes upon his people in the Exodus 19 passage quoted by Peter is not, however, the end of the story in the Old Testament. Israel despised God's covenant love and commited adultery with the gods of the nations.[8] God chose Israel, but Israel chose other gods.[9] The wanton abuse of God's singular love must result in singular judgment: 'You only have I chosen of all the families of the earth; therefore I will punish you for all your sins.'[10] God pours out the vengeance of the covenant.[11]

Must all the promises of God be voided in exile and

---

[1] 1 Cor. 1:29.

[2] Dt. 7:7f. See Dt. 10:14–17; Ho. 11:1, 4; 14:4; Je. 31:2ff.

[3] The 'good pleasure' (rāṣôn) of God is shown in the favour of his grace (Ps. 106:4; Dt. 33:16). The 'men of good will' are the men of God's good pleasure, his elect (Lk. 2:14). *Cf.* Ernest Vogt, 'Peace among Men of God's Good Pleasure' in Krister Stendahl, ed., *The Scrolls and the New Testament* (Harper, 1957), pp. 114–117.

[4] Dt. 32:9.   [5] Dt. 33:3, 12, 27; Lv. 9:5; Is. 49:16.

[6] Ex. 20:5; Nu. 6:22–27.

[7] See the treatment of God's love in the OT in Geerhardus Vos, 'The Scriptural Doctrine of the Love of God', *Presbyterian and Reformed Review* 49 (Jan. 1902), pp. 1–19.

[8] Dt. 32:6.   [9] Jdg. 5:8.   [10] Am. 3:2; but see 9:9.   [11] Lv. 26:25.

destruction? Looking at the valley of dry bones, the prophet Ezekiel might be tempted to think so. But the vision he received gave the answer of the Lord.[1] God's judgment on his people would be neither total nor final. Not total, for God would preserve a remnant. Not final, for God would give renewal.[2] Against the dark background of God's judgment, the reality of God's choosing of his people shines with new glory. The chosen of God are his elect remnant, those whom he will come to gather at last. The scattered flock, exploited by those who should be their shepherds, will be gathered by the Lord himself, the true Shepherd, and brought to the green pastures of his salvation.[3]

God must come to gather his own: they will hear his voice, for they know him. The Old Testament teaching of election points us forward to the election of God's own Servant. Jesus, the true Shepherd, comes to gather the scattered remant flock and to bring in the renewal of resurrection life. 'Fear not, little flock, for it is your Father's good pleasure to give you the kingdom.'[4]

The Old Testament, therefore, presents an election within an election. Israel is chosen, but is unfaithful to its calling. Jesus comes as the elect one, the beloved Son of the Father, and he fulfils the calling of the Servant of the Lord. The elect whom Peter addresses are chosen in Christ who is foreknown before the creation of the world (1:20). As Paul tells us, 'Not all who are descended from Israel are Israel.'[5] Not the son of the flesh but the Son of the Spirit inherits the promises of God. Those who are united to Christ are those the Father has given him. The Good Shepherd holds them for ever in his hand.[6]

There is a vast difference between the election of Christ and the election of believers in Christ. Christ is the chosen of the Father in the sense of choice, the one and only beloved Son. 'Worthy is the Lamb . . . .' We are chosen in the opposite position. We have no status as sons or daughters, for

[1] Ezk. 37:3–6.
[2] The remnant survives (Am. 3:12; 4:11; Is. 1:9; 17:6; Ezk. 11:13–21) and will be righteous (Je. 3:12, 14). The renewal brings not only restoration, but glory (Mi. 7:18; Is. 4:3; 37:31; 28:5; Ezk. 48:35; Zc. 12:8).
[3] Ezk. 34:11–31.   [4] Lk. 12:32, RSV.
[5] Rom. 9:6–8.   [6] Jn. 10:27–29; 17:2, 9–10.

we are no people, enemies of God, unworthy of his love.[1] Yet, as Peter declares, we who were no people are now *the people of God*, chosen in Christ as an elect race, *a holy nation*.

Peter's declaration of our 'peoplehood' in Christ has vast consequences for the life of the church of Christ. The church is not just a religious association formed by saved individuals to give united expression to their faith. Rather, the church is more a people than Israel was under the old covenant. Scattered in the world, indeed, as Israel was in dispersion, but a people nonetheless, bound together in the community of those who are united to one another as surely as they are united to their Lord. Church fellowship is not an optional advantage, to be chosen or ignored, like membership in a social club. It is the calling of every Christian. There is a spiritual 'ethnicity' to the church of Christ; Christians are blood relatives, joined by the blood of Jesus Christ.

Peter declares who we are. He declares also what we are to do. The *holy priesthood* offers up *spiritual sacrifices*, declaring *the praises of him who called* us *out of the darkness into his wonderful light*. The parallel between offering spiritual sacrifices and praising God shows us what sacrifices Peter has in mind. 'Through Jesus, therefore, let us continually offer to God a sacrifice of praise – the fruit of lips that confess his name.'[2] The sacrifices of the Old Testament were ceremonies of worship, glorifying God; they symbolized atonement for sin and the giving to God of the life and devotion of the worshipper.[3] The offering of the blood of Christ on the cross has for ever abolished the bringing of bloody sacrifices in the worship of God. But worship remains, not impoverished, but fulfilled. We present ourselves to God as spiritual sacrifices.[4] The dedication of our lives is presented to God with the confession of our lips. Peter says that we *declare the praises* of the Lord. He is citing Isaiah 43:21, 'the people I formed for myself that they may proclaim my praise'. Peter uses the word for 'praise' that is

---

[1] 1 Pet. 2:9–10; Rom. 5:8,10.   [2] Heb. 13:15.
[3] Th. C. Vriezen: 'In Israel the cult exists in order to *maintain and purify the communion between man and God: the cult exists as a means to integrate the communion between God and man which God has instituted in His Covenant, in other words, the cult exists for the sake of the atonement.'* (*An Outline of Old Testament Theology*, Branford, 1970, p. 255; *cf.* p. 261).
[4] Rom. 12:1–2; 15:16.

found in the Septuagint of Isaiah. The Hebrew term that it translates may mean the 'praises' of God in the sense of the praiseworthy deeds of God.[1] The Greek term, too, applied to deity, meant 'mighty deeds'.[2]

The language of the prophet in this passage is the language of the Psalms. Declaring the praises of God is the great work of worship. Two forms of praise appear in the Psalms: praising God for what he had done, and praising God for who he is. Isaiah used a verb that means to 'count' or to 'tell' in the sense of 'recount'. The praises of Israel are full of the recounting of the mighty works of God.[3]

His deeds of creation excited the marvelling awe of the psalmist: 'When I consider your heavens, the work of your fingers . . .'.[4] God provides the armour of the crocodile and feeds the goats on the mountains.[5] God works in history; he raises up kings and puts them down.[6] But above all, it is God's work of salvation that his people celebrate in praise.[7]

Praise is more than thanksgiving.[8] Praise not only offers the sacrifices of thanksgiving for God's deliverance; praise adores God the deliverer. From declaring the works of God, the sacrifice of praise moves on to praise the name of God. To commemorate the saving deeds of the Lord is a thrilling task, but the pinnacle of devotion is to rejoice in God himself, the doer of those deeds. The supreme prayer of devotion is 'Hallowed be thy name.' When we thank God for who he is and ask him to be God, Father, Son, and Holy Spirit, we enter into the high sanctuary of heaven's praise.

Peter says that we have been brought from *darkness* to *light* and made a *priesthood* so that we may show forth God's *praises*. This spiritual worship has no earthly altar or ark; it has transcended the elaborate ceremonials of Old Testament worship. It is vain to imitate in pageantry the ceremonies that ended when the veil of the temple was torn in two. Yet

---

[1] '$t^e hill\bar{a}h$', KB, p. 1020.

[2] Elliott, *Elect*, p. 42; Bauernfeind in *TDNT* gives the meaning 'self-declaration' or 'fame'.

[3] Ps. 73:28 The Septuagint passage uses the same verb, *exangellō*, to translate the Hebrew *sāpher*, 'count' or 'tell'.

[4] Ps. 8:3.   [5] Jb. 41:1-34; Ps. 104:10-22.

[6] Ps. 33:10-11; 96:9-10; 46:6; 76:12-13.

[7] Ps. 9:14; 13:5; 27:1; 40:10; 62:2, 6; 71:15; *etc.*

[8] See Claus Westermann, *The Praise of God in the Psalms*, tr. K. R. Crim (John Knox Press, 1965), pp. 15-35.

worship remains the central calling, not only of the Christian, but of the Christian church. The worship of God consists not only in hearing and responding to his word, as Peter has been reminding us. It finds its burning focus in lifting the name of God in adoration. This function of the priesthood cannot be delegated. God's praises must rise from the lips of all his people, assembled before his face and joining with the festival assembly of the saints and the angels. If the singing and speaking forth of the praises of God are viewed as 'preliminaries' to the sermon, the meaning of worship has been lost.

Nothing can be put above worship. We adore God not to gain his favour, but because adoration is our response to his grace. We are, to be sure, uniquely blessed through worship, and as God's worshippers we seek his blessing. But the core of our worship is not receiving but giving. Peter reminds us that the inestimable privilege of entering the presence of the Lord contains a yet greater privilege: to lift his name in praise. He lifts us up so that we may lift him up.

Yet our praising of the name of God has another result. We declare before the nations the works and the name of the Lord. Our praises to God bear witness to the world. The heart of evangelism is doxological. Peter emphasizes our offering of praise to God.[1] Yet he is also thinking of the Gentile world in the midst of which we are called to praise. Our hallelujahs do indeed join the anthems of the heavenly host, but here on earth they are heard by our neighbours. They, too, are called to doxology (2:12). In the following section of this letter Peter links the witness of our lives to the witness of our lips as we offer praise to God. His citation from Isaiah reminds us of the call to the nations that springs from doxology in the prophets and Psalms. 'Declare his glory among the nations, his marvellous deeds among all peoples' (Ps. 96:3). Paul in Romans cites the Psalms and Isaiah to

[1] Elliott relates the showing forth of God's praises to missionary witness before the nations. He sees this witness of praise as leading to the witness of life in the following section (*Elect*, p. 180). Balch (pp. 132–135) objects that *exangellō* is regularly used for proclamation in worship rather than in evangelism. He questions whether Peter's reference to Is. 43:21 can bring into view Is. 43:6–9 with its presentation of God's Servant bringing light to the Gentiles. But it is not a question of how immediate the contextual reference is. All the praises of Israel were to be sounded forth in the hearing of the nations.

describe the way in which Jesus Christ has set the Gentiles singing God's praise.[1]

The praises of him who called you out of darkness into his wonderful light. . . . Israel was brought from the darkness of Egypt under the plague to the light of God's glory at Sinai. We are brought by God's mighty deed from the darkness of death and the tomb where Christ was sealed. The rising of the light of salvation is celebrated in the prophecy of Isaiah. Christ's ministry in Galilee brought the dawn of the Sun of righteousness; his transfiguration disclosed his heavenly glory, his resurrection brought his people from darkness to the light of eternal morning. Jesus, our Messiah, is given

> to be a covenant for the people
> and a light for the Gentiles,
> to open the eyes that are blind,
> to free captives from prison
> and to release from the dungeon those who sit in darkness.[2]

God's call does more than invite his people to leave the darkness for the light. As Jesus called Lazarus from the tomb, so God calls us from the darkness into the light of 'his eternal glory in Christ' (5:10). We give thanks to the Father 'who has qualified [us] to share in the inheritance of the saints in the kingdom of light. For he has rescued us from the dominion of darkness and brought us into the kingdom of the Son he loves.'[3] When the designers of the Billy Graham Center in Wheaton, Illinois, sought to provide an architectural parable of conversion, they appropriately planned a passageway through darkness into a room walled with brilliant light. The early church prepared candidates for baptism by instructing them in the enlightenment found in Christ.[4] Few images express more vividly the transformation of God's saving call. Once we were darkness, but now are we light in the Lord, called to walk in the light of Jesus Christ, the light of the world.[5]

Peter had experienced God's deliverance from dungeon darkness when the Lord sent his angel to deliver the apostle

[1] Rom. 15:8–16.   [2] Is. 42:6–7.
[3] Col. 1:12–13.   [4] Kelly, p. 100.
[5] Eph. 5:8; 1 Th. 5:5; Jn. 8:12.

from Herod's prison.[1] Charles Wesley used Peter's deliverance as an image of the dawn of faith:

> Long my imprisoned spirit lay
> Fast bound in sin and nature's night;
> Thine eye diffused a quickening ray –
> I woke, the dungeon flamed with light;
> My chains fell off, my heart was free,
> I rose, went forth, and followed thee.[2]

[1] Acts 12:1–11.   [2] The hymn 'And can it be'.

5. Live as the people of God
II: The new lifestyle

1. The new lifestyle's pattern: freedom in bondage (2:11–17)

Dear friends, I urge you, as aliens and strangers in the world, to abstain from sinful desires, which war against your soul. ¹²Live such good lives among the pagans that, though they accuse you of doing wrong, they may see your good deeds and glorify God on the day he visits us.

¹³Submit yourselves for the Lord's sake to every authority instituted among men: whether to the king, as the supreme authority, ¹⁴or to governers, who are sent by him to punish those who do wrong and to commend those who do right. ¹⁵For it is God's will that by doing good you should silence the ignorant talk of foolish men. ¹⁶Live as free men, but do not use your freedom as a cover-up for evil; live as servants of God. ¹⁷Show proper respect to everyone: Love the brotherhood of believers, fear God, honour the king.

Peter moves to a suprising and urgent application of the teaching he has just given. He has been emphasizing the status that Christians have as the people of God, chosen by him and drawn into privileged fellowship. They are a priestly nation, the recipients of God's grace and favour.

But why should Peter remind them of their status? To be sure, he would have them exercise their priesthood in praising the Lord who bought them; but he has another reason. He would prepare them for lowly service. Just because they are God's royal people they can be servants. The example of Jesus is already before Peter, although he does not yet mention it directly. Knowing who he was, and what he came to do, Jesus could subject himself to people. He came not to be ministered to, but to minister, and to give his life a ransom for many.[1] Called as children of the light, Christians are free. Their freedom, however, binds them to their calling. They are free in bondage to God. They know what it means to fear God in his presence. They are free to love their fellow-Christians. The dark blindness of sinful selfishness is gone; they are free to love. They are also free to honour unbelievers as God's creatures, and to respect the role of authority given to each one.

This whole section is in direct antithesis to the spirit of the world, where every individual and group demands its 'rights' and understands liberty as freedom from responsibility. The apostle describes what is, for our time, a strange liberty. Yet, as Roberto Mangabeira Unger has pointed out, the liberal ideal of liberty is bankrupt.[2] The liberal ideal would free every individual to do what he wants. If there must be curbs to this freedom, they must be neutral and impersonal. But the liberal can find no ground for this neutrality in his own liberal assumptions. The letter of the law cannot provide neutrality, for, on liberal assumptions, the language of law is arbitrary, carrying such meaning as we choose to assign to it. Similarly, if law is viewed as social policy, neutrality is impossible. As Alexander Solzhenitsyn has reminded us, the Soviet Criminal Code of 1926 makes any action directed toward the weakening of state power counter-revolutionary. Only what advances the Soviet state is legal. If there is no standard for values outside of society, there can be no true liberty in social policy.

Peter proclaims liberty in Christ. Because our liberty is under God there is an objective standard of value. But our liberty is not under an abstract deity. It is under the true and living God. It could be no liberty at all if Christ had not died to set us free and to proclaim liberty in the jubilee time of God's favour.[3]

Our freedom is necessarily in servitude to God. Paul delighted to call himself the slave of Jesus Christ.[4] But we

---

[1] Mk. 10:45.
[2] Roberto Mangabeira Unger, *Knowledge and Politics* (Macmillan, ²1984).
[3] Lk. 4:18–21.   [4] Rom. 1:1; Gal. 1:10; Phil. 1:1; Tit. 1:1.

also are called to serve our fellow-Christians and to render proper service to the people of the world. In this section Peter describes our freedom in service: to God, to the church, and to the world.[1]

a. Free in bondage to God: 'Fear God!'

The freedom of God's servants in this world is the freedom of *aliens* and transients. Those who belong to God as his people can have no abiding city here. Like Abraham, they are strangers and pilgrims, even while they live in the world which they will inherit at last.[2] Peter asks his *dear friends* to *abstain from sinful desires*, as *strangers* in a sinful world. The verb *to abstain* fits the calling of strangers. It means literally 'to distance' themselves from fleshly lusts. A temporary resident in a foreign land is not likely to adopt the customs of the land through which he is travelling. His standard of values, his lifestyle, is different.[3] Peter wants Christian pilgrims to remember their heavenly citizenship. Calling his hearers 'transients' or 'pilgrims', Peter returns to a description he used at the beginning of his letter (1:1). He has now shown why they must regard themselves as pilgrims: they are the people of God, a holy nation, and they dare not conform to the wicked conduct of their neighbours. Instead, they must bear witness by their *deeds* to the kingdom of light.

Peter calls the pilgrims *dear friends* to express his affection for them. It expresses as well their belonging to God. They are 'dear' or (better) 'beloved' (*agapētoi*) not only to Peter, but to the Lord, as his own possession. Their alienation from the world is just because they are dear to God.[4] Jesus himself is the Beloved of the Father.[5] (The biblical use of the term goes back to the description of Isaac as the beloved son of Abraham.[6]) Peter's *dear friends* are God's beloved children, adopted in his Son.[7]

Because they are God's children and pilgrims in this world,

---

[1] Peter uses the term 'slaves' only of our service to God. Paul, too, makes it clear that Christians are not the slaves of people, even when they serve them (1 Cor. 7:21–23).
[2] Gn. 23:4.　　[3] Spicq, *Epîtres*, p. 97.　　[4] Jn. 17:16; 1 Jn. 2:15–16.
[5] Mk. 1:11; 9:7; 2 Pet. 1:17; see Eph. 1:6; Gn. 22:2, LXX.
[6] Gn. 22:2, LXX.　　[7] Rom. 1:7; Eph. 5:1.

Christians are also warriors, repulsing the attacks of fleshly lusts that war against the soul. Peter clearly states the opposition between the *desires* of the flesh (literally) and the welfare of the *soul*. This does not mean that our souls are innately good and our bodies innately evil. When Peter lists the 'evil human desires' in the Gentile world, he includes the non-fleshly sin of 'detestable idolatry'.[1] Yet, in our fallen world – Rome in Peter's day, New York or London in ours – the corruption of bodily desires for food, drink, and sex sweeps over us like a flooding sewer. The apostle calls on Christians to be 'out of it', out of the compulsive urgings of hammering sexual music, the seductions of pandering commercials, the sadism of pornographic films and paperbacks. In fleshly temptation the devil promises life, but his assault is against life; he would devour our very souls (5:8). John Stott well points out that the apostolic counter to lasciviousness is thankfulness for sex in loving marriage.[2] God is the creator of our bodies; sex is his gift, not Satan's invention.

Christians have been liberated from sin's bondage, not only to praise God, but to live as his witnesses in the world. Here is an apparent paradox. Christians are not to be *of* the world, but they are to be *in* the world. Peter warns against the desires of the flesh, but instructs us how to live 'the rest of your time in the flesh' (4:2, ASV). In a long section in the middle of his letter, Peter presents the kind of ethical instruction that was common in the early church. We find similar lists of duties within domestic relationships in Paul's letters.[3] But Peter presents these duties in the framework of his special concern. He urges Christians to be the servants of God in the world, and therefore to submit themselves willingly, and even to suffer, so that God might receive the glory.

Peter's instructions tell us how to relate to the world while we are pilgrims in it. On the one hand, we do all before God and for God. (Notice how many times through the rest of this chapter Peter refers to God or Christ.) On the other

---

[1] 1 Pet. 4:2–3. See Paul's list of the deeds of the flesh, Gal. 5:19–21.

[2] Stott, *The Message of Ephesians* (IVP, 1979), pp. 191–193.

[3] Col. 3:18 – 4:1; Eph. 5:21 – 6:9; 1 Tim. 2:8–15; 5:1–2; 6:1–2; Tit. 2:1–10; 3:1. On the Ephesians passage, see Stott, *op. cit.*, p. 214. On the background of the code of household ethics, see Balch.

hand, Christians also live before the world. Some of the duties in the Christian 'household code' were also advocated by Greek or Roman moralists.[1] This is not unintentional on the part of the apostles. To some extent the Gentiles do recognize right and wrong in human relationships (performance being quite another matter!). Surely to that extent Christians must commend themselves to their neighbours and win their grudging respect. When Peter tells his hearers to live *good lives*, he uses a word that can also mean 'beautiful' or 'attractive'. The high holiness of fellowship with God must also produce observable conduct, admirable in its consistency and integrity. This theme of luminous goodness runs like a thread through all of Peter's exhortations.[2] It reflects the word of Jesus, 'Let your light shine before men, that they may see your good deeds and praise your Father in heaven.'[3]

But, given the bias of unbelievers against God, even the good that Christians do will be ill spoken of. That certainly happened. The Roman historian Tacitus remarks that Christians were 'loathed because of their abominations'. Another author, Suetonius, approved of Nero's persecution of Christians, 'a class of people animated by a novel and mischievous superstition'.[4]

Peter knows that the opposition of the Gentile world will not be limited to gossip, calumnies. and fantastic lies. Christians will be accused in the courts; false charges will lead to imprisonment and death. Peter had escaped the sword of Herod, but he would not escape the perverse hatred of Nero.

Yet in spite of pagan injustice, the impact of the Christian witness will not be lost, in Peter's day or ours. The surrounding world will see the *good deeds* of the Christian community (2:12). They cannot avoid it. For some, unbelief will turn to belief as they behold the obedience of the people of God. Unbelieving husbands will see, and be touched by, the godliness of their wives (3:1-2). In the day of God's 'visitation', even those who misrepresented and hated the good works of Christians will *glorify God* for them.

The term 'visitation' in the Old Testament most often

---

[1] See Balch; Spicq, *Epîtres*, pp. 95f.; Goppelt, pp. 163–179; Stott, *op. cit.*, p. 214.
[2] 1 Pet. 1:14–15, 22; 2:9–12, 15–16, 20; 3:1, 10–17; 4:4–5, 17; 5:5–6.
[3] Mt. 5:16; *cf.* v. 12.   [4] Kelly, p. 105.

refers to God's coming in judgment.[1] It is also used, however, of God's coming in mercy. Zacharias praises God for 'visiting' and redeeming his people in the birth of his son John. John is the forerunner of the Messiah, in whom 'the dayspring from on high hath visited us.'[2] If the 'day of visitation' bears a positive sense here, it would mean the conviction and conversion of those who have seen Christian behaviour. However, in view of the emphasis that Peter puts on the coming of judgment in the day of the Lord, it seems more likely that Peter is describing the day when every tongue shall confess that Jesus Christ is Lord.[3] God's searching judgment will then compel the acknowledgment, to his glory, of the faithful living of his true servants.[4]

b. Free in submission to others

Peter draws a radical and difficult conclusion. Christians who would *live as servants of God* in this world (2:16) must be willing to be in submission to others. There is, of course, a vast difference between our submission to God and our submission to other people. He tells us to fear God; he does not tell us to fear people. Peter does not call to us to become their slaves. Even when he addresses those who are slaves, he uses another word, 'household servants' (2:18). Peter does not argue that we should be lowly before others because we are lowly before God. He does the opposite; he stresses the privileged position to which God has exalted us. We have been brought near to God as priests, saints, sons and daughters. Because we are God's own possession, beloved of the Lord, we need not cherish our own dignity. Indeed, we may not. For the Lord's sake, for our fellow-Christians' sake, for the world's sake, we must be ready to subordinate ourselves to others.

We submit ourselves for the world's sake so that our good deeds may be a witness to them or a testimony against them. We submit ourselves for our fellow-Christians' sake out of

---

[1] Jeremiah uses the term most frequently (8:12; 10:15; 11:23, *etc.*). God is said to 'visit iniquity' in judgment (Ex. 20:5; 34:7; Lv. 18:25). God's 'visit' may also bring blessing (Gn. 21:1; 50:24).

[2] Lk. 1:78, AV.   [3] Phil. 2:11.

[4] So Bénétreau, pp. 147f. as against Stibbs, Selwyn, and Goppelt – who mistakenly says 'A forced praise would be absurd' (p. 162).

sacrificial love for them. We submit ourselves for God's sake because we honour his image in our fellow-creatures, and because we respect his ordering of our lives, but especially because we gratefully seek to take up our cross and follow Jesus Christ. In the code of duties that follows, Peter describes Christian living in terms of submission: submission to one another as Christians, and especially to unbelievers.

2. The new lifestyle's practice: submission in role relationships (2:13–14, 18–20)

a. Submission as citizens of worldly kingdoms (2:13–14)

Peter provides almost a title for what follows: *Submit your-selves.* In this whole section the general principle of submission is developed according to the roles that we fill: citizens are to submit themselves to their *governors* (2:14) and servants to their masters (2:18); wives to their husbands (3:1) and, in a yet deeper sense, husbands to their wives (3:7); and Christians to one another (3:8).

It is this link with what follows that helps us to understand what might seem to be a strange expression: literally 'Be subject to every human creature' (2:13). Many interpreters give another meaning to the word for 'creature'. They take it to mean 'order' or 'institution'. (The NIV expands this to *authority instituted*). It is hard to find a clear example of this meaning outside the Bible, and it never means this in biblical usage.[1] Peter is not talking about submission to institutions, but submission to people; to people, however, who have been given roles to fill in God's appointment. Our submission is to creatures of God made in his image. We are to show proper respect to everyone (2:17), recognizing them as God's creatures to whom honour and respect are due. C. S. Lewis has said that if we could see a lowly Christian as he will be in glory, our temptation would be to fall down and worship him.[2] Peter does not call us to worship human beings, of course. Indeed, he may speak of human creatures

---

[1] See W. Foerster, *TDNT* III, pp. 103f.; Kelly, pp. 108f.; Spicq, *Epîtres*, pp. 101f.; Goppelt, p. 182; Bénétreau, pp. 149f.

[2] Clyde S. Kilby, ed., *A Mind Awake: An Anthology of C. S. Lewis* (Harcourt, Brace & World, 1968), p. 125 (excerpt from *Transposition and Other Addresses*).

so as to oppose emperor worship.[1] In spite of the claim of Caesar, he is only a human creature. Such a creature is not to be worshipped, but is to be shown honour; we are to be in submission to him.

There is a submission that is due to every human being, the submission of respect and honour. As Paul says, we are 'to show true humility towards all men'.[2] The particular submission that we owe another will vary according to the role that the person fills in the divine ordering of human life. Peter goes on to describe certain roles. The form of our submission is unique to Christian witness. Christians are called to serve others, to go the second mile, to suffer injustice without demanding their rights, knowing that they have an assured status before God, and that he will vindicate them at last. In this willingness to serve while suffering injustice, Christ himself is the great example for those who bear his name.

It is this submission to suffering, not as something inevitable, but as the Lord's calling, that distinguishes the Christian pattern of loving service. It is true that Stoic moralists had also made lists of duties appropriate to the various stations of life; Jewish authors had similar codes for good behaviour.[3] The same framework appears in Paul's letters, and seems to have been a fixed pattern in Christian teaching.[4] But while Christian instruction followed to some extent a common form of classified duties, the contents were transformed by the teaching and the love of Christ. Peter, in particular, shows the completely new dimension brought to morality by the sacrificial love of the Saviour.

For good behaviour among the pagans, Christians must be subject to the existing rulers. This may seem a commonplace to us: Christians are to be law-abiding citizens. Yet it was a burning issue when the letter was written, and it has become an issue again today. How are God's people to relate to the kingdoms of this world? Israel had been given the land of

[1] Spicq, *Epîtres*, calls attention to this, referring especially to passages in the *Wisdom of Solomon* denouncing the idolatry of worshipping kings (pp. 101f.).
[2] Tit. 3:2.   [3] Kelly cites references, pp. 107–108.
[4] See above, p. 102 n. 1. Kelly gives examples from early Christian writing: the *Didache* 4:9–11; *1 Clement* 1:3; 21:6–9; *Epistle of Barnabas* 19:5–7; Polycarp, *Philippians* 4:2 – 6:2. See *AF*. See also Bénétreau, Excursus III, 'The Social Ethics of 1 Peter', pp. 177–185.

promise through God's blessing on armed conquest. God used Israel to judge the Canaanites and Amorites when the cup of their iniquity was full.[1] David's kingdom was established with victories over the Philistines and other surrounding nations. When Israel sinned, God used the Assyrians and Babylonians as his instruments to judge and punish Israel. The whole nation went into captivity. The prophets, however, promised a vast restoration, including the triumph of the people of God over all their enemies.[2] Fired by the memory of independence under the Maccabees, Zealots in the time of Christ fought as guerrillas and terrorists against the Roman occupation. At least one of Christ's disciples seems to have been a Zealot.[3] Revolt led by Zealots was to bring the destruction of Jerusalem by the Romans in AD 70, a few years after the time that Peter wrote this letter.

The teaching of Jesus, however, cut across revolutionary political expectations. When he refused to claim political kingship and lead revolt against the Romans, the crowds began to desert him. Peter's confession revealed his faith in Christ even when he could not understand the kingdom Christ was bringing in. The Old Testament promises, as even John the Baptist understood them, predicted salvation through judgment. To deliver the poor and the oppressed, the Messiah must judge the oppressor. The Coming One must hew down all unjust power to inaugurate his peace.[4]

In the light of Easter and Pentecost, Peter could remember the delegation of John's disciples who had come to Jesus. 'Are you the one who was to come, or should we expect someone else?' they asked.[5] John, in Herod's prison, had heard of Jesus' power to raise the dead, and was baffled that Jesus did not use his power to bring in his kingdom (and to deliver his forerunner!). Jesus kept John's disciples with him while he performed miracles that directly fulfilled the prophecies of Isaiah. He then sent them back to tell John what was happening, and added the word, 'Blessed is he, whosoever shall not be offended in me.'[6] Jesus was performing signs of kingdom blessing without first inflicting kingdom judgment. John must trust the King to bring in his kingdom

[1] Gn. 15:16.   [2] *E.g.* Zc. 12:1-9.
[3] On the Zealots, see *ODCC*, p. 1510.   [4] Mt. 3:10.   [5] Lk. 7:19.
[6] Lk. 7:23, AV; *cf.* Lk. 7:22; Is. 35:5-6.

LIVE AS THE PEOPLE OF GOD, II

in his own way. That way was the way of the cross. Jesus came not to destroy people but to save them. To accomplish that, he had to defeat the great oppressor, Satan; he had to redeem sinners from the guilt of sin. His hands did not grasp a sword, but were stretched out to be pierced with nails. He did not lift a spear but received the thrust of the spear in his side. He did not come to bring the judgment, but to bear it . . . for us.

Christ's death was his victory over Satan; it was the judgment of the prince of this world.[1] Yet the day of Christ's final judgment will come only when Christ comes again. Peter awaited that coming (1:5, 7, 13; 4:5, 13; 5:1, 4; *cf.* 3:22). Christ had made Peter put up his sword; not in that way would his kingdom be brought in. As Jesus suffered meekly, so must his followers (2:21). His kingdom cannot therefore be one of the kingdoms of this world. His servants cannot use the sword to bring in kingdom justice. Kingdom justice must be absolute; only Christ can bring it.

What, then, of this interval between the first and second coming of Christ? Christ rules in glory, but what of human government on earth? Peter has already given the key to this question when he calls the new people of God the Diaspora (1:1). Just as the Jews in exile were scattered among the nations of the earth, so now are the people of God scattered. In the exile God had shown how his people might live among the nations, praying for the peace of the cities where they were captive.[2] The subjection to Gentile government of the Jewish communities in dispersion paved the way for the pilgrim form of the people of God. New believers from the Gentiles joined believing Jews of the dispersion; they must be taught a similar loyalty to the existing Roman government.

Peter's instruction to this effect has always been needed. There has been no end of confusion about civil and spiritual power. Some have directly challenged the word of the Lord that his servants do not fight because his kingdom is not of this world.[3] Claiming to be Christ's servants they have taken the sword in his name. Often this has not been done directly in the name of the church. Rather the church has summoned the kings of the earth to do its bidding and to carry out its

[1] Jn. 12:31.   [2] Je. 29:7.   [3] Jn. 18:36.

108

crusades.[1] Empires, nations and city-states have identified themselves as the political arm of Christ's kingdom.[2] They have imagined themselves to be the theocratic successors of Old Testament Israel, and have gone to battle singing imprecatory psalms against their foes.[3]

Nations claiming theocratic status are now limited to the Muslim lands dominated by Islamic fundamentalists. The temptation to take the sword in Christ's name is again offered, however, in liberation theology. The error is not the conclusion that there can arise regimes so unjust as to make revolution justifiable. The error is the sanctifying of revolution as the work of God's kingdom, a work of salvation to be pursued in his name.[4] No state, no freedom fighters today can lay claim to Israel's theocratic calling as warriors of God's covenant. The new Israel is the church of Jesus Christ, and he has forbidden the sword to the church. Under the lordship of Christ the kingdom of God does take form in the church, but through mightier weapons than the sword: weapons, as Paul affirms, that can reduce every towering imagination of the rebellious human heart.[5] No other weapons can advance Christ's kingdom. The political renovation of the world awaits his return, for he is the sole monarch of the universe. Until he comes, Christians are to be in submission to the governments that exist in the world.

This, too, is part of God's plan. We submit to the king for the Lord's sake, not just because the king has the force to govern. While Peter does not say explicitly, as Paul does, that the powers that be are ordained of God, he nevertheless recognizes their authority as part of the order that is God's

[1] Pope Urban II and Peter the Hermit launched the Crusades under the motto *Deus vult*, 'God wills it.' The feudal nobility of Europe provided the armies to seek to wrest the Holy Land from the Muslims, but the church issued the call to arms.

[2] Calvin's Geneva distinguished the government of the city from the government of the church. Calvin strongly defended the independence of the church from political control. Yet the civic authorities condemned Servetus. As a Reformed city, it viewed heresy as treason.

[3] Never, perhaps, in a more distressing way than in the battles between the Parliamentary troops under Cromwell and the armies of Scotland, when both sides might sing the same psalms.

[4] It is asserted by the advocates of political theology not only that the church must engage in political action, but that the gospel for today is political. The struggle against the 'principalities and powers' is seen as the political struggle for justice.

[5] 2 Cor. 10:3–6.

will for us.[1] That he does recognize this authority as more than a circumstance of God's providence appears from his summary of this section. There he places the honour we owe to the king beside the fear we owe to God, the honour we owe to all people, and the love we owe to the brethren (2:17).

For the Lord's sake refers not so much to our duty as to the opportunities God gives us in our relationships. We serve and honour the Lord by submitting to others. We honour every 'human creature' and acknowledge the supreme authority of the king and of governors sent by him. This is amazing when we reflect that the supreme king of the Roman empire was the neurotic Nero and that a governor sent by another Caesar was Pontius Pilate! Jesus, however, had justified paying tribute to Caesar, and had recognized the authority of Pilate as given, not merely from Rome, but from heaven.[2]

For the Lord's sake implies, then, that our obedience serves God's purpose. By our civil obedience we *silence the ignorant talk of foolish men*. Christians were often charged with subversion of the established order. They were accused of spreading disloyalty against the government, of disrupting trade, and of all manner of shocking practices, including cannibalism and incest.[3] By their law-abiding conduct they could give the lie to such wild and ignorant accusations.

Peter could speak of the Roman government, in spite of its exploitative economic practices and its curtailing of liberty, as a government that punished those who did wrong and commended those who did right. Clearly he does not imply that the perfect justice of Messiah's reign was executed by Nero. Nor does he encourage civil disobedience until Nero's administration of justice improved. Rather, Peter states the purpose of government in terms that Roman government adequately fulfilled: the restraint of crime and wrong-doing and the encouragement of civic righteousness. No doubt regimes may arise that would be so oppressive and unjust that they can no longer be said to fulfil that function. Peter's description of the function of governments serves indirectly

---

[1] Rom. 13:1–7; Tit. 3:1. Biggs, on entirely insufficient evidence, imagines that Peter is a constitutionalist and Paul a royalist (p. 140).

[2] Mt. 22:21; Jn. 19:11. It is just possible that Peter, in speaking of governors sent 'by means of' the king is suggesting that the king is God's instrument in granting the authority that comes from from God.

[3] Biggs, p. 137.

to limit his command to be in subjection to them.

Peter gives instruction to subjects, not to rulers; to servants, not to masters. He instructs both husbands and wives in a significantly different relationship. Why does he not caution Christian masters? What of Christian rulers? Part of the answer may have been the membership of the churches that Peter addressed. Presumably very few were rulers or wealthy householders. Yet there is clearly another reason. Every Christian needs to learn the secret of freedom, freedom in bondage to the Lord and in humility toward people. Peter never forgot that his Lord had washed his feet. As Jesus girded himself with a towel, we must all gird ourselves with humility in order to serve one another. Peter reminds the proud that they must learn this lesson of humility (5:5). The lesson of submission in freedom is particularly important, however, for those who must bear subjection in their daily life. Theirs is a special privilege: they find that they can serve the Lord in serving others; their humble witness can powerfully show the love of Christ. Peter addresses them in particular to teach the humility that all must learn.

As Paul's letters show us, there is apostolic instruction for those who receive submission as well as for those who render it.[1] The lesson is the same. Particularly in the church, all authority is exercised as a ministry. Jesus' disciples are not to govern the church in the fashion of rule among the nations (5:2–3).[2] Christ's lordship must also transform the way Christians exercise authority in the other spheres of life. They will understand that political authority, too, is service under God. Its purpose is the good of those governed, not the glory of the governor or the profit of the governing class. This principle guides Christians who share in governing authority in democracies. Their goal must also be to serve, to seek the good of the whole people, with special concern for the poor and weak.[3]

[1] Paul instructs husbands (Eph. 5:25–33; Col. 3:19); fathers (Eph. 6:4; Col. 3:21); masters (Eph. 6:9; Col. 4:1).

[2] Mt. 20:25–28; Lk. 22:25–27.

[3] See the discussions in Christopher J. H. Wright, *Living as the People of God* (USA title *An Eye for an Eye*, IVP, 1983); John Stott, *Issues Facing Christians Today* (Marshall, Morgan & Scott, 1984); David Lyon, *Karl Marx* (Lion, 1979), pp. 146–156; Harold O. J. Brown, *The Reconstruction of the Republic* (Arlington House, 1977).

Peter summarizes his teaching of humility in compact and memorable form: 'Honour everyone; love the brotherhood; fear God; keep honouring the king' (2:17).[1] The form of our submission differs greatly, although it is all grounded in the fear of God, who made us in his image. We do not simply honour our fellow-Christians, we love them dearly (1:22). Our continuing respect for the king (2:13) does not worship him as divine, but is of a piece with the respect we owe to all. These brief mottoes summarize again the two commandments that fulfil the law: love for God and love for neighbour.

b. Submission as servants of worldly masters (2:18–20)

Slaves, submit yourselves to your masters with all respect, not only to those who are good and considerate, but also to those who are harsh. ¹⁹For it is commendable if a man bears up under the pain of unjust suffering because he is conscious of God. ²⁰But how is it to your credit if you receive a beating for doing wrong and endure it? But if you suffer for doing good and you endure it, this is commendable before God.

The NIV translation *slaves* is not precise. Peter addresses 'domestics' (*oiketai*), those servants and retainers who would be under the rule and control of an often despotic head of the household. Nevertheless, he seems to have slaves mainly in view: perhaps he wants to reserve the usual Greek word for 'slaves', *douloi*, for our service to the Lord (2:16). Slavery was widespread in Peter's world; it included many who would today be regarded as professionals: managers of estates, physicians, teachers and tutors.[2]

Peter's admonition reveals in pointed fashion the heart of his teaching about submission. Obviously his concern is not social stability or the perpetuation of slavery. He does take for granted faithful service on the part of Christian household slaves. In a sense, this is the least they can do to show their willingness to serve God where he has placed them. If they

---

[1] The same verb for 'honour' is used of the honour towards all and towards the king. The imperative in the first use is aorist, in the second, the present tense. My translation may put too much emphasis on the difference in tenses.

[2] See Kelly, p. 115; Bénétreau, pp. 154f., who notes that the procurator Felix of Acts 23 was a freedman.

are at fault in this service, they should expect punishment and not suppose that such suffering has any particular value. What does have point and value for their Christian testimony is their response to unjust punishment. Such treatment offers a golden opportunity to show the uniqueness of Christian service. By patiently enduring unmerited abuse they show the opposite of a servile attitude. They demonstrate their freedom. In their servitude they may not escape beatings. They may be beaten without cause, or even for good things that they have done; a 'crooked', perverse master may repay evil for good.[1] If the Christian responds in kind – good for good, evil for evil – he becomes merely a victim when he is treated unjustly. In burning resentment he seeks an opportunity to repay the evil. But if he bears the evil patiently he has broken the chain of bondage in the power of the Lord. He shows his confidence in God's justice; he need not avenge himself. He also shows that his service is not really forced but voluntary. He is willing to serve his master for the Lord's sake, even to honour him for the Lord's sake. His master cannot enslave him, for he is Christ's slave; he cannot humiliate him, for he has humbled himself in willing subjection.

Peter is here applying the teaching he heard from his Lord.[2] It is the privilege of those who are sons and daughters of the Most High to imitate the magnificence of their Father's mercy. They rise above simple justice to reflect God's goodness and love. Unthreatened by evil, they can overcome evil with good, and in the midst of suffering show mercy to those who would show no mercy toward them.

'And I thank God that he has given me the love to seek to convert and to adopt as my son the enemy who killed my dear boys.' These were the words of Korean Pastor Yang-won Son. The year was 1948; the place was the town of Soon-chun, near the 38th parallel. A band of Communists had taken control of the town for a brief period, and had executed Pastor Son's two older boys, Matthew and John. They died as martyrs, calling on their persecutors to have

[1] 'Harsh' masters, literally 'crooked' or 'perverse'. The passage does not say explicitly that the suffering is attributable to doing good, only that it is received in the course of doing good.
[2] Lk. 6:32–35.

faith in Jesus. When the Communists were driven out, Chai-sun, a young man of the village, was identified as one who had fired the murderous shots. His execution was ordered. Pastor Son requested that the charges be dropped and that Chai-sun be released into his custody for adoption. Rachel, the thirteen-year-old sister of the murdered boys, testified to support her father's incredible request. Only then did the court agree to release Chai-sun. He became the son of the pastor, and a believer in the grace of Jesus Christ.[1]

How different is the forgiving love of Christ from the best of pagan ethics! Seneca wrote, 'What will the wise man do when he is buffeted? He will do as Cato did . . . He did not burst into a passion, did not avenge himself, did not even forgive it, but denied its having been done.'[2]

The respect that servants show for their masters is not a slavish fear, but the result of their fear of God. The word translated *respect* in 2:18 is *phobos*, which does mean 'fear'. Some think that Peter is here speaking of the fear of God rather than of respect to masters: 'Servants, be in subjection to your masters with all fear [of God].' In favour of this understanding is the fact that Peter has just distinguished between the fear we show toward God and the honour that we give to people (2:17). He also says that we do not share the unbeliever's fear (3:14). But *phobos* may carry many shades of meaning, as Peter's usage shows (3:14). Peter commends *phobos* in a wife's behaviour toward her husband (3:2)[3] Paul shows the connection between 'fear' of masters and fear of God when he tells slaves to be obedient, with fear and trembling, 'but like slaves of Christ, doing the will of God from your heart.'[4] Slavery to Christ transforms servitude into freedom.

For it is commendable if a man bears up under the pain of unjust suffering because he is conscious of God. The translation *conscious of God* interprets the word *syneidēsis* in the general sense of 'consciousness', rather than in the more technical sense, 'conscience', that is usual in the New Testament. The NIV gives the word its usual translation in two other passages where Peter speaks of a good conscience (3:16, 21). The difference is that in 3:21 Peter speaks of a good

---

[1] Yong Choon Ahn, *The Triumph of Pastor Son* (IVP, 1973), pp. 51f.
[2] See Selwyn, p. 178, for the citation.   [3] See Eph. 5:33.   [4] Eph. 6:6.

conscience *toward* God, while in 2:19 his phrase is 'conscience *of* God'. Perhaps Peter is describing the conscience as being of God in its origin, God-given. More likely, he thinks of the conscience as directed toward God. In that case, the difference from 'consciousness' is not great; the translation 'conscience' would stress ingrained and habitual reference to the will of God in the midst of patient suffering for his sake.[1]

The term for *commendable* is *charis*, which means 'grace', or 'gracious' in the sense of 'pleasing' (2:19–20). Could it have the stronger meaning that it has elsewhere in the letter (1:2, 10, 13; 3:7; 4:10; 5:10, 12)? 'This is grace, if a man bears up . . . this is grace before God.' Samuel Bénétreau thinks so: 'Peter dares to claim it: this unmerited suffering takes place in the majestic current of grace. It is a favour of God! Only the light thrown by the christological section which is going to follow could permit the accepting, if not the comprehending, of so demanding a thesis.'[2]

In spite of Bénétreau's appeal, however, the weaker meaning of 'gracious' or 'thankworthy' seems to fit better. The word is used this way in Luke 6:32–34, and this saying of Jesus was evidently in Peter's thoughts as he wrote the passage. Further, Peter puts *charis* in parallel with *kleos*, 'glory' or *credit* (2:20).[3]

Clearly Peter has the submission of Christ already in view as he describes the submission of Christian servants. Christ is the suffering Servant of the Lord. He, too, was beaten. Mark's Gospel, reflecting Peter's preaching, uses the term to describe Christ's beating before Pilate.[4] Now Peter turns to the suffering Lord whom Christians are called to follow.

---

[1] Selwyn, p. 178.   [2] Bénétreau, p. 157.
[3] See Selwyn, p. 176; Spicq, *Epîtres*, p. 109.   [4] Mk. 14:65; 1 Pet. 2:20.

6. Live as people of God
III: The new lifestyle (continued)

3. The new lifestyle's motivation: Christ's suffering (2:21–25)

a. His saving example: in his steps (2:21–23)

To this you were called, because Christ suffered for you, leaving you an example, that you should follow in his steps.

> [22]'He committed no sin,
> and no deceit was found in his mouth.'

[23]When they hurled their insults at him, he did not retaliate; when he suffered, he made no threats. Instead, he entrusted himself to him who judges justly.

To this you were called. Peter has shown the glory of God's calling. Christians have been called out of darkness into God's marvellous light (2:9). They are called as God's elect, his chosen people, heirs of his blessing (3:9). But now Peter says, *To this you were called.* To what? To suffering, to unjust abuse, to patient endurance when they are beaten for doing right! Peter has described our heavenly calling; he does not conceal our earthly calling. 'Many are the afflictions of the righteous,' declares the psalm to which Peter often alludes in this letter.[1] Clearly Peter is thinking not only of Christian servants who were subject to abuse. They have a particular duty to serve the Lord where he has called them; in this, however, they do not differ from their brothers and sisters

[1] Ps. 34:19, RSV.

in other situations. All Christians are called to suffer with Christ before they are glorified with him. Archbishop Leighton comments on the readiness of Christians to claim the peace of Christ while expecting no tribulation in the world. 'They like better St. Peter's carnal advice to Christ, to avoid suffering, Matt. 16:22, than his Apostolic doctrine to Christians, teaching them, that as Christ *suffered*, so they likewise *are called to suffering*.'[1]

Peter does not ask us to view suffering as inevitable in the world under the curse. He does not ask for stoic resignation. A life of suffering is our calling, not our fate. It is our calling just because we are God's people. It is our calling because it was Christ's calling. He calls his disciples to follow him. To be sure, suffering is a flame to burn away the dross so that our tested faith may shine as gold (1:7; 4:12). Some of the suffering that we endure is the direct result of our own sin (2:20; 3:17). But our example in suffering is One who was totally innocent and free from sin (2:22). He suffered, not for his own sake, but for the sake of God's purpose, and for the salvation of others. As we follow him, we suffer for his sake, and for the sake of winning others to his saving gospel (3:1–2; 4:13–16).

Two themes are woven together in this magnificent section of Peter's letter. One is the theme of the *example* of Christ's suffering: *leaving you an example*. The other is the more basic theme of the *saving purpose* of Christ's suffering: *Christ suffered for you*. Some commentators suppose that the cadenced prose of this passage must reflect an early Christian hymn or a credal statement.[2] It has been suggested that the references to the atoning power of Christ's suffering are present here because they were in the source that Peter quoted. Kelly even speaks of 'the stress of the vicarious nature of Christ's sufferings, which is a theme that is strictly irrelevant to the conduct of slaves.'[3]

Far from being irrelevant to Peter's exhortation, the atoning sacrifice of Christ lies at the heart of all that he has to say. The cadences of the passage could well reflect the eloquence with which Peter had preached Christ, the suffering Servant, from the prophecies of Isaiah. The example of Christ

[1] Leighton, p. 216. [2] See the literature in Goppelt, pp. 204f.
[3] Kelly, p. 119.

is a *saving* example. Peter does not hold forth the meekness of Christ simply as an abstract pattern, a pattern that might have been offered by any uncomplaining sufferer. Christ's suffering is our model because it is our salvation. It does not simply guide us; it is the root of all our motivation to follow. Our 'living to righteousness' follows in Christ's steps because we died to sin in his atonement (2:24). Remove Christ's atonement from the passage and its point would be lost.

Knowing that we were redeemed by the precious blood of Christ (1:19), we take up our cross to follow him. He has left us an example, a pattern to follow. Peter's word translated *example* refers to a pattern to be traced. Clement of Alexandria gives samples of Greek sentences containing all the letters of the alphabet (the Greek equivalent of 'The quick brown fox jumps over the lazy dog').[1] They were written out to be traced so that children would learn their ABC. The word could also apply to an artist's sketch to be filled in (our painting-by-number kits).

To the vivid figure in his word for *example*, Peter joins another, the figure of footsteps to be traced. Peter, Christ's disciple, had followed in his Master's footsteps along the narrow paths of the hill country and through fields of grain in Galilee. No doubt Peter also witnessed the dreadful procession that led to Calvary. To save himself from that path he had sworn fearful oaths. Now he is ready to follow Jesus all the way. He calls every Christian to walk that path with him.

The path that Jesus took was the path of meek obedience to the calling of his Father. Peter now presents Jesus as the suffering Servant of the Lord, taking his language from the song of the Servant in Isaiah 53. Jesus advances toward Calvary as a lamb that is led to the slaughter (Is. 53:7). He is without sin or deceit; here Peter quotes directly from Isaiah 53:9. The sufferings of the Servant are not for his own faults, but for the sins of others. He suffers to fulfil the will of God: 'It was the Lord's will to crush him and cause him to suffer' (Is. 53:10). He is a willing sacrifice: 'he poured out his life unto death' (Is. 53:12). His meekness appears in his silence – before the high priest, before Pontius Pilate, and

---

[1] *Stromata* V, 675, cited in E. K. Lee, *NTS* 8 (January 1962), pp. 172f.

before Herod.[1] On the cross he answered nothing to the mockery of his enemies as they cursed the King of the Jews, or to the taunts of the thief crucified with him. Peter had cause to remember all too vividly the silence of Jesus before the high priest. He can bear witness: *When they hurled their insults at him, he did not retaliate.* Oppressed and afflicted, he was silent: 'as a sheep before her shearers is silent, so he did not open his mouth' (Is. 53:7).

The meekness of Christ not only showed his submission to his Father's will; it showed also his confidence in his Father's righteous judgment. He did not revile or threaten because he *entrusted himself to him who judges justly.* He had no need to vindicate himself. Paul writes to Christ's followers: 'Do not take revenge, my friends, but leave room for God's wrath, for it is written: "It is mine to avenge; I will repay," says the Lord.'[2]

Perhaps there is even a deeper sense to Peter's description of Christ's meek commitment to God. The verb translated *entrusted* is used twice in the Greek version of Isaiah to describe the 'delivering up' of the Servant for our sins (Is. 53:6, 12). It is also used in the gospels for the delivering up of Christ to Pilate. Stibbs says of the term, 'Here in the phrase *committed himself* it is used to describe our Lord's own surrender of Himself to bear the penalty of sin – not His own sin but ours (cf. Rom. iv. 25), and not at the hands of men, but at the hands of God, the righteous Judge.'[3]

Certainly the way of Christ's meek suffering, so well remembered by Peter, is the way of redeeming love. By the welts of his scourging we were healed: Isaiah foresaw it, and Peter witnessed it. The very torture that Peter wanted Jesus at any cost to escape was the torture that Jesus came to endure. In Isaiah's songs, the Servant is both identified with the people of God and distinguished from them. He suffers for them, stands in their place, and bears the judgment of their sins.[4] The example of Christ's meekness is drawn from the mystery of Christ's sacrifice.

---

[1] Mk. 14:61; 15:5; Mt. 26:62–63; 27:12, 14; Lk. 23:9; Jn. 19:9–10.
[2] Rom. 12:19, quoting Dt. 32:35.
[3] Stibbs, p. 119, commenting on the AV text.
[4] For a clear and moving exposition of the Servant songs see Henri Blocher, *Songs of the Servant* (IVP, 1975).

b. His atoning sacrifice (2:24)

He himself bore our sins in his body on the tree, so that we might die to sins and live for righteousness; by his wounds you have been healed.

Jesus is far more than our example; he is our sin-bearer. As Leighton says, 'This was his business, not only to rectify sinful man by his example, but to redeem him by his blood.'[1] In one brief sentence Peter uses the prophecy of Isaiah to interpret what he had seen: Jesus going to his death. Jesus' predictions of rejection, suffering and death had contradicted the expectations of the disciples. But they did not contradict the words of the prophet. Isaiah had said, 'He bore the sin of many.'[2] Now Peter understands those words; they convey the heart of the gospel.

The background for Isaiah's prophecy and Peter's teaching is the symbolism of sacrifice that God appointed for Israel. Sin was pictured as a burden to be placed upon the head of a sacrificial animal before it was killed. Death was the penalty for sin; the sacrificial animal died in the place of the sinner, who confessed his sin with his hands on the head of the animal.[3] That action graphically pictured the transfer of the weight of his sin from himself to the substitute. The sprinkling of the blood of the sacrificed animal marked atonement; the penalty of sin had been paid.[4] Isaiah describes the mysterious tragedy of the righteous Servant of the Lord: his astonishing agony, his scornful rejection, his submissive meekness. Then he discloses the meaning of the apparent tragedy. The suffering Servant offers himself as a sacrifice for sin. He was stricken with death for the transgression of his people. His soul was made an offering for sin. He bore the sin of the many.[5]

We lack Peter's preparation for understanding Christ as the sacrifice, the lamb whose precious blood redeems us (1:19). We have not witnessed, as Peter did, the offering of lambs, bulls and goats on the altar of sacrifice; the symbolism is not vivid in our minds. Yet Peter knew that the sacrifices

---

[1] Leighton, p. 223. [2] Is. 53:12.
[3] Lv. 4:4, 15. [4] Lv. 17:11.
[5] See Blocher, *op. cit.*; 2 Cor. 5:21; Rom. 8:3.

at Jerusalem had not cleansed his heart from sin. Faced with the divine power of Jesus on the Lake of Galilee, he had fallen on his knees in his fishing-boat to cry, 'Go away from me, Lord; I am a sinful man!'[1]

Peter, who had slept through his Lord's agony in the garden of Gethsemane, now knows what cup it was that Jesus had to take; he knows why Jesus cried out in his abandonment, *'Eloi, Eloi, lama sabachthani?'*[2] When Jesus went to Calvary, 'he bore the sin of many'. The wood of his cross could be put upon another; the weight of sin was his alone to bear. Should anyone think lightly of his sin – and Peter could not – then to see the agony of the Son of God must call him to think again. Jesus bore our sins personally, in his own body. Only he could do so, for only he was sinless, God's lamb without spot (1:19; 3:18). Only he could do so, for only he was who Peter confessed him to be: no mere man, not even the greatest prophet, but the Lord's Anointed; indeed, the Lord himself, the Son of God, now crowned with glory (3:22; 4:11). If our death does not confront us with the wages of sin, then his death must. That such a price was paid, by the Son who gave his life, by the Father who gave his Son, is the measure of the measureless love of God.

The priests of old put away sin in the symbolic ritual of sacrifice; Jesus put away sin through the sacrifice of himself. The author of Hebrews reminds us of the words of Psalm 40:

'Sacrifice and offering you did not desire,
  but a body you prepared for me;
with burnt offerings and sin offerings
  you were not pleased.
Then I said, "Here I am – it is written about me in the scroll –
  I have come to do your will, O God." '[3]

The expression Peter uses seems to describe not simply Christ's bearing of sin *on* the cross, but his carrying the burden of sin *to* the cross.[4] In any case, it is the death of Christ, the shedding of his precious blood, that accomplishes

---

[1] Lk. 5:8; see Ps. 38:3–4.
[2] Mk. 15:33.   [3] Heb. 10:5–7.
[4] The preposition *epi* with the accusative usually expresses motion towards. But see Kelly, pp. 122–123.

121

our redemption. Peter's expression emphasizes the dreadful extent of Christ's sin-bearing. He suffered not only to the point of death, but to death as one accursed. Peter is well aware of the law's curse upon one who died as a criminal *on the tree*.[1] To Pharisees like Saul, before his conversion, Christ's death on the cross refuted any claim to Messiahship. The Messiah could not die as one accursed of God. The astonishing prophecy of Isaiah shows the very opposite; only the One who becomes a curse for us can be the true Messiah, for his accursed death in our place paid the price of sin. Peter had proclaimed to the Sanhedrin the horror of their offence in killing Jesus, 'hanging him on a tree'.[2] Yet the wicked hands of men had fulfilled the counsel and will of God. God raised up Jesus, and by his death brought forgiveness of sins to all who trust in him.[3]

By bearing our sin Jesus brings healing as well as atonement. The curse of sin includes suffering as well as death. From this, too, Jesus saves us. Peter again quotes from Isaiah: *by his wounds you have been healed*. Slaves who had been beaten bore the scars of the lash to which *wounds* ('welts') refers. Jesus had been tied to a post on the 'Pavement' of the palace where Pilate administered justice. There he had been whipped with the Roman scourge, a lash with multiple thongs, weighted with lumps of lead or bone.[4] How did Christ's wounds bring healing to slaves who might also have felt the lash? Did not Peter call them to follow in Christ's steps, to imitate him in receiving wounds for his sake?

The apparent contradiction reveals the heart of Peter's message. That which is to be feared is not the wrath of men, but the wrath of God.[5] That which is to be desired is not the passing comforts of the world, but the blessing of God's eternal inheritance. This is not just a matter of suffering now and glory to come: the promised blessing is already the possession of believers in Christ. They now taste the joy of heaven, for they taste the Lord's grace (2:3). They know Jesus, the great Physician. Peter well knew the healing power

---

[1] Dt. 21:22–23; Gal. 3:13.   [2] Acts 5:30; *cf.* Acts 10:39.
[3] Acts 2:23–24, 38; 5:31; 10:43.
[4] Mk. 15:15; Mt. 27:26; Jn. 19:1. See J. D. Douglas, ed., *The Illustrated Bible Dictionary*, Part 3 (IVP, 1980), pp. 1402f.
[5] Mt. 10:28.

of Christ. As an apostle he had power to declare, 'Jesus Christ heals you.'[1] In hope of the resurrection, Peter could promise the final healing of all the people of God. But here Peter speaks of healing, not by the hands of Jesus, but by the wounds of Jesus. Christ's wounds heal suffering at its root: the curse of sin. Not only do they plead the sinner's case in the judgment; they transform his present suffering. No longer is it the bitter legacy of unrighteousness; it has become fellowship in the steps of Jesus. The pain that remains for the Christian is not the penalty of sin: Christ has suffered that in his place. The pain that remains is Christ's calling to follow in his steps, sharing his reproach.

c. His saving claim (2:24–25)

... so that we might die to sins and live for righteousness; by his wounds you have been healed. For you were like sheep going astray, but now you have returned to the Shepherd and Overseer of your souls.

Christ's atoning sacrifice has accomplished our salvation. We were like sheep going astray, but now we have been brought back to the Shepherd and Overseer of our souls. Jesus is not only the Good Shepherd who gives his life for the sheep; he is also the seeking Shepherd, the Lord who gathers his remnant flock.[2] He bore our sins with a marvellous purpose: 'that we, having died unto sins, might live unto righteousness'. (This translation in the ASV is to be preferred to that in the NIV.[3])

Peter here speaks in a way that is close to the language of Paul. Central for Paul is the doctrine of union with Christ.

[1] Acts 9:34.

[2] The verb for 'turning back' may be taken as passive or reflexive: 'you have been returned' or 'you have returned.' The passive seems closer to Peter's expressions in 3:18 and 4:1, as well as the assertions of 1:3–5, 9, 18–19. His exhortations to obedience are always grounded on affirmations of what God has done for us in Christ. Further, the image of the seeking Shepherd found in John 10:16 and Luke 15:5–7 is grounded in the Old Testament promise in Ezekiel 34 where God condemns the false shepherds for not seeking the lost (34:6, 8) and pledges to seek and gather his scattered sheep (34:11–13). The verb is used in the active to describe turning to the Lord in Acts 11:21; 1 Thes. 1:9.

[3] The ASV reflects better the form of the aorist participle. The aorist indicates a completed action in the past. It is true that the tense of a participle does not always indicate a sequence in relation to the main verb, but it does emphasize the punctiliar form of the action.

We were united to Christ in his saving death; when he died to sin, so did we. When he rose, we rose with him. We are therefore to live in accord with our new position.[1] Peter, too, stresses what Christ has accomplished for us. He makes Christ's finished work the ground of his exhortations to live for righteousness. While he does not develop the theme of our union with Christ in the way that Paul does, he presents the same conviction from a different perspective, using particularly the Servant songs of Isaiah.[2] In this passage he is showing us the meaning of the death of Christ from Isaiah 53, a passage in which the Servant suffers for the sins of the people because he is identified with them. In affirming that Jesus bore our sins, Peter teaches that Jesus is identified with us as our representative. That enables Peter to say that because of Christ's sin-bearing in our place, we have died to sin. Peter makes it clear that Christ has done more in his death than enable us to die to sin. By his death in our place 'once, the righteous for the unrighteous', he has brought us to God (3:18). We have ceased from sin in Christ's suffering and death for us, and therefore we are to live to God (4:1–2).

Peter had begun this section by addressing servants, speaking to them of their calling to follow Christ. But now he speaks in the first person plural, not 'you' only, but 'we'. Peter's hope is one with theirs, remission of sin through the death of Christ and freedom for a new life of righteousness.

By his atoning death Jesus puts his saving claim upon us. We *have returned to the Shepherd and Overseer of our souls.* The title *Shepherd* for the One who is the suffering Servant of the Lord is suggested in Isaiah 53:6, the passage that follows the statement that we are healed by his wounds: 'We all, like sheep, have gone astray, each of us has turned to his own way; and the Lord has laid on him the iniquity of us all.' David's confession, 'The Lord is my shepherd . . .', presents one of the major images of the Old Testament describing the Lord's care for his covenant people.[3] The Lord, the true shepherd, promises to gather and care for his

---

[1] See Rom. 7:4; Col. 1:22. Paul, too, contrasts death with life. Rom. 6:2, 10–11; Gal. 2:19.
[2] Paul speaks of himself as the servant of the Lord, like Moses. Christ is the Lord whom Paul serves.
[3] Jeremias, *TDNT* 6, pp. 485–502.

scattered flock.[1] In the prophet Zechariah the figure of the shepherd and that of the sufferer are brought together. The shepherd, the one who was pierced, is identified with the Lord himself,[2] yet distinguished from him as his 'fellow', the man close to him:

> 'Awake, O sword, against my shepherd,
>> against the man who is close to me!'
>> declares the LORD Almighty.
> 'Strike the shepherd,
>> and the sheep will be scattered,
>> and I will turn my hand against the little ones.'[3]

Peter would well remember that passage. He had heard Jesus quote it as he led the disciples from the last supper to the garden of Gethsemane. Jesus used it to warn the disciples of their scattering, their falling away, when he, the Shepherd, would be struck down. Peter had replied, 'Even if all fall away, I will not.'[4] Yet Peter, too, had forsaken Jesus and fled. When he later followed from a distance, he had been prepared to swear that he never knew Jesus. What joy filled Peter's heart to receive forgiveness and blessing from his risen Lord! Peter had returned to the Shepherd and Overseer of his soul. His own calling as an apostolic shepherd had come from the Lord, the good Shepherd, who had reclaimed Peter from his desertion.[5]

The Zechariah passage goes on to describe how the Lord will purify his people, refining them as silver or gold in fire. This image, too, is in Peter's thoughts (1:7; 4:12). The Lord who is now gathering his own from the nations of the world leads them through suffering to know him.

> They will call on my name
>> and I will answer them;
> I will say, 'They are my people,'
>> and they will say, 'The Lord is our God.'[6]

Our Shepherd is also our *Overseer*, the 'Bishop ' (AV; Greek, *episkopos*) of our souls. The overseer is one who

[1] Ezk. 34. [2] Zc. 12:10. [3] Zc. 13:7. [4] Mk. 14:27–29.
[5] Lk. 22:31–32; Jn. 21:15–19; 1 Pet. 5:4; Jn. 10:27–28. [6] Zc. 13:9.

125

watches over a charge to protect and preserve it. A shepherd is the overseer of his flock. The elders of the church are to exercise oversight as they tend the flock of God (5:2). Yet the oversight of the 'Chief Shepherd' (5:4) has majestic breadth and depth; it goes far beyond the care of any under-shepherd. The Lord who knows the secrets of our hearts watches over our souls.[1] So Jesus was the Overseer of Peter's soul, warning him, calling him to watch and pray, praying for him that his faith should not fail, and searching his heart in order to restore him to his calling.[2] Household slaves, designated as 'things' by the Romans and 'bodies' by the Greeks, are in Christ a kingdom of priests; Jesus the Lord is their Shepherd, the guardian of their precious souls.[3]

4. More on the new lifestyle's practice: submission for the Lord's sake in role relationships (3:1–7)

a. Submission of wives to husbands (3:1–6)

Wives, in the same way be submissive to your husbands so that, if any of them do not believe the word, they may be won over without words by the behaviour of their wives, ²when they see the purity and reverence of your lives. ³Your beauty should not come from outward adornment, such as braided hair and the wearing of gold jewellery and fine clothes. ⁴Instead, it should be that of your inner self, the unfading beauty of a gentle and quiet spirit, which is of great worth in God's sight. ⁵For this is the way the holy women of the past who put their hope in God used to make themselves beautiful. They were submissive to their own husbands, ⁶like Sarah, who obeyed Abraham and called him her master. You are her daughters if you do what is right and do not give way to fear.

Both Greek philosophy and Roman custom required order

---

[1] In the Old Testament the oversight of God is described as his 'visitation', bringing judgment or mercy (*pequddāh*). The Septuagint uses *episkopos* for God once, Jb. 20:29.

[2] Lk. 22:31–32; Mk. 14:27–31, 37; Jn. 21:15–19.

[3] Spicq, *Epîtres*, p. 114.

in the household as the foundation of order in the state.[1] In calling for the submission of wives to their husbands Peter is requiring behaviour that would be approved in society at large. Such conduct would put to shame the slanderers of Christian lifestyle (3:16). Plutarch, the Greek biographer and moralist, wrote in his *Advice to Bride and Groom* (not much later, perhaps, than Peter's letter):

> So it is with women also; if they subordinate themselves to their husbands, they are commended, but if they want to have control, they cut a sorrier figure than the subjects of their control. And control ought to be exercised by the men over the women, not as the owner has control over a piece of property, but, as the soul controls the body, by entering into her feelings and being knit to her through goodwill.[2]

But Peter is by no means urging Christian wives to pattern their lives on even the best traditional values of their society. He has already condemned the 'empty way of life handed down to you from your forefathers' (1:18). The distinctive behaviour of the Christian wife is signalled at once by the word translated *in the same way*. Peter refers us back to the whole pattern of Christian conduct he has described, the life of Christian pilgrims in this world. This style of life will force hostile pagans to recognize Christian genuineness (2:12). Christians fear God; they are his slaves, therefore they do not fear people. They are free, because they are the royal people of God. Free in slavery to God, free as followers of Christ, they submit themselves to others freely. No-one else has the status and honour of Jesus Christ, whom Peter confessed to be the Son of God. Yet Jesus had washed Peter's feet like a domestic slave. His girding himself with a towel for that humble task was as nothing compared to his bowing beneath the cross to bear Peter's sins. It is Christ's example that Peter calls us to follow in all the relationships of life. We need not be concerned about maintaining our rights. Jesus trusted his Father, the righteous Judge, to do that; and

---

[1] On the historical and cultural background and setting of this passage, see Balch. Balch shows that even the Stoic philosophers who argued for a greater recognition of sexual equality assumed the subordination of wives to husbands in practice (Appendix V, pp. 143–149).
[2] Cited in Balch, p. 99.

so should we. The Christian who follows Jesus does not grasp for privilege; he or she is already privileged beyond imagination. The Christian seeks rather opportunities to imitate Christ in willing subjection to service.

Christian women submit to their husbands, and particularly to non-Christian husbands, not because they are in some way inferior, for they are God's elect. Rather, they submit for the Lord's sake, with the particular purpose of winning their husbands to the Lord by their unselfish example. The key expression, *in the same way*, is applied to the husband as well as the wife (3:7). Both follow Jesus, the suffering Servant. Although the husband does not fulfil the same role in relation to his wife as his wife does to him, there is a fundamental identity of attitude: both are servants of God, seeking to serve others for Christ's sake.

Peter shows how all social relationships are transformed by following Jesus Christ. These relations differ in their nature. The honour that we give to civil rulers recognizes the appointment of God. They have been authorized by him to restrain evil-doers and encourage civil peace (2:14, 17). In contrast, no divine warrant or approval is given to slavery; rather it is assumed that slave-masters may be guilty of despotic and wicked treatment of their slaves. The submission that Christian servants give is presented as a privilege, the privilege of glorifying God by submitting willingly to an unjust situation (2:19–20). In the case of wives also there is the possibility of mistreatment. Christian wives are to remain faithful to God under pressure; they are not to deny the Lord for fear of their unbelieving husbands (3:6).

But the submission that wives are to yield to their husbands represents more than an opportunity to endure unjustice for the sake of Christ. Peter presents this submission as an adornment of the Christian woman, the *beauty* of a meek and quiet spirit that is pleasing to God. The *spirit* of which Peter speaks is not here the Holy Spirit, but it is the fruit of the Spirit in the heart of the Christian. The *gentle and quiet spirit* is not presented as distinctively feminine, for Jesus described himself as 'gentle and humble in heart.'[1] He entered Jerusalem, not like a proud conqueror on a war charger, but

[1] Mt. 11:29.

'gentle and riding on a donkey'.[1] Meekness or gentleness is one of the principal fruits of the Spirit.[2] The 'quietness' of a woman is linked with her submission in 1 Timothy 2:9–12, a passage that is similar to Peter's exhortation. But Paul also urges quietness upon all, as a Christian virtue, in 1 Thessalonians 4:11. The role of the wife gives her an opportunity to display Christian love and humility in a distinctive way, but Peter makes it clear that Christian men and women are alike called to reflect toward others the meekness they find in following Christ.

Peter points Christian wives to the example of *holy women of the past* who, *like Sarah*, were submissive *to their own husbands*. While Peter does not expand on God's creation ordinance of marriage as Paul does, he clearly assumes that wives have a role to fulfil in marriage that pleases God.[3]

While Peter's exhortation applies as well to wives of Christian husbands, he has particular concern for the witness of women married to unbelievers. This flows from his burden in this part of his letter. In 2:11 he begins the section with a plea for behaviour that will be a witness to the pagans. In 3:16 he is still speaking of how the good behaviour of Christians will put to shame those who slander them. Peter sees the 'impossible' position of the Christian as a remarkable opportunity to bear witness to Christ.

In the Roman world it was assumed that wives would conform to the religious practices of their husbands.[4] This became an issue in Roman history when many women were attracted to the cult of Bacchus or to the worship of the Egyptian goddess Isis. The rituals of Bacchus had been banned by the Roman Senate; the senators saw a threat to the state in the participation of women in bacchanalian revelries at night in the mountains.[5] These suspicions were later directed against Christians. In the eyes of imperial Romans, here was another subversive Eastern religion threatening the stability of the home and of the state.

Peter's letter might certainly have been shown to pagan

[1] Mt. 21:5.　　[2] Gal. 5:23.
[3] Eph. 5:21–33; 1 Cor. 11:3–12; 1 Tim. 2:11–13. For a treatment of Paul's teaching, see James B. Hurley, *Man and Woman in Biblical Perspective* (IVP and Zondervan, 1981). See also John Stott, *The Message of Ephesians* (IVP, 1979), pp. 215–226.
[4] See Balch, pp. 61–69, 84; Best, pp. 116–117.　　[5] Balch, p. 67.

rulers, masters, or husbands as evidence of the falsity of the charges made against Christians.[1] But Peter is not writing to suspicious non-Christians. He is writing to encourage Christians to accept suffering and reproach for the sake of Jesus Christ (4:16). Christian wives can have an important part in the church's witness. That witness may not be easy. Their husbands have resisted the claim of the gospel. They may ridicule the message and insult their wives. So strong may be their hostility that it is no longer possible for their wives to speak of the Lord to them. Even then the Christian wife must not despair. She still possesses a mighty weapon for winning her husband to the faith; it is the testimony of her life. Her husband has refused to heed the word; very well, let him be won *without words*.[2] The silent eloquence of his wife's pure and reverent behaviour can preach daily the transforming power of Jesus Christ. No-one could be more emphatic than Peter has been about the place of the word of God in conversion (1:23). Yet there are situations in which the silent witness of Christian love must support and prepare for the presentation of the truth.

Augustine describes the faithful witness of his Christian mother Monnica to his pagan father Patricius:

> She served her husband as her master, and did all she could to win him for You, speaking to him of You by her conduct, by which You made her beautiful . . . Finally, when her husband was at the end of his earthly span, she gained him for You.[3]

The deep and growing beauty of a woman who trusts in the Lord will have its effect on her husband, but, above all, her spiritual beauty will be precious in the sight of God. Peter's contrast between the outward vanities of fashion and inward spiritual adornment calls to mind the catalogue of beauty aids that Isaiah denounces in proclaiming God's judgment against the idle luxury of the daughters of Zion.[4]

Peter's teaching may be misunderstood in two directions. On the one hand, the positive thrust of his contrast may be

---

[1] Balch, ch. VI, pp. 81–109, describes an apologetic value that the household code would have.

[2] *Without words* but not without *the* word. It is important to note that Peter does not use the article with 'word' the second time. Kelly, p. 128.

[3] *Confessions* 9:19–22. Cited in Kelly, p. 128.   [4] Is. 3:16–25.

missed. Later church fathers interpreted the passage as banning all aesthetics in women's dress, attributing such desires to the work of fallen angels.[1] If the 'literal' force of Peter's warning is taken out of context, he could be made to say that the wearing of clothing is prohibited as outward adornment (3:3)! The point is not a legalistic ban on beauty of attire. (The father of the prodigal welcomed his returning son with the best robe and a ring!) The point is the vastly superior value of inward beauty and the danger of extravagant and sensual fashions in dress.

The opposite misunderstanding is much more popular. Peter's warning can be brushed aside; it was conventional for the times. Did not Plutarch say,

That adorns a woman which makes her more decorous – not gold, emeralds, scarlet, but whatever invests her with dignity, good behaviour, modesty.[2]

Indeed, the same author opposed gaudy clothing and the equivalent of rock music (cymbals and drums) in connection with the cults that attracted women:

Those who have to go near elephants do not put on bright clothes, nor do those who go near bulls put on red; for the animals are made especially furious by these colours; and tigers, they say, when surrounded by the noise of beaten drums go completely mad and tear themselves to pieces. Since, then, this is also the case with men, that some cannot endure the sight of scarlet and purple clothes, while others are annoyed by cymbals and drums, what terrible hardship is it for women to refrain from such things, and not disquiet or irritate their husbands, but live with them in constant gentleness?[3]

We must not discount Peter's warnings, however, just because pagan moralists warned against some of the same things. The contrast that Peter makes is real. Enslavement to fashion by men or women runs counter to growth in spiritual holiness. Coiffure, jewellery, dress: the categories have not changed since Peter's day, as any shopping centre demon-

---

[1] With reference to Jewish exegesis of Gn. 6:1–4. See Bénétreau, p. 171.
[2] Plutarch, *Moralia* 141e. Cited in Kelly, p. 129.
[3] Plutarch, *Advice to Bride and Groom* 144DE, cited in Balch, p. 85.

strates. Ornate hairstyles were prevalent in the high society of the Roman world:

> Curl climbs on top of curl and over the forehead there arose something which at its best looked like the *chef d'oeuvre* of a master pastry cook and, at its worst, like a dry sponge. At the back the hair was plaited, and the braids arranged in a coil which looks like basketwork.[1]

Today's hairstyles are less ornate, but the time and expense demanded have hardly decreased. The issues of stewardship are pressing: Christian expenditures for beauty aids, jewellery, and modish costumes increase while church funds go begging and thousands starve. Nor is the cost the only factor. Open licentiousness sweeps in and out of the fashion world: modesty as well as restraint should mark the Christian style.

The submission of a Christian wife must always be first to God. Worldly husbands may wish to flaunt the beauty or even the sexuality of their wives. Christian women will seek to please their husbands, but they cannot avoid the issue of obeying God rather than men. Peter calls for the fear of God that dispels the fear of men (3:6, 14).

Knowing how precious to the world are the gold and gems of outward show, Peter displays that on which God puts a high-price tag: the hidden but unfading beauty of the heart.[2] The contemporary world resists the aging process at all costs, yet the youthful body that it idolizes quickly fades. Christians need God's values to reject the futility of the worldly search for beauty. Can real beauty still be blooming along with wrinkles? Peter offers the answer of a long-established beauty school: the daughters of Sarah (3:5–6).

Peter names *Sarah* as an example of a class of godly women who cultivated the beauty of spirit that he has been describing, and who were *submissive to their own husbands*. He calls attention to the fact that Sarah spoke of Abraham as her *master* (the reference is to Gn. 18:12). The Greek term

[1] J. Balsdon, *Roman Women, Their History and Habits* (The Bodley Head, 1962), p. 256, cited in Hurley, *op. cit.*, p. 258.
[2] Peter's expression is compact: 'but the hidden man of the heart in the incorruptibility of a meek and quiet spirit'. In these words the phrase 'of the heart' explains 'the hidden man'. See Rom. 2:29. The inward is also the real, the authentic, as against the apparent. See Bénétreau, p. 172. See also 1 Sa. 16:7.

kyrios was used in polite address, rather like our 'sir' or 'Mr'. It indicates the respect with which Sarah spoke of Abraham. Certainly Sarah's submission to Abraham was not slavish.[1]

It would be misleading to think of a separate line of 'children of Sarah' like the 'seed of Abraham'; nevertheless the Lord insisted that Isaac, the son of the promise, be born of Sarah, not Hagar. Sarah, like Abraham, was a chosen believer, and theirs is the line of the promise from which Christ was born. In speaking of Sarah and her 'children', Peter indicates her calling and dignity. Her willing submission to Abraham was therefore freely given. Like Sarah, Christian women of the new covenant are believers, doing what is right, and not giving way to fear.[2] It is better not to put an *if* in the translation of verse 6, but to follow the Greek more closely: 'of whom you have become children, doing good and not being afraid of any terror'. Peter consistently begins with the privilege we have and moves on to the behaviour we show.

b. Consideration of wives by husbands (3:7)

Husbands, in the same way be considerate as you live with your wives, and treat them with respect as the weaker partner and as heirs with you of the gracious gift of life, so that nothing will hinder your prayers.

Husbands, in the same way . . . The path of Christian living is no different for the husband than for the wife. Both are called to follow Christ in humble and compassionate love, accepting rebuffs with forgiving grace (3:8–9). Since the husband's role is different, the form of his service is different. The wife is called to be submissive to her husband; the husband is called to honour his wife. That honour includes considerate understanding.

The husband is to live with his wife considerately, literally 'according to knowledge'. The expression describing their living together is not limited to sexual intimacy, but it has

[1] She insisted, for example, on the exclusion of Hagar and Ishmael from the household – to Abraham's dismay. Yet her request was supported by God's command to Abraham (Gn. 21:10, 12).
[2] Peter's exhortation to be doing good without fear is drawn from Pr. 3:25, 27.

133

particular reference to it. In all their life together, and particularly in their sexual union, the husband is to relate to his wife 'according to knowledge'. Does Peter mean knowledge of the wife, or knowledge of God and his calling?[1] The close connection with the description of the wife as *the weaker partner* favours the specific sense: the husband must dwell with his wife as one who knows her needs, who recognizes the delicacy of her nature and feelings. On the other hand, Peter has warned against 'the evil desires you had when you lived in ignorance' (1:14). Knowledge of God distinguishes Christian love from pagan lust. That saving knowledge enables the husband to love his wife as Christ loved the church and gave himself for it.[2]

Peter describes the wife as *the weaker partner*. The word translated *partner* in the NIV means 'instrument' or 'vessel'. Again it is possible that the sexual relation is particularly in view.[3] The description of their bodies as 'instruments' might suggest that *the gracious gift of life* of which the man and wife are *heirs* together is not eternal life, but the gift of new life in children. Peter's description of the inheritance of Christians (1:4), however, is a persuasive argument for holding to the traditional interpretation. In any case, whether the gift in view is of physical life or of spiritual life, Peter is stressing the mutuality of the relationship. While the wife is of the weaker sex in muscular strength, her role in the gift of physical life is surely not less! In relation to the gift of spiritual life, the woman is in no sense weaker, for in Christ there is no longer male and female.[4] No less then her Christian husband, the Christian wife is a living stone, 'being built into a spiritual house' in the Lord (2:5).

The husband gives to his wife the 'honour' that is her due. *Respect* is not strong enough. Peter uses the word translated 'precious' in 2:7; literally it means 'preciousness'. The honour or preciousness that the husband must bestow on his wife is not only the recognition of her place in God's ordinance of marriage; it is the honour that is hers as one of God's precious

---

[1] The word is found in the list of Christian graces in 2 Pet. 1:5–6; *cf.* Col. 1:9; 3:10.
[2] Eph. 5:24.
[3] See the argument for this by Christian Maurer in *TDNT* VII, pp. 362–367.
[4] Gal. 3:28.

and holy people. If husbands fail to give that honour, their fellowship with their wives will suffer; so will their fellowship with God. Their prayers will be 'hindered', a strong word.[1] The prayers of the husband will be blocked, will lose their effectiveness. Probably Peter also has in view the joint prayers of the couple. Husband and wife are to pray together; their home becomes a temple where they together approach God in the worship of a holy priesthood, offering up spiritual sacrifices.[2] Paul, too, emphasizes the importance of prayer in the marriage relationship. He counsels consideration in the sexual expression of marriage; marital intercourse is not to be unduly denied by either partner. But he makes special note of times of mutual continence 'so that you may devote yourselves to prayer'.[3] Piety becomes hollow and false if it is not expressed in the closest of human relationships. Marriage is not a sacrament conveying divine grace, but it is the human relationship that God has designed to mirror the love of Christ for the church, and of the church for Christ.

[1] Spicq, *Epîtres*, p. 125.   [2] *Ibid.*   [3] 1 Cor. 7:5.

3:8–22

7. The blessing of living with Christian suffering

1. Response to suffering in a life of blessing (3:8–12)

Finally, all of you, live in harmony with one another; be sympathetic, love as brothers, be compassionate and humble. ⁹*Do not repay evil with evil or insult with insult, but with blessing, because to this you were called so that you may inherit a blessing.* ¹⁰*For,*

> *'Whoever would love life*
> *and see good days*
> *must keep his tongue from evil*
> *and his lips from deceitful speech.*
> ¹¹*He must turn from evil and do good;*
> *he must seek peace and pursue it.*
> ¹²*For the eyes of the Lord are on the righteous*
> *and his ears are attentive to their prayer,*
> *but the face of the Lord is against those who do evil.'*

a. Called to a life of blessing

Peter has concluded the section of his letter in which he has encouraged Christians to display their freedom in submission for Christ's sake, as citizens, servants, wives, and husbands. He has encouraged them to bear unjust treatment as part of their calling. Now he turns to deal with the issue of suffering at greater length. He has spoken of trials from the very beginning of the letter (1:6), and has presented the example of Christ to show Christians how to submit to suffering for doing right (2:19–24). In 3:8–9 he summarizes what he has been saying and prepares for what will follow. As al-

136

ways, he begins with what God has done. God calls us to be heirs of his blessing (3:9). That calling commits us to a life of blessing, a life that responds to the free grace of God. Peter thinks of God's blessing as it is proclaimed in Psalm 34 (quoted in 3:10–12). Does he not also remember the Beatitudes pronounced by Jesus?[1] Certainly he reflects Jesus' teaching regarding the love and meekness of the heirs of the kingdom, especially as it is shown toward enemies.

Peter names five characteristics of the life that brings blessing: like-mindedness, sympathy, brotherly love, compassion, and humility. These are not virtues chosen at random. Like the fingers of the hand, they radiate from one centre and work together. The key to them all is the love of grace: they reflect the grace, love, and compassion of Jesus Christ. The teaching and example of Jesus have become the teaching of the apostles.[2]

Live in harmony with one another. The NIV translation paraphrases one word, 'like-mindedness'. Greek and Roman philosophers spoke of the need for such harmony in the home and in the state.[3] In Peter's letter, however, the word has new depth. It is interpreted by the parallel terms, and by the focus of the letter on Jesus Christ. Peter describes the 'clear mind' in which Christians are to be united (4:7–11). It is the mind of those who prayerfully await the coming of the Lord and serve one another in fervent love. They prepare their minds for action by setting their hope on Christ (1:13). When Peter had urged Jesus not to speak of the cross, Jesus had rebuked him for minding the things of men rather than the things of God.[4] Christians find oneness of understanding in the gospel of the cross.

The unity of mind that Christians are to show includes harmony of attitude as well as of understanding. It relates directly to the humility and love that Peter goes on to mention. When Paul urged the Philippians to be 'of the same mind', he added 'having the same love', and continued, 'Have

---

[1] Mt. 5:3–12.
[2] See Rom. 12:9–19; Eph. 4:1–3, 31–32; Col. 3:12–15; 1 Thes. 5:13–22. The similarity of these lists would seem to reflect patterns of instruction in the apostolic church.
[3] Kelly, p. 136. [4] Mt. 16:23.

this mind among yourselves, which is yours in Christ Jesus.'[1] The magnificent passage that follows describes how Christ humbled himself, even to the death of the cross. Being of one mind means having a common understanding of the truth, but it means more. When the truth of Christ is affirmed in arrogance it is denied. The 'like-mindedness' that Peter requires manifests the mind and love of Christ. It is precisely willingness to submit ourselves to others for Christ's sake that undercuts the misunderstandings and hostilities that can divide the Christian community. That willingness flows from the love of Christ.

Christ's love also shines in the *sympathy* that marks the Christian life of blessing. The author of Hebrew describes Christ as the high priest who sympathizes with our weaknesses.[2] Peter has just spoken of the sympathetic understanding that husbands must show to their wives (3:7). Sympathy means readiness to rejoice with those who rejoice and to mourn with those who mourn.[3] In his vivid image of the body of Christ, Paul reminds us of the sympathy that exists among bodily parts: when one member suffers, the other members suffer with it.[4] The love that binds the body of Christ together not only seeks the other's good, but enters into the other's needs and concerns. Such identification begins in the heart, but it is seen, often enough, in the event. Peter could remember the event that exposed his failure to 'sympathize', to suffer with Christ, who had come to suffer for him. Much contemporary research into human motivation and psychology has the purpose of manipulating people for economic or political advantage. Christian sympathy does not exploit; it shares and supports.

Love as brothers. Like these other graces, brotherly love is specifically Christian. It is not simply a sense of comradeship, but the knowledge that we have been given new birth. We are children of the heavenly Father and therefore brothers and sisters in Christ. As we have been loved by God, so we must love our fellow-believers. Here Peter returns again to the theme of the 'family' love of the Christian community (1:22; 2:17). Jesus Christ is not ashamed to

[1] Phil. 2:2–5, RSV. See also Rom. 12:5.   [2] Heb. 4:15.
[3] Rom. 12:15.   [4] 1 Cor. 12:26.

call us brothers, since he has taken part in our flesh and blood.[1]

Each of these graces reflects the love of Christ. In none is this clearer than in the case of compassion: *be ... compassionate*. It is God who has in Christ shown compassion to us. Paul urges us: 'Be kind and compassionate to one another, forgiving each other, just as in Christ God forgave you.'[2] The root of the word refers literally to one's inner organs, and therefore to one's feelings. The Greeks associated inner organs with courage (*cf.* our use of 'guts').[3] But in the Bible these inner organs are linked with mercy and concern (the 'bowels of mercy' in the AV).[4] The prophet Isaiah uses the term as he seeks the mercy of the Lord. His cry is accurately, though euphemistically, translated, 'Your tenderness and compassion are withheld from us.'[5]

The Gospels speak of the compassion of Jesus for the crowds, and for the sick.[6] Jesus describes the compassion of his Father in the parable of the prodigal son.[7] In the parable of the good Samaritan Jesus binds that compassion upon his disciples.[8] He contrasts the tender care of the Samaritan with the indifference of the priest and Levite. The Samaritan had *compassion* on the critically wounded man. The priest and Levite would surely be considered 'neigbours' to the victim. The Samaritan would not. No-one would hold a Samaritan accountable to nurse a wounded Jew at his own expense. Yet the Samaritan showed a love that could not be demanded, the love of mercy. He made himself a neigbour in the love of compassion.

The burden of the Lord's teaching is the burden of Peter's letter. We have received the free compassion of Christ's grace. Jesus himself bore our sins; he suffered, the righteous for the unrighteous (2:24; 3:18). The love that he now requires of us as his people is not a self-righteous, legalistic love, working to score points for heaven. Rather, as those who are made heirs of the blessing of life eternal (3:9), we

[1] Heb. 2:11–12, 14.   [2] Eph. 4:32.   [3] Stibbs, p. 129.
[4] See BAGD on *splanxnon*, p. 763. Col. 3:12, AV.
[5] Is. 63:15. 'Where is . . . the sounding of thy bowels and of thy mercies toward me? are they restrained?' (AV).
[6] Mt. 9:36; 14:14; 15:32; 20:34; Mk. 1:41; 6:34; 8:2; Lk. 7:13.
[7] Lk. 15:20.   [8] Lk. 10:33.

THE BLESSING OF LIVING WITH CHRISTIAN SUFFERING

must model our love on the love of God in Christ. God's compassion demands love like his, love that cannot be demanded, the love of free grace. Only God's love, poured out in our hearts by the Holy Spirit, can move us to show his compassion.

The last of the graces that Peter mentions is humility: *be . . . humble*. Friedrich Nietzsche scorned this biblical virtue. He called the Jews 'a people "born for slavery" ', and accused them of inverting values by making the word 'poor' synonymous with 'saint' and 'friend'.[1] The Scriptures do, indeed, give place to the poor and humble in contrast to the rich and proud. The remnant of God's people, redeemed by his grace, are the poor and lowly. In Greek literature, by contrast, the word that Peter uses is often taken in a derogatory sense: 'low-mindedness'.[2]

For this grace, too, Christ is our model. He called disciples to him as one who is 'gentle and humble in heart'.[3] The word is a compound, like the first in this list, and the two are in close harmony, for if there is to be 'like-mindedness' there must also be 'lowly-mindedness'. Peter will return to this theme, urging Christians to 'clothe yourselves with humility', to serve one another (5:5). Clearly Peter had learned humility the hard way. His pride had been crushed by the denials that shamed his boasting. But Peter sees humility as deeper than the levelling of pride. He finds it in the free humiliation of his Lord, not only in taking the towel and basin, but in taking the cross. This is the lowliness that calls us to humble service. Christian humility will be mocked, as Jesus' humiliation on the cross was. But it will be honoured by God in the triumph of the returning Lord.[4] Even before that day, the power of Christian humility bears witness. Our world has seen the outworking of Nietzsche's 'master-race' in Nazi Germany. Does it yet recognize the power of what Nietzsche scorned?

[1] *The Philosophy of Nietzsche* (Random House, 1937), 'Beyond Good and Evil' 1937, p. 106.
[2] See Cranfield, p. 94; citations in BAGD, pp. 804.
[3] Mt. 11:29.   [4] Mt. 23:12.

b. Called to bless in response to cursing

God's calling of the Christian appears in a marvellous contrariness. Opposition and hatred cannot thwart the life of blessing. Even when Christians are cursed, they bless. This is how Christians 'get even'. They pay back evil with good, insults with blessing. This, of course, was the teaching of Jesus, as well as his example (2:23). 'But I tell you: Love your enemies and pray for those who persecute you, that you may be sons of your Father in heaven.'[1] Christians are free from vindictiveness because they trust God's justice; but they are free for blessing because they know God's goodness. Again, this was standard apostolic instruction.[2] It is not only in the world that Christians must repay evil with good; they must do it in the church, too. Certainly this attitude of loving humility will provide the strongest rebuke to the conscience of a fellow-Christian.

The blessing with which a Christian meets insults cannot, of course, pronounce God's favour on those who blaspheme his name. In the psalm that Peter quotes we read that 'the face of the Lord is against those who do evil' (3:12). Our blessing of evil-doers and persecutors must take the form of a prayer that seeks their salvation and good. Yet this does not reduce blessing to mere well-wishing words. Stephen prayed for those who stoned him, 'Lord, do not hold this sin against them.'[3] A young Pharisee named Saul was one of those for whom Stephen prayed. The Lord who stood at the right hand of God received Stephen and answered his prayer.

c. Called to bless as heirs of blessing

Peter joins our calling to bless with our calling to receive God's blessing (3:9). His words may be taken to mean 'You have been called to this, to bless, to the end that you may inherit a blessing'. Alternatively, the 'this' may refer to what follows: 'Bless, because you have been called to this, that you might inherit a blessing.' As we have seen, Peter regularly appeals to what the Lord has done for us in order

[1] Mt. 5:44.   [2] Rom. 12:17; 1 Thes. 5:15; 1 Cor. 4:12.
[3] Acts 7:60.

to encourage us to live for him. According to the second interpretation, this is what Peter now does again.[1] But he cites Psalm 34 to support his statement, and this favours the first interpretation. The psalm summons the righteous to keep their lips from evil that they may see good days. Peter, of course, does not understand the psalm to present a 'works' religion, suggesting that we can *earn* God's blessing by guarding our tongues. He speaks of God's gracious calling, and of the inheritance of blessing that we receive (1:4). Yet the Lord who keeps the inheritance for us keeps us for the inheritance by keeping us in the faith, and by leading us in the paths of righteousness. God who calls us to inherit his blessing calls us to follow the path of peace that leads to blessing (3:11). The Christian's knowledge of the blessing that he will receive from the Lord encourages and enables him to bless others, even his enemies.

Peter quotes from Psalm 34 without any introductory phrase. He has alluded to it already (2:3–4); it may have been used regularly in the instruction of new Christians and in the worship of song.[2] Peter cites the psalm to describe the blessing of the life to which Christians are called. Those who practise the love of compassion, refrain from speaking evil, and pursue peace are blessed by the Lord. His *eyes are on* them; he hears *their prayer* (3:12). The blessing that they inherit reaches to eternal life, but it also fills this life with *good days*. Peter affirms this, although he knows that days of suffering will come (3:14). Yet the blessing of the Lord will make days of suffering 'good days' in his favour. A 'good day' in a television beer commercial pictures friends imbibing in the sunset at a fishing-lodge. 'It doesn't get any better than this,' they say. A 'good day' in the book of Acts shows Paul and Silas in a Greek prison, their backs bleeding and their feet in stocks. They are singing psalms at midnight – perhaps Psalm 34![3] Silas, now sitting beside Peter, would remember with him the word of Jesus, 'Whoever wants to save his life will lose it, but whoever loses his life for me and for the gospel will save it.'[4]

---

[1] The second interpretation is favoured by Kelly, p. 137, and Bénétreau, p. 195.
[2] Selwyn, p. 190.   [3] Acts 16:25.   [4] Mk. 8:35.

2. The blessed witness of suffering for righteousness (3:13–22)

a. The opportunity for witness in word (3:13–15)

Who is going to harm you if you are eager to do good? 14*But even if you should suffer for what is right, you are blessed. 'Do not fear what they fear; do not be frightened.'* 15*But in your hearts set apart Christ as Lord. Always be prepared to give an answer to everyone who asks you to give the reason for the hope that you have. But do this with gentleness and respect . . .*

Peter has moved to the issue that is central for the rest of the letter: the issue of Christian suffering. He has shown how the love of God turns the problem upside down. Christians are free from the need of vindication, and filled with humility as heirs of grace. Suffering has become an opportunity to meet evil with good and cursing with blessing. Peter describes the triumphant witness of this response.

'Who, then, will *harm you if you are eager to do good?*' This question could be taken to mean that, on the whole, Christians who heed the counsel of Psalm 34 need not expect any harm. Governments are instituted to commend those who do right, masters do not usually punish servants who do what they are told, spouses of pagans may win their grudging respect. No doubt there is truth in this observation. God's blessing may give many 'good days' in this sense to those who are zealous for doing good.

But it is likely that Peter is saying much more than this.[1] The 'and' at the beginning of the sentence (omitted in the NIV) has the force of 'then'. It ties the statement to what has just been said, that the eyes and ears of the Lord are fixed on the righteous, while his face is against those who do evil. Further, the word 'evil' at the conclusion of the psalm quotation is picked up again in the verb for *harm* (3:13). 'Who, then [in the light of the Lord's care, and his control of evil], will do you evil . . . ?' Peter is not encouraging Christians to suppose that their chances are better than

---

[1] See Kelly, pp. 139f.; Spicq, *Epîtres*, p. 130.

average for escaping persecution. He is assuring them that, under God's care and blessing, no evil can befall them. Peter's words express Paul's affirmation: 'If God is for us, who can be against us?'[1] The psalmist had the same conviction: 'In God I trust; I will not be afraid. What can mortal man do to me?'[2]

'But if, indeed, *you should suffer for what is right, you are blessed.*' No harm, to be sure, can come to us at last. God's vindication and protection will preserve the heirs of his blessing. Christ prayed that the Father would protect his own for the evil one. But he did not pray that they be taken out of the world.[3] Jesus warned his disciples, 'In this world you will have trouble. But take heart! I have overcome the world.'[4] Peter writes to those who feel the mounting pressure of opposition in their society. 'Indeed, the spectacle of moral beauty does not disarm all the wicked; they are often even irritated by the radiance of a virtue that condemns them.'[5]

Christians should therefore not think it strange that they are called to endure persecution (4:12). Yet they must understand that suffering is not the opposite of blessing. Jesus had declared those to be blessed who suffer for righteousness. He promised them a reward in heaven: 'Blessed are you when people insult you, persecute you and falsely say all kinds of evil against you because of me. Rejoice and be glad, because great is your reward in heaven.'[6] That word of Jesus is more than a promise. It pronounces blessing. Those who will receive a heavenly reward are already blessed by the Lord. Peter emphasizes this. Those who suffer receive the benediction of Christ as a present possession. Their time of suffering has been made a time of blessing.

Paul knew the blessing of Christ's grace given in the midst of suffering. 'That is why, for Christ's sake, I delight in weaknesses, in insults, in hardships, in persecutions, in difficulties. For when I am weak, then I am strong.'[7] Tertullian, an African church father at the beginning of the third century, said that 'Prison does for the Christian what the desert did for the prophet. Call it not prison but the place of retirement.

[1] Rom. 8:31; see Is. 50:9.   [2] Ps. 56:4; *cf.* 118:6.   [3] Jn. 17:15.
[4] Jn. 16:33b.   [5] Spicq, *Epîtres*, p. 130. He cites Jn. 3:20; 15:19.
[6] Mt. 5:11–12.   [7] 2 Cor. 12:10.

144

The body is shut in, but all is open to the spirit: it may roam abroad on the way to God . . . The leg does not feel the chain if the mind is in heaven.' It was Tertullian who said that the blood of martyrs is indeed the seed of the church.[1] Peter writes at the outset of centuries of persecution that the church of Christ has endured, a chronicle that is still being written today in the labour camps and prisons of a world that rejects the gospel.

If you should suffer . . . , he writes.[2] The imperial persecutions that would sweep across the Roman world had not yet come. Christians were not yet being compelled to affirm the deity of Caesar. No doubt there were already those who had given their witness as martyrs (see 4:6), but much more was to come. Yet it was already time to prepare. Churches today that experience little persecution need Peter's instruction; in a future nearer than they suppose they may find themselves suffering with the rest of Christ's afflicted church in the world.

Peter would prepare the church, not simply to endure persecution, but to find in persecution an opportunity for witness. Both the boldness and the humility needed for witness come about through a fundamental exchange. Christians must exchange the *fear* of men for the fear of the Lord. Peter gives the secret of boldness as one who had found it after failure. Waiting in the courtyard of the high priest's house while Christ was being examined, Peter had failed miserably. Rembrandt's painting captures the scene: Peter has just denied Christ for the third time, swearing with fearful oaths that he was no disciple of Christ, was not with him, did not know him.[3] In the background shadow stands Jesus. He has just turned to look at Peter.

Contrast Peter, filled with the Spirit as the apostle of the risen Lord. He is no longer huddled by the fire in the outer courtyard. Now he is the accused. He stands before the same tribunal that had examined Jesus. He who had feared to confront a maidservant now confronts the high court. He

[1] Herbert B. Workman, *Persecution in the Early Church* (Oxford University Press, 1980), pp. 117, 143.

[2] For the use of the optative here and the relation of this passage to the apparently more extreme language of 4:12, see Kelly, pp. 140f.

[3] Rembrandt's painting of Peter's denial is in the Rijksmuseum in Amsterdam. See Lk. 22:61.

accuses them of crucifying Jesus, and refuses their order to be silent. 'We must obey God rather than men!'[1]

Peter had lost the fear of men by gaining the fear of the risen Lord. He had set apart *Christ as Lord* in his heart. Yes, Peter knew the meaning of fear. He remembered the panic that unmanned him when, by the fire in the courtyard, he was recognized as a Galilean. His accent had given him away![2] Peter also knew the secret of a boldness that conquers fear. That secret was announced long ago in the prophecy of Isaiah:

> 'Do not fear what they fear,
>   and do not dread it.
> The Lord Almighty is the one you are to regard as holy,
>   he is the one you are to fear,
>   he is the one you are to dread.'[3]

Peter quotes from that passage to share his secret of boldness. No doubt the Lord's words through Isaiah had strengthened his own heart. He had already quoted from this section of Isaiah concerning the stone of stumbling (2:8). *Do not fear what they fear*, writes Peter. (His statement could also be read, 'Do not be afraid with fear of them.'[4]) In Isaiah's prophecy the Lord calls his true disciples not to share the fears of the people: they see only the armed power of the enemy. The antidote to the fear of men is awareness of the glory of the Lord himself. Peter's words *But in your hearts set apart* – literally, 'sanctify' – *Christ as Lord* echo Isaiah's words 'The Lord Almighty is the one you are to regard as holy', literally 'Sanctify the Lord' (AV). When the Lord sanctifies us, he makes us holy (1:2; 2:9); when we sanctify the Lord, we set him apart as the Holy One. We recognize his lordship and confess his transcendent deity. Jesus taught his disciples to pray to the Father, 'Hallowed be your name.' That petition asks God to set apart his own name, to be the God that he is in all his glory.

To break the throttling grip of fear we must confess God's

---

[1] Acts 5:29; *cf.* 4:19.   [2] Mt. 26:73.   [3] Is. 8:12–13.
[4] The Septuagint has 'Do not fear *him*', referring to the king of Assyria (Is. 8:7). Peter may have paraphrased this translation, changing 'him' to 'them', or he may have returned to the meaning of the original Hebrew.

lordship with more than mental assent. We must confess
it with our heart's devotion. Setting him apart as Lord
means bowing before him in the adoration of praise. A
praising heart is immune to the fear of other people. Fear
of another sort takes possession of our hearts and minds:
a fear that does not flee in terror, but draws near in awe and
worship.

We are amazed, then, at the force of the addition Peter
makes. He says, literally, *Do not fear what they fear,...
But in your hearts* sanctify the Lord, the *Christ.* He repeats
the words of Isaiah, 'Sanctify the Lord', but adds, 'the
Christ'. He does not hesitate to identify the Lord of hosts
with Jesus Christ. More than that, he does so in a passage
that calls for our total devotion to the Lord in his transcendent deity. Peter is not making a merely verbal connection
between two meanings of 'Lord', as applied to God and men.
He is explicitly identifying the One who slept in the stern of
his fishing-boat with the almighty Creator of heaven and
earth. Nor is Peter simply stating the orthodox theology of
the earliest period of the church. He speaks from his own
experience. The Father in heaven had enabled him to confess
the deity of Christ as the Son of the living God. The reality
of the resurrection had confirmed his conviction: Jesus who
could command the storm and the demons had conquered
death and ascended to the right hand of his Father. The Spirit
of Christ, given from the throne of glory, worked in Peter
awe and reverence for his Lord and Saviour. Filled with that
awe, he scorned all that men might do to him. In prison he
could sleep securely; on trial he could accuse his accusers.
His secret was not simply that he had been with Jesus, but
that the Lord Jesus was with him.

Peter had heard Jesus say, 'Do not be afraid of those who
kill the body but cannot kill the soul. Rather, be afraid of
the One who can destroy both body and soul in hell.'[1] Jesus
had followed that solemn warning with words of supreme
assurance to his disciples. Their Father in heaven has
numbered every hair in their heads; nothing can happen to
them outside of his care.

For the Christian, the fear of death has been removed

[1] Mt. 10:28.

by Christ's resurrection. He no longer shares the dread that shadows mortal life: fear of atomic holocaust, of terrorist attack or wasting cancer. Certainly he does not fear those who may persecute him for Christ's sake. Indeed, he can understand that their very persecution is fear-driven, the fear of the light on the part of those who live in darkness.

Yet the conquest of fear does not yield pride or smugness. The Christian must not taunt his enemies, but bear witness to them. This, too, will be the fruit of sanctifying the Lord in his heart. The fear of the Lord in the heart of the Christian is not the terror of the guilty under judgment. It is awe before the love of God as well as before his holiness. Awareness of the Lord's presence means tasting afresh that the Lord is good (2:3). We adore the Lord Jesus Christ who redeemed us at the cost of his life's blood (1:19). Peter has already joined our fear of God with our knowledge of his redeeming love (1:17–19). The Lord whom we sanctify in our hearts is the Lord who died for us.

Our courage before those who persecute us is born of *hope* in the Lord as well as fear of the Lord. In our response to those who may interrogate us we give a reason for our hope. Peter's letter is of hope. Hope is not substituted for faith; it *is* faith as it looks to the future of the Lord's salvation. As we have seen, it is a sure hope, not wishful thinking, and it is firmly grounded in the redemption that Jesus Christ has established for us. Hope is the form that faith takes under the threat of death. Stephen's hope lifted his eyes to Christ in glory as he finished his defence before his accusers. They viewed his hope as blasphemy, and stoned him in their fury.[1]

Peter shows us that our hope provides both the courage for our witness and the content of our witness. Our hope is in our risen Lord. We sanctify the Lord Christ in our hearts; there is the end of fear. We sanctify Christ in our words; there is the start of witness. In the Greek, Peter does not begin a new sentence when he tells us to be always ready to give a reason for our hope. Rather, he says, 'Set apart the Lord, the Christ, ready always for answer.' Our devotion to

[1] Acts 7:55–60.

148

Christ the Lord makes us ready, not only in attitude but in rationale. The word that Peter uses for *answer* is our word 'apology'. We use the word exclusively in the sense of 'excuse', to express regret for a wrong. In the New Testament, however, the word is used to describe a 'defence', usually in a formal or courtroom context.[1] (That meaning survives when we speak of an 'apologist' for the Christian faith.) Paul, for example, speaks of his right, under Roman law, to meet his accusers face to face and to make his 'defence' against their charges.[2] Jesus had promised the presence of the Holy Spirit to enable his disciples to state their case before authorities.[3] Peter well knew what it meant to stand accused in court and give answer.

As Peter speaks of Christian readiness to defend their hope, he is certainly allowing for situations in which they might be haled before Roman magistrates. His encouragement is not limited to Christians in court, however. He speaks of readiness to make a defence to all who might ask a reason for their hope. Persecution was not as intense as it would become; Peter could still speak of *if* rather than 'when' times of trial and suffering would come (3:14). Yet Christians must be ever ready, not only because they would be called to face Roman courts one day, but because they might be accused or challenged by suspicious or malicious pagans any day. It is true, of course, that the witness of a godly life can evoke questions of another sort. Unbelievers may become inquirers, asking with more than curiosity about the distinctive Christian hope. But Peter is here speaking of suffering for Christ's sake. He is arming Christians against attacks, showing them how such confrontations can be turned into occasions for witness.

How, then, does setting apart Christ as Lord prepare Christians to make defence of their hope? The formal speeches of defence in the book of Acts provide the answer; so, indeed, does the whole New Testament. For the Christian faith, a strong offence is the best defence; indeed, it is the only defence. Christians defend their faith by proclaiming the gospel, declaring the reality of the resurrection of Jesus Christ in the plan and power of God. That which is foolish-

[1] BAGD, p. 95. [2] Acts 25:16; see 22:1; Phil. 1:7, 17; 2 Tim. 4:16.
[3] Lk. 12:11–12; 21:12–14.

149

ness to the Greeks and an offence to the Jews is the saving wisdom of God.

Paul's defence before Agrippa shows us why Peter speaks of giving a reason for the *hope* that we have.[1] Paul declares, 'And now I stand and am judged for the hope of the promise made of God unto our fathers.'[2] 'Why should any of you consider it incredible that God raises the dead?' he asks. Peter and Paul both centre on the reality of the resurrection, and they both proclaim the resurrection as the fulfilment of Scripture. Paul summarizes his defence: 'I am saying nothing beyond what the prophets and Moses said would happen – that the Christ would suffer and, as the first to rise from the dead, would proclaim light to his own people and to the Gentiles.'[3] In this letter, Peter has proclaimed the same gospel to those who have been given 'new birth into a living hope through the resurrection of Jesus Christ from the dead.' (1:3). Peter, too, presents this salvation as the fulfilment of what the prophets have spoken (1:10–12, 25). The apostolic gospel bears witness to the historical fact of Christ's death and resurrection, and proclaims the meaning of that fact from the word of God.[4] The reality of the resurrection and the rationale of the resurrection are joined under the authority of God. Apart from the testimony of God's word, the fact of the resurrection could be discounted as a strange and unexplained fact of history. The chief priests who bribed the soldiers to lie about the empty tomb were in full possession of the evidence, yet they did not submit to the word of God.[5] Conversely, there is no lack of contemporary theologians who display their skill in reconstructing apostolic Christianity so that an empty tomb is no longer necessary.

When Paul gave the reason for the Christian hope, Festus, who with King Agrippa heard Paul's defence, declared that he had lost his reason.[6] (Festus, indeed, shouted his charge, betraying by his emotion the offence that the gospel aroused!) Yet, in spite of hatred or scorn, the Christian presents his

[1] Acts 26:1–23.
[2] Acts 26:6, AV. The NIV, by inserting 'my', loses the force of Paul's declaration. The hope for which he is tried is the hope of Israel (v. 7), not just his personal hope.
[3] Acts 26:22–23. See Acts 23:6. [4] 1 Cor. 15:3. [5] Mt. 28:11–15.
[6] Acts 26:24.

hope, humbly proclaiming God's work and word. As we acknowledge the deity of the risen Lord in our hearts, we bear witness to our hope in doxology; we declare the praises of him who called us out of darkness into his light (2:9). Worshipping the Lord, we set our hope fully on the grace to be given us when Jesus Christ is revealed (1:13).

Peter has made it clear that Christians are to be bold in their witness. Hallowing the Lord in their hearts, they are ready at all times to confess his name before others. But now Peter returns to his major theme, the other side of the coin. Humility of life is as important as boldness in word. This is the other result of glorifying Christ as Lord. We are unafraid to press his claims, but we do so as his servants. It has been said that the corruption of the best is the worst; certainly no pride is more offensive than pride in being trophies of grace. The *gentleness* or humility that we are to show is far more than politeness of manner. It reflects the fear of the Lord in which the gospel is presented. *Respect* seems to be the wrong translation here. It suggests a proper attitude toward those who question us. Peter may have used the Greek word *phobos* in that sense when he described the attitude of servants to their masters (2:18), but he has just used it to speak of our fear of God rather than of man (3:14). It seems unlikely that he is now reversing this to ask that we fear man, even in a lesser degree. Rather, Peter is teaching us that it is our fear of the Lord that enables us to bear witness in humility.

b. The opportunity for witness in life (3:16–17)

... keeping a clear conscience, so that those who speak maliciously against your good behaviour in Christ may be ashamed of their slander. [17]It is better, if it is God's will, to suffer for doing good than for doing evil.

Bold words will not honour the Lord if they are not supported by a consistent life. Consider the bitterness of a wealthy old man: he was orphaned as a boy, but his father had made provision for him by entrusting funds for his support to the minister of his church. The minister made off with the money. Through a long life the victim of that injustice saw Christianity as financial exploitation of the gullible. The lives of Christians must reflect the gospel message to those outside the church. That consistency is not less needed in the church and in the heart of the believer. The witness of a good *conscience* is crucial for the witness of a good word. Again, Paul's defence illuminates Peter's words. Standing trial after his arrest on false charges of desecrating the temple, Paul could say, 'So I strive always to keep my conscience clear before God and man.'[1]

Conscience has been defined as a person's 'inner awareness of the moral quality of his actions'.[2] Pagan moralists recognized this inner awareness of behaviour, but apostolic teaching transformed its meaning. The presence of the Holy Spirit in the heart of the believer brings his conscience before God, with radical results. On the one hand, the Christian conscience is informed and reshaped by the light of God's righteousness. No longer is it insensitive to sin, like scar-tissue seared by a hot iron.[3] On the other hand, because God is Lord of the conscience, the Christian is delivered from false guilt, and from the condemnation of sin that God has forgiven. Robert Leighton, with Puritan wisdom, traces the care and nurture of the Christian conscience, growing in the light of the Lord's presence and cleansed by his blood.[4]

In this passage Peter is speaking of our clear conscience as obedient saints rather than simply as forgiven sinners.[5] The clear conscience of a justified sinner indeed frees him for witness, but the impact of his witness will require the outward evidence of a consistent life. By maintaining a clear conscience before God we will be able to show a godly life to others. The Walt Disney version of Pinocchio has given us the cartoon image of conscience as a friendly cricket, an effort, perhaps, to reduce the hostility with which people are inclined to view the promptings of conscience. Christians are called to do much better: to cultivate conscience rather than to stifle its occasional chirps. Suspicious observers are quick to detect hypocrisy in a Christian's life; if we are to avoid self-deception we need a conscience that is both informed and clear.

A clear conscience gives stamina and faithfulness to a

---

[1] Acts 24:16.   [2] Kelly, p. 144.   [3] 1 Tim. 4:2.
[4] Leighton, pp. 333–335.   [5] See Maurer, *TDNT* VII, pp. 918f.

Christian's witness. He knows that the malicious slander that he hears is untrue; he can therefore wait patiently for the truth to win out. His detractors may be ashamed sooner than he thinks. It may be, however, that their shame will be evident only when Christ returns to judge. In any case, even if persecution and suffering do not end, he knows that he is in God's will and that to suffer for doing good brings blessing. To invite the scorn and hostility of others by doing evil would be quite another matter (3:17).

Christians with tender consciences may be dismayed by Peter's words. Aware of their sins and shortcomings, they may despair of having a clear conscience. They may find the suspicions of others confirmed by their suspicions of themselves. Peter shows that he knows our need of forgiveness and cleansing, for he goes on to describe again Christ's atonement (3:18). He also shows the source of power for holy living and a clear conscience. He expresses it in the telling phrase *your good behaviour in Christ* (3:16). Peter uses the phrase *in Christ* that is a keystone of Paul's teaching. Like Paul, Peter glories in the fact that Christ represented us in his death and resurrection. He suffered, the righteous for the unrighteous (3:18), bearing our sins in his body on the tree (2:24). We are given new birth because we are joined to Christ in his resurrection (1:3). We are therefore 'in Christ' as our representative: he died and rose for us. But our union with Christ does not stop there. We are 'in Christ' also because he gives us life. The Spirit of Christ joins us to our Lord as we hallow him in our hearts. We are in no sense alone as we seek to show by our lives that the gospel is true. Without the assurance of sins forgiven, we could not bear witness to those around us. Christians may rightly plead on bumper-stickers, 'Christians are not perfect: just forgiven.' Yet, because the Lord who forgives us also makes us new creations, we are able by grace to show in our lives the reality of his salvation. The God of all grace has called us to his eternal glory in Christ, and will restore and strengthen us (5:10).

Peter again summarizes by saying that *it is better ... to suffer for doing good than for doing evil* (3:17). We are reminded of his word to servants in a section that parallels this (2:20). In both passages this statement leads into a declaration about the sufferings of Christ, who did only good. One commentator suggests that Peter may also be warning those who might seek martyrdom through mistaken zeal in oppposing the pagan government. 'It is unworthy of Christian believers to court martyrdom through deeds of violence, as for instance, the Jewish zealots did.'[1] Peter, however, seems concerned to encourage Christians to endure suffering; he does not speak of their seeking it. In any case, the application of Peter's teaching does have importance for some forms of Christian protest today. Suffering for provocative acts in the name of Christ is not to be commended, but rather suffering that follows our Lord's example in doing good.

c. The victory of Christ's suffering (3:18–22)

For Christ died for sins once for all, the righteous for the unrighteous, to bring you to God. He was put to death in the body but made alive by the Spirit, [19]through whom also he went and preached to the spirits in prison [20]who disobeyed long ago when God waited patiently in the days of Noah while the ark was being built. In it only a few people, eight in all, were saved through water, [21]and this water symbolises baptism that now saves you also – not the removal of dirt from the body but the pledge of a good conscience towards God. It saves you by the resurrection of Jesus Christ, [22]who has gone into heaven and is at God's right hand - with angels, authorities and powers in submission to him.

Again Peter returns to the cross. Our willingness to suffer for the sake of Christ is grounded in the wonder of Christ's willingness to suffer death for our sake. This passage stands in close relation to 2:21–24. There, too, we read of Christ's atoning death as our substitute. There, too, the merciful purpose of Christ's suffering is declared (that we might die to sins, live for righteousness, and be healed, 2:24). Yet Peter now presents the suffering Christ as the Victor. He adds to his teaching about the saving power of Christ's *death* a fresh emphasis on the saving power of his *resurrection*. In the

[1] Reicke, p. 108.

154

earlier passage, Peter points us to the example of Christ's meekness in suffering. We are called to imitate him as we suffer for his sake. In this second passage, Peter tells us that Christ who suffered and died was made alive again, has gone into heaven and is at God's right hand. He is the Conqueror; we share his triumph.

Persecuted and suffering Christians need to remember both the humiliation and the exaltation of Christ. His patient suffering will show them meekness when they are interrogated. His glorious triumph will give them courage to face their accusers. Undergirding both the meekness and the boldness of the Christian is the saving work of Christ.

Christ died for sins once for all. Christ's saving victory flows from the fact that his sacrifice was perfect, final, and therefore not to be repeated in history or in symbol. If Christ's sacrifice were not complete, it would have to be offered again, as the Old Testament sacrifices were. But, as the author of Hebrews teaches us, Christ's sacrifice was of a different order. If he had offered no better sacrifice than the priests, and had entered no better sanctuary than they, then he would have had to 'suffer many times since the creation of the world'. But he is the Son of God, his royal priesthood is heavenly, his sacrifice is his offering of his own blood. 'But now he has appeared once for all at the end of the ages to do away with sin by the sacrifice of himself.'[1] When the Protestant Reformers understood this, they could no longer participate in the mass, for the mass is celebrated as a bloodless sacrifice in which Christ is again offered for sin.[2]

Christ suffered and died to pay the price *for sins*, fully and

---

[1] Heb. 9:26–28; *cf.* 10:10, 14.

[2] This was a crucial factor in John Calvin's separation from the Roman Catholic church. Why should Calvin leave the church when the prophets had remained in apostate Israel? Calvin replied that the prophets never participated in an act of worship that was sacrilegious (*Institutes*, IV: 2:9). The issue remains; see 'Instruction on the Worship of the Eucharistic Mystery' in 'The Constitution on the Sacred Liturgy', *Vatican Council II*, ed. Austin Flannery, OP, (Costello 1975): 'Hence the Mass, the Lord's Supper, is at the same time and inseparably: a sacrifice in which the sacrifice of the cross is perpetuated . . .' (p. 102); 'For in it Christ perpetuates in an unbloody manner the sacrifice offered on the cross, offering himself to the Father for the world's salvation through the ministry of priests' (p. 103). See the decree of Trent 'On the Holy Sacrifice of the Mass' in P. F. Palmer, ed., *Sacraments and Worship* (Longmans, Green, 1957), pp. 304–309.

finally.[1] The phrase 'for sin' appears in the phrase for the sin-offering in the Greek Old Testament.[2] He who was righteous and without sin took the place of unrighteous sinners. His purpose, Peter tells the Christian 'pilgrims and strangers', was *to bring you to God*. Apart from Christ's saving work they were without hope and without God. The judgment of God against their sins separated them from fellowship with him. But now those who were far off are brought near.[3] They may approach God in worship and fellowship, for he has claimed them as his own. On earth they are journeying pilgrims; Christ, their shepherd, is leading them home.

By his death Christ won life for his own. His resurrection brings triumph after suffering, a triumph that is the hope of suffering Christians. Notice the credal or confessional content of this section (a form that resembles the credal hymn of 1 Timothy 3:16): *For Christ died for sins once for all . . . He was put to death in the body but made alive by the Spirit . . . has gone into heaven and is at God's right hand – with angels, authorities and powers in submission to him.*[4]

That Peter is describing Christ's triumph is clear. His death was not defeat, but the once-for-all sacrifice that atoned for sin. It was followed by the resurrection and the ascension. In that context, Peter writes about Christ's preaching to *spirits in prison*. His words were no doubt clear to those who first heard them, but they have been hard for later generations to understand. Martin Luther writes in his commentary: 'A wonderful text is this, and a more obscure passage perhaps than any other in the New Testament, so that I do not know for a certainty just what Peter means.'[5] Study of the passage may have progressed since Luther's day, but his confession still warns us against overconfidence!

Three major interpretations have been given to Peter's

---

[1] A variant textual reading is 'suffered for sins' rather than 'died for sins'. This would not affect the sense; it is the mortal suffering of Christ on the cross that is in view. Both readings are also found in 2:21.

[2] Lv. 5:6, LXX. [3] Eph. 2:11–13.

[4] See Best, pp. 135f., Bénétreau, p. 204, n. 1.

[5] Luther, p. 168.

words, each with various modifications.[1] According to the first, Jesus descended into hell and preached to the spirits of those who perished in the flood in the time of Noah. Some who hold this view also think that what Jesus proclaimed to the dead was the gospel, offering them a further opportunity to repent. Others would have Christ preaching to the righteous dead, proclaiming their release from the prison where they awaited his coming. Still others would understand his preaching to be the heralding of the doom of the wicked dead.

The second major interpretation was presented by Augustine, who objected to the first view as presented by Origen and others. Augustine held that Christ's preaching was done in the Spirit through Noah. Peter says that it was the Spirit of Christ who preached through the Old Testament prophets (1:11); Christ's preaching through Noah would be a case in point. Those to whom Noah preached were not in prison literally, but they could be described as in prison spiritually. (Or, it might be said that those to whom Noah once preached are *now* spirits in prison.)

A third interpretation would understand *spirits in prison* to refer to fallen angels rather than to human beings. Jesus proclaims to them his victory and their doom. This is seen by some as taking place after his resurrection. As he ascends into heaven, Jesus confronts the principalities and powers, showing his victory and power over them.

None of these explanations is free of difficulty; to weigh them we must answer several key questions. First, when did Christ preach to the spirits in prison? Was it long before the incarnation, in the time of Noah? Was it after his death, but before his resurrection? Or was it after his resurrection (either before he appeared to the disciples, or in the course of his ascension)?

To answer the question we must understand the words, 'having been *put to death* with respect to the flesh, *but made alive* with respect to the spirit' (3:18).[2] Martin Luther

[1] For accounts of the history of interpretation, see Selwyn, Essay I, pp. 314–362; and Reicke, *Spirits*, pp. 7–51, and Dalton. See also Feinberg, pp. 303–336; Grudem, Appendix, 'Christ Preaching through Noah: 1 Peter 3:19–20 in the Light of Dominant Themes in Jewish Literature'.

[2] The dative case is used for both 'flesh' and 'spirit' in the sense of 'with respect to'. See BDF, par. 197, p. 105. See R. T. France, 'Exegesis in Practice: Two

explains these words as expressing the same distinction that Paul makes in 1 Corinthians 15:45, 49.[1] Paul contrasts our present 'natural' bodies with the 'spiritual' bodies that we shall receive at the resurrection. It is Christ's resurrection that is the source of the spiritual: 'The first man Adam became a living soul. The last Adam became a life-giving spirit'.[2]

Peter is not saying that Christ's body died but that his spirit continued to live. He is saying that Christ died as to the natural, physical sphere of existence, and that Christ was given life as to the spiritual sphere of existence. If Peter were distinguishing between the death of the body and the continuing life of the soul, he would not have said that Christ was *made* alive. 'Thus the second phrase does not refer to Christ *disembodied*, but to Christ *risen* to life on a new plane.'[3]

This explanation would also help us understand somewhat similar language in 1 Peter 4:6. There Peter speaks of those to whom the gospel was preached so that they might indeed have been judged 'according to men with respect to the flesh', but might live 'according to God with respect to the spirit' (my translation). If those spoken of are the Christian dead, then the life that they receive through the gospel should not be thought of as the continued existence of the soul, but as the resurrection life of Christ they receive.[4]

The phrase 'he was raised as to the spirit' rules out the thought of an underworld descent by the disembodied soul of Christ in the time between his death and resurrection. It does not settle the question, however, as to the time of Christ's preaching. Christ's death was physical, but his resurrection was in the realm of the spiritual, that is, in the power

---

Samples' in I. H. Marshall, ed. *New Testament Interpretation* (Paternoster and Eerdmans, 1977) p. 280, n. 35.

[1] Luther, p. 167. For an exposition of the spiritual form of the resurrection see R. B. Gaffin, Jr. *The Centrality of the Resurrection: A Study in Paul's Soteriology* (Baker, 1978).

[2] 1 Cor. 15:45, ASV.

[3] R. T. France, *op. cit.*, p. 267. See Selwyn, p. 197: 'The phrase clearly embodies a familiar NT contrast between Christ dead and Christ living (cf. Rom. xiv. 9, 2 Cor. xiii.4, 1 Tim. iii. 16).'

[4] See the comments on 4:6. Compare 1 Thes. 5:10 where 'live together with him' refers to the resurrection. BDF, par. 369 (2), p. 187.

of the Holy Spirit.[1] The NIV translation, *made alive by the Spirit*, may well capture Peter's meaning. It allows for Augustine's interpretation: Christ who rose 'spiritually' also preached 'spiritually' through Noah.

What, then, is the connection between Christ's death and resurrection and his proclamation to the spirits in prison? There are two possibilities. The Greek phrase which the NIV renders *through whom* (3:19) means 'in which'. It may refer directly to the word 'spirit' or it may be more indefinite, 'in which time'. If it is the latter, the preaching spoken of must have taken place after the resurrection. It could then have been before Christ appeared to the women, as Lutheran interpreters have held.[2] It could also have been during the forty days, or in the course of Christ's ascension. If, however, 'in which' refers to 'spirit', then the preaching of the Spirit of Christ through Noah remains a possibility.[3]

The next key question is: To whom did Christ make proclamation? Who are *the spirits in prison*? The phrase 'spirits in prison', taken by itself, could refer to fallen angels.[4] In 2 Peter 2:4–5 fallen angels are described as imprisoned; the passage then goes on to speak of Noah and the judgment of the flood:

> For if God did not spare angels when they sinned, but sent them to hell [literally, 'Tartarus'], putting them into gloomy dungeons [literally, 'pits of darkness'] to be held for judgment; if he did not spare the ancient world when he brought the flood on its ungodly people, but protected Noah, a preacher of righteousness, and seven others . . .

In the letter of Jude similar language is found:

[1] See Rom. 1:3–4.
[2] Martin H. Scharlemann, ' "He Descended into Hell": An Interpretation of 1 Peter 3:18–20', *Concordia Theological Monthly*, 28:2 (February, 1956). Cited in Traver, p. 50.
[3] See Selwyn, Bénétreau and (for the case against Selwyn's view) Grudem.
[4] For example, Heb. 1:14; Lk. 10:20; Rev. 1:4; 3:11. See Reicke, *Spirits*, p. 54. See also the discussion in Selwyn, pp. 198–200. Note the distinction between 'spirits' and 'flesh' in 1 Enoch 15:8. In 1 Enoch, 'Lord of Spirits' as a title of God refers to angels (R. H. Charles, *The Apocrypha and Pseudepigrapha of the Old Testament in English*, vol. II: *Pseudepigrapha*, Oxford University Press, 1913, note 'Lord of Spirits', p. 209). Grudem, however, shows that 'spirits' can mean human spirits, depending on the context: Ec. 12:7, LXX; Mt. 27:50; Lk. 23:46; Jn. 19:30; Acts 7:59; 1 Cor. 5:5; Heb. 12:23. He also cites 1 Enoch 20:6; 22:6–7.

And the angels who did not keep their domain, but abandoned their own dwelling, he has kept in everlasting chains, under darkness, for judgment on the great Day.[1]

Both the term *spirits* and the reference to *prison* fit well with these passages that describe the doom of fallen angels. But could angels be described as spirits *who disobeyed long ago . . . in the days of Noah?* A case can be made for this by taking account of Jewish traditions and writings that were current when Peter wrote, especially the book of *Enoch.* (A prophecy of Enoch contained in this book is quoted in Jude 14–15.) In Genesis 5:24 are the striking words, 'Enoch walked with God; then he was no more, because God took him away.' These words contrast with the concluding formula of the Genesis genealogies, 'and then he died'. Enoch's walk with God links with the righteousness of his descendant Noah, and contrasts with the wickedness that abounded on earth before the flood.

What happened to Enoch when the Lord took him? Where did he go? Jewish traditions and writings speculated about this. In the version now designated as *1 Enoch*, we are told of Enoch's travels as he was shown the secrets of the universe. In particular, he went to the place where the fallen angels were kept under judgment. In *1 Enoch* and in some other Jewish traditions, it is assumed that the 'sons of God' in Genesis 6:2 were angels who took wives as they pleased from the 'daughters of men'.[2] Their progeny, the 'Nephilim', were thought to be demons. The angels who had disobeyed and had left their place were imprisoned in a 'burning valley'. Enoch describes the place:

'Beyond that abyss I saw a place which had no firmament of the heaven above, and no firmly founded earth beneath it: there was no water upon it, and no birds, but it was a waste and horrible place.'[3]

This is supplemented by a further description of 'another

---

[1] Jude 6, my translation.

[2] Meredith Kline has argued persuasively for viewing the 'sons of God' as royal figures, and the sin as polygamy ('Divine Kingship and Genesis 6:14', *WTJ* XXIV, 1961–1962, pp. 187–204.

[3] 1 Enoch 18:12. Imprisonment of the angels in the 'burning valley', 1 Enoch 67:4.

place, which was still more horrible than the former', a place
cleft as far as the abyss, having descending columns of fire.
'This place is the prison of the angels, and here they will
be imprisoned forever.'[1] In *1 Enoch* this prison for fallen
angels is distinguished from the places where the souls of
men await judgment.[2] Another writing, *2 Enoch*, locates
the place of detention for the fallen angels in the second
heaven.[3]

It would be a great mistake to read into 1 Peter the fanciful
descriptions of *1 Enoch*. But the use of *1 Enoch* in Jude
14–15 and the passage about the doom of fallen angels in 2
Peter 2:4 show us that the language of the 'Enoch' literature
could help us to understand the terms used in 1 Peter. Since
the disobedient angels and their offspring were viewed as
instigators of lawlessness in the antediluvian world, it might
be possible to speak of them as those *who disobeyed long
ago when God waited patiently in the days of Noah* (3:20).[4]
On this understanding, Peter is claiming for Christ a mission
that far transcends the journey that tradition ascribed to
Enoch. Enoch was sent by God to pronounce doom upon
the rebellious angels. They asked Enoch to present a petition
to God to cancel their sentence. Enoch did so, but God sent
him back with the same message.[5] Peter's word for *preached*
(3:19) means 'heralded' or 'proclaimed'. It could carry the
meaning of announcing judgment rather than offering
salvation. In view of the description of Christ's victory in
3:22, that meaning is possible here. Christ's 'preaching' to
the spirits in prison would then be his proclamation to the
'angels, authorities and powers' of his resurrection victory
and their doom. Christ is the true Enoch: he walks with God
and is taken up to be with his heavenly Father. Not Enoch,
but Christ, is the one who confronts the angelic and demonic
forces of evil.

[1] 1 Enoch 21:1–2.　[2] 1 Enoch 22:1–14.

[3] 2 Enoch 7:1–3; 18:3–6. See the discussion in R. T. France, *op. cit*, p. 270.

[4] See 1 Enoch 6:1 – 10:3; 106:13–15. Note the mention of Jared in 6:1; 106:13.
Bénétreau holds that the disobedience could have preceded the proclamation. He
notes that 'who had been disobedient' would be a proper translation of the aorist
participle in 3:20 (p. 109).

[5] Enoch does not find them in prison at this time, however. Rather they are near
Mount Hermon, where they covenanted together to engage in their sin (13:10, *cf.*
6:6). Apparently the angels are bound in 'valleys of the earth' until the day of
judgment when they will be consigned to the abyss for ever (10:13).

Yet, attractive as this explanation may be, it is not completely satisfying. To speak of those *who disobeyed long ago . . . in the days of Noah* recalls at once the generation that perished in the flood. In *1 Enoch* the disobedient angels are said to have sinned, not in the days of Noah, but in the days of Jared, the father of Noah.[1] Even if angelic disobedience were thought of as continuing in the days before the flood, why would it be described as taking place while God was waiting patiently during the building of the ark? God's patience during the time before the flood is obviously like the patience he now shows in postponing judgment: 'The Lord is not slow in keeping his promise, as some understand slowness. He is patient with you, not wanting anyone to perish, but everyone to come to repentance' (2 Pet. 3:9).

While the ark was being built, the possibility of escape from judgment existed for human beings, not for fallen angels.[2] The patience of God was directed to the sinners of Noah's generation, those to whom Noah preached righteousness (2 Pet 2:5). This refers so clearly to human beings, not angels, that some who favour the reference to angels have concluded that human beings must also be included.[3] Further, if angels were in view, it would seem strange that Peter should use the word that he does for *disobeyed*. It is a term that describes the disobedience of unbelief.[4]

Yet another consideration supports the view that the 'spirits in prison' are the sinners of Noah's generation. A recent commentator has pointed to a better translation of 1 Peter 3:19–20: 'He went and preached to those who are now spirits in prison when they disobeyed formerly when God's patience was waiting in the days of Noah.'[5] This preferred translation shows that the disobedience was going on along with the preaching. It is a perfectly natural

[1] 1 Enoch 6:6; 106:13.
[2] Grudem cites extra-biblical Jewish literature to show a unanimous emphasis on God's waiting for sinners to repent, and connecting his patience specifically with the time of the flood. Indeed, the *Enoch* literature also emphasizes that there can be no mitigation of the judgment on the angels; this is reaffirmed by Enoch's visit.
[3] So Selwyn, pp. 199, 323; Reicke, p. 69.
[4] 1 Pet. 2:7–8; 3:1; 4:17.
[5] Grudem, pp. 233–236. The word describing their disobeying, used without the article, should be taken with the verb 'to preach' rather than with 'spirits'.

expression if Peter is thinking of Christ's preaching through Noah, and does much to relieve the usual objection to referring the preaching to the days of Noah. In the time that the ark was being built, it is true, the people of that generation were not in prison. (Augustine's explanation that they were spiritually imprisoned is unconvincing.) But the shift in translation underscores the fact that we are to understand that the spirits are *now* in prison. These sinners, now under condemnation, were those who were disobedient when the Spirit of Christ preached to them *long ago* through Noah (3:20; 1:11). This understanding gives the same interpretation to *in prison* that is given to 'dead' in 1 Peter 4:6. In both cases Peter is referring to people in terms of their present state. (The NIV translates 1 Peter 4:5 'to those who are *now* dead', adding the word to convey the meaning.)

An objection to this understanding of the text appeals to the word *went* in verse 19. The same verb is used in verse 22 (*has gone*) to describe Christ's going to heaven in the ascension. 'How,' it is asked, 'can Christ's preaching through Noah be described as his "going" in the Spirit?'[1] This is not a compelling objection. God's interventions in Old Testament revelation are often described in terms of his going or coming.[2] The verb *went* may also be used with little or no emphasis, as in colloquial English speech: 'He went and told him.'[3]

The strong case for regarding the 'spirits in prison' as the spirits of those who were disobedient to the preaching of Noah can settle the question as to what was preached. On this assumption, what was preached is identified in 2 Peter 2:5, where the same word-stem is used in the phrase 'Noah, a preacher of righteousness'.[4] It is the proclamation of God's righteousness, and therefore of the need for repentance. That message was addressed through Noah to those disobedient sinners during their lifetime. The passage describes no second

[1] Dalton, *op. cit.*, p. 35. Note the reply by Grudem, pp. 236–237.
[2] Grudem calls attention to Gn. 3:8; 11:7; 18:21, and to Christ as the Rock following Israel in the wilderness (1 Cor. 10:4). Since the same verb for 'going' is used of Christ's ascension (1 Pet. 3:22), it has been argued that his 'going' to preach must be a similar or even identical journey. As Grudem points out, however, some such expression would be needd to indicate the preaching of Christ through Noah in contrast to a spiritual address from heaven.
[3] BAGD, p. 692.   [4] Grudem, pp. 233–235.

163

chance for repentance after death. Even less does it promise universal salvation.[1]

In this whole passage Peter continues to give reassurance to Christians who must endure suffering and persecution. Christ has conquered by the power of his resurrection. He has prevailed to bring them to God. The devil may still be on the prowl like a roaring lion (5:7), but he cannot destroy those whose refuge is the Lord. Peter reminds suffering Christians of the period before the flood. The power of evil might then have been greater, the number of the elect even fewer. But God was in control. He withheld judgment, then as now, only to display his longsuffering grace. But his judgment did come: Noah and his family were delivered from that evil age by the judgment, the waters of the flood. Yet the judgment of the flood was only provisional, and the deliverance of Noah but a prefiguring, or 'type', of the final and full salvation of Jesus Christ. The doom of death in the flood pictures the doom that Christ suffered for us. He was put to death in the flesh. But he was made alive in the power of the Spirit. It was in that power that he preached through Noah to those whose disobedience brought eternal condemnation. It is in that same power that he now saves us. Those who reject the gospel put themselves under the judgment that will come when Christ comes. But those who are united to Christ are saved by the same promise that delivered Noah and his family.

Peter continues to relate the time of Noah to that of the church by appealing to typology. The inspired authors of the New Testament find in the Old Testament history not merely instances of God's saving power, but also anticipations of his final salvation in Christ.[2] By providing the ark, God saved Noah and his family from the judgment of the flood. That deliverance, however, did not in itself give eternal life to the eight persons that were spared. Like the exodus liberation, it was a symbol of God's final salvation from all sin and death. Peter uses the term 'antitype' to describe the

[1] Goppelt considers that this apostolic tradition needs to be demythologized – relieved of its mythical form – but that it presents the universal salvation of Christ's sufferings and death (p. 254).

[2] See Richard M. Davidson, *Typology In Scripture* (Andrews University Press, 1981); Leonhard Goppelt, *Typos: The Typological Interpretation of the Old Testament in the New* (Eerdmans, 1982).

relation of the new to the old (3:21; NIV's verb *symbolises* translates the Greek noun *antitypos*). This use of 'type' and 'antitype' is itself figurative, drawn from the striking of coins or the impression of seals. 'Type' describes either a matrix from which an impression is made, or the image created.[1] In the letter to the Hebrews, the typology is vertical. That is, the heavenly realities are called the 'type' and the earthly symbols the 'antitype'. The tabernacle in the wilderness was therefore the antitype of the heavenly sanctuary.[2] In Paul's letters and here in 1 Peter, the typology is horizontal in history: the Old Testament symbol is the type, and therefore Christ's fulfilment is the antitype.[3]

What is the 'antitype' to which Peter refers? Apparently it is *baptism*, although the construction of the passage is difficult. (The antitype could be *you*: that is, Noah and his family were types of Christians: they were saved through water, and Christians are also saved through the water of baptism.[4]) In any case, Peter would have us understand that the God who delivered Noah will also deliver us, and that ours is the final salvation.

That full and final salvation is sealed to us in Christian baptism. It may seem strange that Peter finds the fulfilment of Old Testament symbolism in New Testament symbolism. The symbol of the type points us to the symbol of the sacrament. Indeed, to prevent misunderstanding, Peter at once adds that he is not speaking of the outward application of *water, the removal of dirt from the body*. Rather, he is speaking of the new existence that we have through *the resurrection of Jesus Christ*. Baptism as an outward sign marks the putting off of the pollution of sin, and the beginning of new life in Christ.

Yet Peter also calls our attention to an analogy between the type and the sacrament. Both involve water in the context of gaining life out of death. The *eight* persons in the ark *were saved* 'by' or *through* water. 'By' would be the more usual

---

[1] See the summary in Davidson, *op. cit.*, pp. 115–132.

[2] Heb. 9:24; *antitypos* = 'copy' in NIV.

[3] Rom. 5:14 (*typos*, NIV 'pattern'); 1 Cor. 10:11 (*typikōs*, NIV 'as examples'). See Davidson, *op. cit.*, pp. 191–397.

[4] *Antitypos* may be an adjective, modifying 'you'. Selwyn translates 'And water now saves you too, who are the antitype of Noah and his company, namely the water of baptism' (p. 203).

translation of the preposition. We might think of the water of the flood as the means by which Noah's family was delivered from the threatening wickedness of their generation.[1] But the verb for *saved* has the same preposition attached to it; there it must mean 'through'. Noah and his family, then, were saved 'through' water. Why does Peter not say 'saved *from* water'? Perhaps because the water that destroyed the wicked also bore up the ark. But more probably Peter is already pointing forward to the analogy that he has in mind. Meredith Kline has pointed out that covenants in the ancient Middle East, and in the Scriptures, are sealed by an oath.[2] A powerful example is the oath that God himself takes in Genesis 15. There the divided parts of the animals symbolize the malediction that God calls down upon himself if he should not be faithful to his pledge.[3] So, too, the blood shed in circumcision implies not only cleansing, but an oath involving one's descendants. In baptism, Kline reasons, the same element remains. When baptism is compared to the waters of the flood or to the waters of the Red Sea, the threatening symbolism of water is brought into view.[4] Israel was brought through the waters of the sea and of the Jordan; Noah was brought through the waters of the flood. Christians are brought through the waters of death, the flood of destruction, in order that they might be established upon the rock, secure in the resurrection life of Christ.[5]

It is significant that Peter goes on to speak of the pledge made in baptism, *the pledge of a good conscience towards God*. The word for *pledge* implies an undertaking made in reponse to formal questions.[6] Peter underscores the solemnity of the commitment made by these new Christians. They pledge the life of a good conscience. (Or, they make the

[1] See Reicke, *Epistles*, p. 113.

[2] See M. G. Kline, *By Oath Consigned: a Reinterpretation of the Covenant Signs of Circumcision and Baptism* (Eerdmans, 1975).

[3] See Je. 34:18–20. The terms describing the fire or lightning that passes between the pieces are repeated to describe God's appearing at Sinai. In the symbol of the fire, God passes between the pieces.

[4] 1 Cor. 10:2.

[5] The figure of the church established on the rock has in view the floods of destruction issuing forth from the gates of death (Is. 28:14–18; Ps. 18:4–5; 42:8).

[6] For a defence of the translation 'pledge' for a much disputed term, see Kelly, pp. 162f.; France, *op. cit.*, p. 275.

pledge of baptism sincerely, out of a good conscience.[1]) In that pledge Christians agree with God's judgment on sin, and on their own sinful past (4:3). They acknowledge that to turn from their commitment would be to bring upon themselves God's just judgment. Yet Peter's words stress the wonder of the sacrament even more than its solemnity. As Noah was delivered by the grace of God, although only in symbol, so have they been delivered in fact. Christ has saved them, for he died for their sins and gave them life through his resurrection (3:18, 21).

Like circumcision, baptism does symbolize cleansing. Indeed, when Peter says that we are not saved by the 'putting off' (NIV *removal*) of impurity, he uses language that seems even more appropriate to circumcision than to baptism.[2] But baptism means much more. It means union with Jesus Christ in his death and resurrection.[3] Christians have set apart Jesus Christ as Lord; they have been participants in his victory over death and all the powers of darkness. Christians need never fear their enemies; their concern must rather be to live in good conscience toward God.

Christ's conclusive death for our sins was accomplished *to bring* us *to God* (3:18). The victory of his atoning death is seen in his resurrection, and in his triumphant ascension to the right hand of God. He died to bring us where he now is. Peter has called Christians to lives of submission for Christ's sake, following the example of his humiliation (2:21). Yet the submission of Christians is not that of defeated captives, brought into hopeless slavery. It is the willing and joyful service of those who know that they are victors with Christ. Once he submitted himself, but now all the *angels* are *in submission to him* (3:22). So, too, Christians are called to submit themselves, but in the sign of baptism they are already participants in Christ's resurrection victory. Peter had witnessed the ascension of Christ; he had proclaimed from Psalm 110 the seating of Christ at the Father's right

[1] Bénétreau and Selwyn prefer the latter interpretation; Kelly and France the former.

[2] Kelly points out that the noun translated *removal* is unusual to describe washing. It fits better the removal of the foreskin as a symbol of defilemen˙ ˙n circumcision (p. 161).

[3] Rom. 6:1–11. See below on 1 Pet. 4:1–2.

hand.[1] Here in his letter he stresses the authority that Jesus has over all the powers of creation. Christians need not fear the sword of Roman magistrates or the fury of Satan. They belong to the Lord in glory.

[1] Acts 1:9; 2:34–35.

8. The blessing of living as stewards of grace

1. Union with Christ in death to sin (4:1)

Therefore, since Christ suffered in his body, arm yourselves also with the same attitude, because he who has suffered in his body is done with sin.

At first sight, it might seem that Peter is presenting a general truth: bodily suffering inhibits sin. Accordingly, Christians should not regret suffering, since suffering will advance their sanctification.[1] Yet it seems clear that this cannot be Peter's meaning. An immediate difficulty for this interpretation is that Peter does not begin with suffering in general, but with Christ's suffering. Christians are to have the same insight, the same perception that Christ had.[2] Are we to suppose that Peter is telling us that Christ embraced suffering to avoid sinning? Did the Lord seek the sanctifying power of suffering?

Further, the forms of the Greek verbs tell against this interpretation. The verbs for *suffered* and *has suffered* have a form that describes a definite event, not an ongoing process. The same form is used in 3:18 to describe the once-for-all suffering of Christ on the cross. There it is a synonym for his death, and indeed the NIV translates it 'died'. The phrase *is done with sin* describes a present condition determined by a past event. This phrase does not describe an ongoing process, either, but rather a new situation. Peter is speaking of one

---

[1] This is the view of Leighton.
[2] Or the same insight that understands Christ's suffering. On either interpretation Christ's suffering is made a means of avoiding sin.

act of suffering that results in a situation where sin is stopped or finished.[1]

What, then, is the 'suffering in the body' that Peter has in view? Surely, in the case of Christ, it is his suffering for sins once on the cross (3:18). The result was that sin was done away. He was finished with it. Peter does not mean, of course, that Jesus was sinning, and that the cross put a stop to it. He affirms that Jesus did no sin (2:22). But although Jesus did no sin, he bore our sins in his own body to the tree (2:24). The burden of our sin was on him; he carried it up to Calvary. But there it ended. His death finished his involvement with our sin.

Indeed, it is possible that in the last half of 4:1 Peter is still speaking of Jesus: *he who has suffered in his body is done with sin*.[2] In any case, Peter applies this principle to us. We are to arm ourselves with a thought that is decisive for our new manner of life. Christ's mortal suffering ended his conquest of sin and ushered in his resurrection life. Peter has already shown the connection with us: Jesus bore our sins in his body on the tree so that we, having died to sins, might live to righteousness (2:24). In that passage, too, Peter spoke of an event in the past that marks the end of sin and the beginning of a life of righteousness.[3] When Christ died to sin in our place, we died to sin, just as when he rose, we were given new birth (1:3). Our decisive 'suffering in the body' is that death which we share with Christ who suffered in the body for us. Baptism marks our union with Christ in his death and resurrection (3:21). It is nothing less than death that separates us from a life of sin. When Peter encourages us to arm ourselves with this thought, he is saying in his way what Paul, too, tells us:

> Now if we died with Christ, we believe that we will also live with him . . . The death he died, he died to sin once for all; but the life he lives, he lives to God.

[1] 'Is done with sin' – the verb is either reflexive or passive, and is in the perfect tense. See Kelly, pp. 166–168.
[2] The thesis of A. Strobel, 'Macht Leiden von Sünde frei?', *ThZ* XIX, 1963, pp. 412–425, cited in Bénétreau, p. 217; Kelly, p. 167.
[3] See the comments on 2:24 above. The arguments for the explanation given here are concisely stated in Kelly, pp. 165f., and Stibbs, pp. 147f. Bénétreau builds the case in careful detail; pp. 214f.

In the same way, count yourselves dead to sin but alive to God in Christ Jesus. Therefore do not let sin reign in your mortal body so that you obey its evil desires.[1]

2. The liberty of salvation (4:2–6)

As a result, he does not live the rest of his earthly life for evil human desires, but rather for the will of God. [3]For you have spent enough time in the past doing what pagans choose to do – living in debauchery, lust, drunkenness, orgies, carousing and detestable idolatry. [4]They think it strange that you do not plunge with them into the same flood of dissipation, and they heap abuse on you. [5]But they will have to give account to him who is ready to judge the living and the dead. [6]For this is the reason the gospel was preached even to those who are now dead, so that they might be judged according to men in regard to the body, but live according to God in regard to the spirit.

The decisive death to sin that is marked by baptism ushers in a new time of life. You have heard it said that 'Today is the first day of the rest of your life'. For the Christian the rest of his life begins with the faith that unites him to Christ. Having died to sin, he is alive to God; the rest of his life is no longer to be shaped by the desires of sin, but by the will of God. Peter is not teaching that the Christian is now perfect, and that sin is no longer a problem for him. Indeed, he writes to urge Christians to forsake sin. Yet there is a decisive difference. They have died to sin and have gained the freedom to live according to the will of God. Their lives are different.

Peter shows the difference by a vivid contrast. There are two ways of life. One is determined by *the will of God*. The other is marked out by the will of the Gentile nations, *what pagans choose to do*. The two cannot be blended: no-one can serve two masters. Those who have been given new life through Christ will look with fear and revulsion at the lifestyle that once swept them along with the crowd. Equally, those living in the licentious fast lane will look with scorn and contempt at the pious life of 'born-again' Christians. Yet

[1] Rom. 6:8–12.

the Christians addressed by Peter had a sad advantage. They knew well what life in the fast lane was like. They had been Gentile pagans; wild drinking parties, sexual perversion, idolatrous cults – they had drowned in that *flood of dissipation*. But they now knew a better way, a way that their scornful friends could not imagine. Fervent love of brothers and sisters in Christ had replaced lust, alert awareness of the times had replaced drunken stupor, but above all, the joyful adoration of the risen Lord had replaced the folly of idolatry.

For you have spent enough time ... *doing what pagans choose to do*, writes Peter. Enough indeed! Those converted pagans would wince at Peter's irony. How they would wish to erase those wasted years from their memory! But now they have a new life, and Peter reminds them that there is no turning back.

In listing the vices of pagan immorality Peter makes vivid the 'evil desires you had when you lived in ignorance' (1:14), the 'empty way of life' in the pagan tradition (1:18). Paul gives similar descriptions.[1] Peter is accurate; his hearers would not dispute his description of their past. But there were pagan moralists who condemned many of the same vices. Has not Peter overdrawn the picture? Paul answers that question in Romans 2. The moralists are themselves hypocrites, practising in one way or other exactly what they condemn. The forms of sin may differ, but all have sinned and come short of the glory of God. The division of the city of Berlin after World War 2 brought contrasts of many kinds: the freedom of the West expressed itself in the flaunting of commercialized sex. In contrast to the neon glitter of flesh shows in the West, the drab avenues of the East seem puritan in their restraint. Yet the Communist effort to legislate morality without God has opened other floodgates of repression and murder.

Peter draws the line for those who have died with Christ to the life of sin. That life went on long enough. The new life, *the rest of* our *earthly life*, is before us. How long that will be we do not know. Some who earlier trusted in Christ have already gone to be with him. 'The end of all things is near' (4:7). We do not know when the Lord will return. But,

[1] Rom. 13:13; Gal. 5:19–21. See also the description of the 'ways of the spirit of falsehood' in the Community Rule of the Dead Sea sectarians (1QS 4:9–11, in *DSS*).

by Christ's resurrection power, we may be rid of that old life of selfish indulgence. We may live for the will of God, the Father of our Lord Jesus Christ. How different the will of God now seems! Once it loomed like a dark prison, curbing our desires, threatening our freedom to do as we pleased. Now we find that his yoke is easy and his burden light. The law of love is the law of liberty.

Drawing the line in a new life will antagonize former friends. They will find our new behaviour bizarre, even threatening. Charles Colson had gained notoriety in the Watergate scandal as a close associate of President Richard Nixon. When he was converted in the midst of the Watergate proceedings, the press greeted his 'born-again' witness with hoots of derision. Cartoonists had a field day picturing a cover-up by this instant. saint. With the passing years, however, Colson's genuineness in caring for prisoners made its mark. The cynical laughter died down, and Colson's conversion began to command respect. Something had happened in his life.

Peter has already urged Christians to make their new manner of life a witness (2:11–12; 3:1). Some may be brought to glorify God in repentance as they see the changed lives of Christians. But this will not always be the happy outcome. Rather, Christians who will no longer join the pagan parties can expect to have *abuse* heaped on them. (The one Greek word for *they heap abuse on you* is literally 'blaspheming'. It may link with the idolatry of the pagans, and describe blasphemy, not against Christians, but against their God.[1]) In the Wisdom of Solomon, an apocryphal book from before the time of Christ, the author cites the words of the wicked against the good life of a righteous person:

> He professes to have knowledge of God,
> and calls himself a child of the Lord.
> He became to us a reproof of our thoughts;
> the very sight of him is a burden to us,
> because his manner of life is unlike that of others,
> and his ways are strange.[2]

The passage goes on to describe how the wicked plan to

---

[1] Bénétreau, p. 221.   [2] Wisdom 2:13–15, RSV.

put the righteous man to the test 'with insult and torture' to see how well his profession will hold up. Yet even if Christian testimony meets with this response, the Christian must not despair. Those who persecute him because of his faithfulness must one day give account to the Lord, *who is ready to judge the living and the dead*. Peter has twice reminded us of God's just judgment (1:17; 2:23), and he may be speaking of the Father's judgment again.[1] On the other hand, the New Testament often speaks of the Father's committing his judgment to the Son.[2] Peter has brought Christ's role as Judge into view by describing his exaltation to God's right hand (3:22); the phrase *to judge the living and the dead* is used particularly of Christ to express the inclusiveness of the judgment given to him.[3] The word *ready* also seems to point to Christ. By his finished work and his exaltation he has accomplished everything; he is now ready to judge.

The people of this world may haul Christians before judges, and demand that they give account of themselves. Christians must be ready in every situation to give a reason for their hope (3:15). But their persecutors are themselves accountable to Christ, the Lord. The thought of that contrast, and of the Lord's vindicating judgment, leads Peter to add 4:6.

This verse has been as much debated as 3:19, and for some of the same reasons. Those who see the earlier passage as teaching Christ's preaching *the gospel* to the *dead* find confirmation in this text. Some take it to say that Christ preached the good news to all the dead in his descent to hell; he gave them the opportunity to repent, so that while their death has judged them in *the body*, they may live in *the spirit*.[4] Others have held that the dead to whom the gospel was preached are the saints of the Old Testament, who were brought from their confinement in Hades by Christ.[5]

There are sound reasons, however, for interpreting this text in quite a different way. It does not speak of 'spirits' as

---

[1] See Rom. 2:6; 3:6; 14:10.
[2] Jn. 5:22, 17; Mt. 25:31–33; Acts 10:42; 17:31; 1 Cor. 4:5; 2 Tim. 4:1.
[3] Acts 10:42; 2 Tim. 4:1; see Jn. 5:28. [4] See Spicq, *Epîtres*, p. 138.
[5] For example, Odes of Solomon 42:15. See the summary in Selwyn, Essay I, pp. 314–362, especially 337ff.

does 3:19, but of the *dead*. These cannot be the spiritually dead, as has been proposed,[1] for the dead mentioned in 4:5 are physically dead. Further, the verb for *the gospel was preached* (all one word in Greek) is passive; literally, 'it, or he, was-preached-as-good-news'. Verse 6 is closely tied with what goes before: *For this is the reason* . . . Since Peter has just spoken of the Lord's judgment of the living and the dead, the simplest translation would be: 'For this is why he was-preached-as-good-news to those who are dead also . . .' From Peter's words it is much more natural to think of Christ as the content of the preaching than as the preacher.[2] Other New Testament passages also speak of Christ's being preached (1 Cor. 15:12; 2 Cor. 1:19; 1 Tim. 3:16).

Who, then, are the *dead* to whom Christ was preached? Evidently Peter speaks of them to encourage the Asian Christians. That is why Peter refers to the judgment: persecutors will be held accountable (4:5), and Christians will be vindicated. Peter's reassuring word fits the context perfectly if we understand him to be speaking of the dead who will be vindicated by Christ in the judgment; that is, the Christian dead. Peter connects verses 5 and 6 with *For*. 'The point of *For*, therefore, is not to suggest reasons why Christ should judge the living and the dead, but rather to draw out and underline an aspect of His judgment which will comfort and sustain the Asian Christians, viz. that because he is a righteous judge their converted brothers who have died have not believed in Him in vain.'[3]

We must remember that the death of Christians created a problem for the church in the time of the apostles. Paul had to write to reassure the Thessalonians: those who had died had not missed out on the promise of the return of Christ.[4] Perhaps the opponents of the gospel also used the death of Christians to mock the Christian hope. They said, 'Where is this "coming" he promised? . . . everything goes on as it has since the beginning of creation.'[5] The death of Christians seemed to confirm their scepticism. This would surely be heightened if some of the Christians who had died had been

[1] So Clement of Alexandria and Augustine. See Kelly, p. 173.
[2] This point is clearly made by Kelly, pp. 173f.
[3] Kelly, p. 175. [4] 1 Thes. 4:13–18.
[5] 2 Pet. 3:4.

martyred. They then would have died under human judgment.

Peter gives a strong answer. Christ the Judge was preached to those who are now dead.[1] He was preached, and they believed. That preaching brought about a decisive change. Although they might be judged in the flesh in the eyes of human beings, they live in the spirit in the eyes of God.

We saw that Peter's statement about the reaction of the wicked to the new behaviour of the converted had a close parallel in the Wisdom of Solomon. What he now says also has a parallel in the same Wisdom passage:

> But the souls of the righteous are in the hand of God,
> and no torment will ever touch them.
> In the eyes of the foolish they seemed to have died,
> and their departure was thought to be an affliction,
> and their going from us to be their destruction;
> but they are at peace.
> For though in the sight of men they were punished,
> their hope is full of immortality.[2]

The connection seems more than coincidence. If Peter does not have the Wisdom passage directly in mind, he certainly is following the same familiar line of thought: the wicked scorn the behaviour of the righteous, but the righteous dead are justified in spite of the accusations of the wicked. For Peter, to be sure, this thought is transformed through Jesus Christ: the righteous are those who have been redeemed by his blood; their hope is sure in his resurrection.

Indeed, it is the confidence of Peter and of the Christian church in the greatness of Christ's salvation that makes these words of his necessary. Since death is God's judgment on sin, and since Christ has paid the price of sin, it might seem that Christians should not die, but live until the second coming. Peter explains that even though they are judged in the body *according to men* ('in the eyes of men'), they live in the spirit *according to God*.

---

[1] The NIV translation 'even to those who are now dead' gives the right interpretation, but by adding the crucial word 'now' not found in the text.

[2] Wisdom of Solomon 3:1–4.

3. Understanding the time of our stewardship (4:7)

The end of all things is near. Therefore be clear minded and self-controlled so that you can pray.

Peter presents the positive side of the contrast in lifestyle. Not drunken debauchery and licence, but sober clearheadedness, marks the Christian (4:7). Love, not lust, fills his heart (4:8); the Christian home is open for hospitality, not orgies (4:9). Ministry replaces exploitation (4:9–11). The dissolute life of the pagan fails to recognize his accountability to the Lord in the day of judgment, a day that is fast approaching. This is exactly what the Christian does recognize. *The end of all things is near.* Peter had seen the Lord ascend from the Mount of Olives until he vanished in a cloud. He had heard angels repeat the promise of the Lord that he would come again. The whole New Testament emphasizes the expectation of the Lord's return; Peter's hope in the Lord look to that event, and to the salvation ready to be revealed with Christ (1:5, 8–12; 4:13, 17; 5:4, 10).[1]

'The end is near': our contemporaries expect to see that warning crudely lettered on a sandwich-board carried by a figure with long hair and dirty sandals. The figure appears often enough in cartoons and advertising, but rarely on city streets. Yet the smug assumption that only a 'crazy' would prophesy the end has begun to ring hollow in our atomic age. How different is the Christian expectation of the end from the foreboding that sees atomic annihilation! The Christian looks for the Lord who will bring judgment, justice, and the wonder of a new creation.

That realization brings sobriety to the Christian's use of time. (*Self-controlled* is literally 'sober'.) Three times in this short letter Peter exhorts the Asian Christians to be sober (1:13; 4:7; 5:8). Obviously this includes literal sobriety in contrast to drunkenness, but it also indicates the attitude of mind that is the opposite of drunken stupor or delusion. Sobriety means watchful waiting for the Lord's return, realistic living. (See the comments on 1:13.) *Clear minded*

---

[1] Kelly notes, for example, Rom. 13:12; 1 Cor. 7:29; Heb. 10:25; 1 Jn. 2:18.

describes the practical wisdom that comes from the knowledge of the Lord. In Greek use the term was contrasted with
mania; the demonized man healed by Jesus was found seated,
clothed, and 'in his right mind'.[1] Preoccupation with the
second coming, particularly by those who have set a date for
it, has often led to hysteria rather than sober wisdom. 'Faced
by the imminent end of all things the community must not
give way to eschatological frenzy. In such excess it would fall
victim precisely to this world.'[2] Jesus described the faithful
servant as 'dressed ready for service' and busy as he waited
for the returning Lord.[3]

Sobriety and a clear mind have one value above others.
They equip us for prayer. Peter does not think of prayer as
an effort to induce ecstasy, but as sober, direct, profoundly
thoughful communication with the Lord. His whole letter
points us to the depth and glory of our fellowship with
Christ. We have not seen him, but we love him; we set him
apart as holy in our hearts. Peter's love for Christ is intensely
personal; he is overwhelmed by the glory of the Lord. He
does not, therefore, advocate prayer as a cold, rational exercise. But we might say that he advocates it as a *fervent*,
rational exercise. Fervent love, agonizing intercession, these
are marks of true prayer. Peter knew of Christ's agony in
the garden of Gethsemane. Prayer tastes the agony of struggle
or the delight of communion with God. Yet prayer seeks
the Lord, not a transformation of consciousness.[4] Prayer
demands alertness. Peter failed in Gethsemane. He slept
when Jesus had charged him to watch and pray.[5] Peter goes
on to speak of the fervent love for others that we should
show, and of the service of love. Thoughtful and earnest
prayer will seek God's blessing on those whom we love and
serve.

4. Serving in the grace of our stewardship (4:8–11a)

Above all, love each other deeply, because love covers over a

[1] Mk. 5:15; Lk. 8:35.
[2] Ulrich Luck, '*sōphrōn*', *TDNT* VII, p. 1102.
[3] Lk. 12:35–43.
[4] See E. P. Clowney, *Christian Meditation* (IVP USA, 1980).
[5] Mk. 14:37.

multitude of sins. 9*Offer hospitality to one another without grumbling.* 10*Each one should use whatever gift he has received to serve others, faithfully adminstering God's grace in its various forms.* 11*If anyone speaks, he should do it as one speaking the very words of God. If anyone serves, he should do it with the strength God provides* . . .

New life in Christ is lived in a community of loving service. Peter brings this section of his letter to a climax by appealing again to the fervency of love that binds together the new people of God (see 1:22). Jesus taught that love for God and for our neigbour fulfils the law, and Peter, with Paul, puts love first in our walk of obedience and fellowship.[1] *Love each other deeply* . . . The word translated *deeply* can also mean 'constant'. 'Keep love constant' would be a good translation.[2] The word describes something that is stretched or extended. The love of the saints keeps stretching, in both depth and endurance, 'to grasp how wide and long and high and deep is the love of Christ, and to know this love that surpasses knowledge. . . .'[3]

It is the reach of God's love that stretches our love. We love because he first loved us.[4] Our love, kindled by God's love, is stretched by exercise. If love collapses at its first test, it is not worthy of the name. 'Love never fails.'[5] A parent's love for a child grows as it is tested. Someone has said that a toddler steps on your feet and a teenager on your heart. Maturing children, in turn, may grow in love for their parents. As adults they perceive the faults and sins of their fathers and mothers in a new perspective; their love is tested, and grows.

We do not love others if we take delight in finding and exposing their faults and sins. Rather, *love covers over a multitude of sins* (4:8). Peter reflects the language of Proverbs: 'Hatred stirs up dissension, but love covers over all wrongs.'[6] Unless love can stretch to forgive many sins, it will not avail among us sinners. Peter had asked Jesus how many times he must forgive his brother. He proposed a generous seven times. Jesus was not impressed. He replied, 'I tell you,

[1] Mt. 22:37–40; 1 Cor. 13; Gal. 5:22.   [2] BAGD, p. 245.
[3] Eph. 3:17–19.   [4] 1 Jn. 4:19.   [5] 1 Cor. 13:8.
[6] Pr. 10:12.

not seven times, but seventy times seven.'[1] Love does not keep score, but grants forgiveness freely to every brother or sister who seeks it.

Some have taken this text to mean that it is our own sins that are covered by love.[2] They appeal to the Lord's Prayer, 'Forgive us our debts, as we also have forgiven our debtors.' But our forgiving does not gain our forgiveness. Rather, Jesus, after answering Peter's question, went on to tell of the servant who had been forgiven, and who must therefore forgive.[3] The love that covers our sins is the love of God, as Peter teaches in this letter (1:3; 2:24; 3:18). But our love, modelled on Christ's love, can also cover sins in his name. Our love cannot, of course, pay the price of sin. Christ did that. But our love can imitate the mercy of God; our love can forgive, and forgiveness always pays a price.

But lest we begin to commend ourselves on forgiving others (or at least on tolerating them), Peter reminds us that love must go further. Jesus took a towel and basin to wash his disciples' feet. Love for our brethren moves us to *serve* them. It is the love of God that brings us to our brother's feet; it is the *grace* of God that fills our basin for service. We are ministers of the rich and variegated grace of God. Early in his letter Peter spoke of the varied trials Christians must face (1:6). Here he presents variety of another kind: the varied grace of God. The term translated *in its various forms* is sometimes used of varied colours, the colours of precious stones.[4] The rainbow colours of spring flowers can only suggest the richness of the gifts of God's grace.

Deep in the Luray Caverns of Virginia stands the console of a unique organ. Ages of seeping water have created thousands of stalactites, icicles in stone, hanging from the vaults of the caves. Each stalactite resonates, when struck, with a slightly different tone. The organ builder explored the cavern till he found the right stalactite for each note in the full range of an organ console. Some had to be 'tuned' by chipping away a bit of their length. He then wired an array of motor-

[1] Mt. 18:21–22, mg.

[2] So (with qualification) by Kelly, p. 178, and Spicq, *Epîtres*, p. 150. Tertullian and Origen think of the sins covered as our own, but the love that covers them as love for God (Selwyn, p. 217). Selwyn tries to hold together both meanings. See Bénétreau, p. 243.

[3] Mt. 18:21–35.   [4] BAGD, p. 690.

ized mallets so that each stalactite could be struck from the keyboard of the organ. Visitors who have heard the music long remember the deep, throbbing echoes of the singing rocks. If such melodic variety may be found in calcium deposits, what varied tones has God's Spirit given to the heirs of Christ's glory?

We must respect the rich variety of gifts that God has granted to our Christian brothers and sisters. To be sure, some may be spoken of as 'spiritual' in the sense that they have been more evidently granted beyond the 'natural' range of a Christian's abilities. Such gifts have a certain priority in equipping the saints for ministry. Yet we must not forget that God's Spirit is the creator Spirit, and that the Spirit renews us in the image of Christ.[1] Every gift that is ours by creation has been touched by the Spirit in our re-creation.

Peter does not list the gifts of the Spirit; he mentions only two broad categories of ministry: speaking and serving. On the side of service, hospitality is to be given high priority. Such service employs both 'natural' and 'spiritual' gifts. Peter speaks of gifts of the Spirit to focus not on ourselves, but on God and on others. He would have us look to the Lord for the gifts we need to serve him and others in his name. Peter's focus is often lost today. Christians eagerly discuss spiritual gifts, but in a way that would surely distress the apostle. Their concern is not how they can serve others and bring glory to the Lord. Rather they seek self-fulfilment. They want to discover their gifts so as to establish their own identity. In a Christian context, they want to 'do their own thing'. That gifts are granted for service is lost from sight.

Peter does not offer a sample list of spiritual graces, as Paul sometimes does.[2] (It would be a mistake to suppose that Paul's lists are intended to be exhaustive.) Peter evidently does not fear that a Christian will miss his calling if he cannot find his gift classified in Scripture. Indeed, the rich variety of God's gifts of grace makes close classification impossible. When Peter distinguishes speech and ministry, he obviously indicates two areas of special importance, but areas that could include a great variety of gifts. Individual gifts may be classi-

[1] Col. 3:10; Eph. 4:24.　[2] 1 Cor. 12:7-11, 28-29; Rom. 12:6-8.

fied, but they remain individual. Jesus promised to those that overcome, a white stone engraved with a name known only to the overcomer and the Lord.[1] The name the Lord has for us is entirely personal, and it describes the calling we have received from him. Jesus named Peter the 'rock', and granted him spiritual gifts to become a rock in the apostolic company. So, too, his call names every believer, and grants the spiritual gifts that equip each individual to serve God and other people.

The gift, or pattern of gifts, that each believer receives determines his or her function in serving the Lord. When Paul speaks 'by the grace given me' he is speaking as an apostle.[2] To speak of his gift is to speak of his office and calling. Some gifts imply a measure of authority in the community of Christ. They require public recognition for their proper exercise.[3]

Peter affirms that as *each one* has received a *gift* he is to *serve* with it (4:10). Gifts are discovered in service. We may rightly ask about the gift we have received, but we will not gain the answer by introspection. Indeed, the gift that we have received may not be all that the Lord has for us. We may seek greater gifts, as Paul reminds us.[4] We must ask, however, 'Why do I want a greater gift?' If the answer is that, like the sons of Zebedee, we are looking for places of honour in Christ's kingdom, we cannot expect our prayer to be answered.[5] Jesus came to serve, and calls us to serve in his name. It is in humble service that we discover the gifts that we have and the greater gifts that we may need.

If the testing of gifts in service is ignored, disappointment and calamity may follow. Some candidates for the gospel ministry in Britain and America move through an academic programme of preparation, and present themselves for a pastoral call with little or no record of service other than academic achievement. In contrast, most Third World pastors seek further preparation after their gifts for ministry have been shown in years of service. William Carey went to India

[1] Rev. 2:17.
[2] Rom. 12:3; 15:15–16; 1 Cor. 3:10; 15:10; Gal. 2:7–9.
[3] Paul had to plead, at times, for his calling and gift: Gal. 2:7–9; 1 Cor. 14:37–38.
[4] 1 Cor. 12:31.   [5] Mt. 20:20–28.

182

under the compulsion of his missionary vision, but he had demonstrated his gifts as a linguist by mastering Latin, Greek, Hebrew, Dutch, and French, and had shown his pastoral gifts in caring for a little church. His gifts as a missionary statesman and educator became evident as he carried forward his own challenge: 'Expect great things from God and attempt great things for God.'[1]

Peter calls us 'stewards' or administrators' of the grace the Lord gives us. The term describes a servant who has the administrative responsibility for household affairs. Joseph, sold into Egyptian slavery by his brothers, became the household manager for Potiphar. He refused the advances of Potiphar's wife so as to remain faithful to his stewardship.[2] The steward's office has two doors. On the one hand, he is accountable to his master. He administers the goods and affairs of another. All that he has, he has received. On the other hand, he is an administrator, put in charge of his master's affairs and exercising authority in his master's name. Peter returns to this key of stewardship when he addresses the elders of the church (5:2–3).

Peter may already have the elders and deacons of the church particularly in view. His reference to *speaking the very words of God* surely has special reference to the 'shepherds of God's flock' (5:2). But that makes it the more important that he has expressed himself in general terms. It is not only the elders who have the responsibility of stewards in the house of God. Rather, the vast variety of gifts that God has poured out on the church are all to be administered in his name.

Hospitality, in particular, is a gift to be cultivated in every Christian home. No doubt hospitality had a special importance for the church at the time of Peter's writing. The inns of the time were few in number and unsavoury in reputation. Travelling evangelists and teachers were dependent upon the hospitality of the churches. Without the grace of hospitality the expansion of the church would be severely limited. Then, as now, hospitality had its problems. We are struck by the realism of the *Didache*, a Christian document perhaps as early as the first century. Speaking of travelling 'apostles'

[1] *ODCC* p. 239.   [2] Gn. 39:8–9.

(missionaries) and prophets, the *Didache* gives these instructions:

> But concerning the apostles and prophets, so do ye according to the ordinance of the Gospel. Let every apostle, when he cometh to you, be received as the Lord; but he shall not abide more than a single day, or if there be need, a second likewise; but if he abide three days, he is a false prophet. And when he departeth let the apostle receive nothing save bread, until he findeth shelter; but if he ask money, he is a false prophet.[1]

Caution and wisdom are needed in the exercise of hospitality, though hardly in the legalistic way indicated in the *Didache*. John commends Gaius for his hospitality to brothers who were strangers to him, but who travelled for the sake of Christ's name.[2]

The emphasis of the New Testament on the grace of hospitality goes back to the promise of Jesus. He will say to those on his right hand, 'I was a stranger and you invited me in.' What we do for one of the brothers of Jesus, we do for him.[3] While Christians are charged to do good to all as they have opportunity, the provision of hospitality is particularly directed towards fellow-Christians.[4] Peter calls for hospitality *to one another.*

Do we need the grace of hospitality as hotels, motels and credit cards multiply? The question is absurd in the eyes of any Christian who has offered or received hospitality in the name of Christ. The early church often met in the homes of its members; the fellowship of Christians in the setting of the home has a quality that can be duplicated nowhere else. Equally important is the function of our homes in aiding the homeless and those in crisis or trouble. In New Testament times evangelism, too, went from 'house to house', not by organized canvassing, but by the hospitality of Christian homes.

The whole community can participate in showing hospitality. Peter thinks also of the special gifts of individuals. Like Paul he emphasizes the ministry of the word of God in

---

[1] 'The Teaching of the Lord to the Gentiles by the Twelve Apostles' sec. 11 (*AF*, p. 127).   [2] 3 Jn. 6–8.
[3] Mt. 25:35, 40. See Lk. 14:12–14; Rom. 12:13; Heb. 13:2.
[4] Gal. 6:10.

the church.[1] *If anyone speaks, he should do it as one speaking the very words of God* (4:11). Peter is not describing casual conversation. He has in view the preaching and teaching of the word of God. So Peter spoke the words of God to the household of Cornelius.[2] Paul said of his own teaching, 'Unlike so many, we do not peddle the word of God for profit. On the contrary, in Christ we speak before God with sincerity, like men sent from God.'[3]

Peter stresses the grace that is needed to speak the word of God. Inspired apostles and prophets provided the foundation on which the house of God was built.[4] Others join in the ministry of the word, building on their foundation. Those who now speak the word must depend upon the gift of the Spirit to proclaim the 'oracles' of God (4:11, RSV), the very word of God in the gospel. Preaching God's word is not a mechanical task; human eloquence is ineffective apart from the blessing of the Spirit. By the Spirit, ministers of the word speak 'as though God were making his appeal through us. We implore you on Christ's behalf: Be reconciled to God.'[5]

It is true that every Christian must handle the word of God with reverence, and seek the help of the Spirit to make it known to others. Yet there are also those with special gifts of the Spirit for the preaching and teaching of the word of God. They have a special charge to tend and feed the flock of God (5:2). There is some danger that, in reacting against clericalism, the church may forget the importance of the ministry of the word of God by those called to be undershepherds of the flock.

If anyone serves, he should do it with the strength God provides. The serving ministry that Peter has in mind may be especially that of deacons in the church, here set beside the teaching ministry. In any case, Peter uses the same term for service here that he used in 4:10. We 'minister' or 'administer' God's grace in our service of others. The same Greek root appears in our word 'deacon'. It could describe those who waited on tables or performed other menial tasks. Jesus applied it to himself, as one who came not to be served, but

[1] Rom. 12:6–8; 1 Cor. 12:8, 28; Eph. 4:11.   [2] Acts 10:44.
[3] 2 Cor. 2:17.   [4] Eph. 3:5; 2:20.   [5] 2 Cor. 5:20.

to serve.[1] It is used in the New Testament for Christian service in general, as well as for diaconal service in the official sense.[2]

Peter's exhortation is no less needed for service than for teaching. Christians may be more tempted to undertake diaconal service in their own strength. They may agree that the ministry of the word needs special grace, but waiting on tables, collecting money, or caring for the sick is just a matter of rolling up one's sleeves and getting the job done. Not so. If God is to be glorified by ministry in his name, it must be ministry performed in his *strength*. Paul speaks of the cheerfulness that God gives for showing mercy.[3] This is very different from grumbling hospitality or condescending benevolence. Anyone who has served in a ministry of mercy will know the need for patience and strength to carry on. Peter would have us look to the Lord from the very beginning of every such ministry. Only when it is performed, not just in the name of Christ, but in the Spirit of Christ, does it bring praise to God.

5. The purpose of our stewardship (4:11b)

. . . so that in all things God may be praised through Jesus Christ. To him be the glory and the power for ever and ever. Amen.

Why does Peter so emphasize our calling to minister as stewards, servants who recognize our dependence on God's gifts? Because only so will we give God all the glory. Anyone who has begun a ministry in Christ's name finds it perilously easy to shift the ownership of the enterprise. It becomes his ministry, her organization. Success demonstrates one's own organizational skill and entrepreneurial genius. The leader gives lip-service to God's enabling grace, but trusts management techniques. He looks to professional consultants more than to the Lord. The 'success' of such a ministry may be a graver judgment from God than its failure.

---

[1] Mt. 20:28.
[2] See C. E. B. Cranfield, '*Diakonia* in the New Testament', in J. I. McCord and T. H. L. Parker, eds., *Service in Christ* (Eerdmans, 1966), pp. 37–48.
[3] Rom. 12:8.

186

Peter insists that we must minister in the strength that God provides, *so that in all things God may be praised through Jesus Christ.* God is to be praised not only for the new birth from which our service begins, but for the continuing grace that enables us, in serving others, to serve him. Peter was keenly conscious of the gifts he had received from Christ with the coming of the Holy Spirit. He had been granted the miraculous signs of an apostle and could bid a lame man to walk in the name of Jesus.[1] He had also been given grace to speak the word with boldness, proclaiming the exalted Christ as Prince and Saviour.[2] Jesus' disciples had once argued about who would be first in Christ's kingdom.[3] But such thoughts are now remote from Peter's experience. Not his own leadership skills, but the gifts of Christ's Spirit, were the secret of his apostleship. Peter is jealous for God's glory. In everything (or, perhaps, 'in everyone') God is to be glorified.

All is to be done to God's *glory* because his are the glory and power for ever. Peter's exhortation becomes an affirmation: God is to be praised in everything.[4] Does Peter ascribe the glory and power to God or to Christ? Since he says that God is glorified *through* Christ, either interpretation is natural. (Either, God has the glory and power, and receives it through Christ; or, Christ has the glory and power, and God receives it through him.[5]) Again we see Peter's conviction as to the deity of Christ.

It has been thought that this doxology marks the end, or the intended end, of the letter, and that the rest is an addition, occasioned perhaps by fresh news of persecution – 'painful trial' (4:12). But it is natural for the inspired authors of the New Testament to pause to declare God's glory when they are brought to consider the wonder of God's grace.[6]

The *Amen* reflects the response of the people of God to the glory and power that are his. By affirming 'So be it',

[1] Acts 3:6; 4:30; 2 Cor. 12:12; Heb. 2:4.
[2] Acts 5:31–32.   [3] Mk. 9:33f.
[4] The verb translated *be* (subjunctive in the English) is indicative, not optative, though Peter does use the optative form.
[5] Bénétreau, with appeal to 2 Tim. 4:18; 2 Pet. 3:18; Rev. 1:6, takes the 'to whom' with 'Jesus Christ' immediately preceding. Kelly takes the reference to be 'God'.
[6] Rom. 1:25; 11:36; 2 Cor. 11:31; Gal. 1:5; Eph. 3:21; Phil. 4:20; 1 Tim. 6:16; Jude 25; Rev. 1:6; 5:13; 1 Pet. 5:11. Kelly gives convincing reasons against viewing this as the intended end of the letter (pp. 182–184).

they declare, in effect, 'Hallowed be your name'. The 'Amen' of the new-covenant people of God echoes that of the old.[1]

[1] Ne. 5:13; 8:6; Pss. 41:13; 72:19; 89:52; 106:48; 150:6.

9. The blessing of suffering for Christ's sake

1. The joy of fellowship with Christ in suffering (4:12–16)

Dear friends, do not be surprised at the painful trial you are suffering, as though something strange were happening to you. [13]But rejoice that you participate in the sufferings of Christ, so that you may be overjoyed when his glory is revealed. [14]If you are insulted because of the name of Christ, you are blessed, for the Spirit of glory and of God rests on you. [15]If you suffer, it should not be as a murderer or thief or any other kind of criminal, or even as a meddler. [16]However, if you suffer as a Christian, do not be ashamed, but praise God that you bear that name.

Should Christians be surprised when painful trials come? Peter speaks tenderly, for he can understand the question. Has he not assured them of the victory of Christ over all the powers of darkness and death? Has he not called them the holy people of God, living stones in God's own temple, heirs of heaven? Yet the more firmly Peter grounds their hope, and the more eloquently he states their privilege, the more strange it must seem that they should have to suffer. Given the resurrection victory of Christ, why should those who bear his name be abused, mocked and arrested as criminals?

Peter reminds confused Christians that suffering for Christ's sake is not unexpected or unaccountable. Indeed, if we understand why suffering comes, we will not only accept it, but rejoice in it. Peter shows the meaning of our suffering from two sides. First, our suffering for Christ finds its significance in Christ's suffering for us. We share now in

189

suffering for him as we shall one day share in glory with him (4:13; 5:1). Secondly, our suffering does not destroy us, but purifies us. The fire of God's judgment that we endure is not the fire of wrath that will consume the unbelieving. It is the purging fire of his discipline. God will destroy all sin from his new creation; he has begun that work in us. The trials that we experience show us that God is already beginning his great work of renewal.

Consider first what Christ's sufferings mean for our sufferings. Peter is a witness of Christ's sufferings (5:1). He testifies not only to the events of Gethsemane and Calvary, but also to their meaning. Christ, the righteous one, suffered for us, the unrighteous, to bring us to God (3:18). The fact that the righteous suffer is the enigma posed in the book of Job and in many Psalms. Peter answers the question just as the Old Testament does. God is sovereign; we suffer according to the will of God (4:19). But God's will for our suffering must now be understood in the light of God's will for Christ's suffering. Only Christ is truly righteous, yet he suffered for our sins. The key to the mystery of the suffering of the righteous is the mystery of the suffering of Christ. The prophets testified of his suffering and of the glory to follow (1:11). In the wonder of God's design, it was his purpose that Christ should suffer for us, and by his suffering save us. Knowing his suffering for us, we may rejoice when God wills that we should suffer for him. We cannot add to his atoning sufferings, for he bore our sins in his own body on the tree (2:24). Christ suffered for sins 'once' (3:18). Yet when we suffer as Christians there is a sense in which we share in the sufferings of Christ. Made righteous by him, we suffer as the righteous with him.

The phrase *the sufferings of Christ* may refer to the sufferings that Christ endured or to the sufferings that we endure in his name.[1] Since Peter speaks of suffering for *the name of Christ* (4:14), and *as a Christian* (4:16), we might take *the sufferings of Christ* to mean 'Christian sufferings'. Peter also says, however, that he is a witness of the sufferings of Christ and a partaker of the glory to be revealed (5:1). There he has

---

[1] In 2 Cor. 1:5 Paul speaks of abounding suffering and comfort, both in relation to Christ. 'Sufferings of Christ' in that context refers to suffering for Christ. This may also be the sense in Col. 1:24.

in view *Christ's* sufferings and glory.

It seems best, therefore, to understand *the sufferings of Christ* as the sufferings that he endured. We partake of his sufferings, not by contributing to his atonement, but by following in his steps (2:21). As we suffer for Christ, we are linked to him. Our sufferings witness to his. We did not see Jesus on the cross as Peter did, but like Peter we understand the meaning of his atoning death. Because he suffered for us, we can rejoice when we are counted worthy to suffer for him.

The reality of our suffering for Christ becomes a pledge to us of the reality of our belonging to Christ. That in itself brings joy to our hearts. It also strengthens our hope. If, like Christ, we suffer according to God's will, we know that, like Christ, we shall enter the glory of the Father. Joy lies before us, the joy of seeing Christ in his glory in the great day when he will come again (4:14). Suffering, then, is not a threat, but a promise. The pattern of Christ's life is the pattern of our lives, too.

From the earliest centuries the church has treasured accounts of the joy with which martyrs have endured suffering for Christ's sake. The letter from the church of Smyrna in the second century describes the martyrdom of Polycarp, bishop of Smyrna. After the old man had been arrested and brought to the arena, the proconsul urged him to offer incense to Caesar. 'Take the oath,' said the proconsul, 'and I shall release you. Curse Christ.'

Polycarp replied, 'Eighty-six years I have served him, and he never did me any wrong. How can I blaspheme my King who saved me?' Tied to the stake, Polycarp prayed to be received by the Lord 'as a rich and acceptable sacrifice'.[1]

Believers who suffer for Christ are filled with hope. They know that they will *be overjoyed when his glory is revealed* (4:13). The glory of Christ is more than a future hope, however. It is also a present possession. In the Holy Spirit Christ's glory is already revealed, for the Spirit is sent from his throne (4:14). Peter had proclaimed the coming of the Spirit at Pentecost.[2] God's glory was represented in the

[1] Cyril C. Richardson, ed., *Early Christian Fathers* (Westminster, 1953), pp. 152, 154.
[2] Acts 2:3, 33.

191

tongues of fire, but the reality is the person of the Spirit, the Spirit of divine glory.[1] *The Spirit of glory and of God rests on you*, Peter says (4:14). Insults, of course, cannot drive the blessing of the Spirit from Christ's disciples. Indeed, that blessing is specifically joined to being insulted and persecuted. Peter had heard Jesus pronounce blessings upon those who would be persecuted for his name's sake.[2] When he had first experienced the wrath of the high priest, he prayed with the others for boldness. The room itself shook with the power of the Spirit's answer.[3]

Peter, no doubt, remembers that Jesus promised to provide the help of the Spirit in answering accusers.[4] Christians in Galatia or Bithynia are not promised tongues of fire; they are not told that they will have Stephen's vision of Christ at the right hand of God when they are insulted. But they are reminded that they do have Christ's Spirit from his throne. In that glory they can rejoice.

Suffering for Christ leads to glory and tastes of glory; it also gives glory to God. When believers suffer because they are Christians, God is glorified. Satan's accusations against God and Job were proven false; God was vindicated.[5] Christians are given an understanding not granted to Job; all the more are they to glorify God in the midst of suffering for Christ's sake. Paul and Silas sang praises in the prison at Philippi; Peter glorified the name of Jesus before the very rulers who had delivered the Saviour to Pilate; through the centuries Christians have defied their persecutors to praise the Lord. Armando Valladares, for twenty-two years a prisoner of Castro's regime in Cuba, tells of how he came to a living trust in Christ: 'Those cries of the executed patriots – "Long live Christ the King! Down with Communism!" had wakened me to a new life . . . The cries became such a potent and stirring symbol that by 1963 the men condemned to death were gagged before being carried down to be shot. The jailers feared those shouts.'[6]

[1] See M. G. Kline, *Images of the Spirit* (Baker, 1980).
[2] Mt. 5:11; Lk. 6:22. See Mk. 13:13; Acts 9:16.   [3] Acts 4:29.
[4] Mt. 10:19f.
[5] See M. G. Kline, 'Trial by Ordeal', in W. R. Godfrey and Jesse L. Boyd III, eds., *Through Christ's Word* (Presbyterian & Reformed, 1985), pp. 81–93.
[6] *Against All Hope: the Prison Memoirs of Armando Valladares*, translated by Andrew Hurley (Hamish Hamilton, 1986), p. 17.

The suffering that brings glory to God is not, of course, suffering that is the consequence of crimes that we commit (4:15). If we do evil and suffer for it, we do not bring glory to God (2:20). Peter mentions murder and theft, not because he expects Christians to be guilty of such crimes, but because they are crimes that carry a death penalty, the penalty that Christians may have to face for the sake of Christ. Perhaps the offence of 'meddling' is added as one that Christians might be more likely to commit. Kelly suggests that Christians may have 'meddled' through excessive zeal in attacking pagan habits.[1]

As he describes suffering for Christ, Peter makes references to the *name* (4:14, 16). It is possible that the term is used in the sense of 'account' rather than 'name': 'if you suffer on account of Christ (4:14); 'let him glorify God on this account' (4:16).[2] The name of Christ is so strongly emphasized in the New Testament, however, that we may well read 'for the name of Christ' and 'in this name'.[3] (*That you bear that name* in the NIV translation takes the 'name' to refer to 'Christian' and paraphrases to explain this.)

2. The confidence of commitment to God in suffering (4:17–19)

The Christian who loves the Lord rejoices that he may suffer for the sake of the One who suffered for him. He patiently waits for the day when he will see the Lord and share his glory.

Yet suffering itself is a grim experience. Peter knew threats and imprisonment; his own martyrdom was soon to come. He therefore takes account of the judgment of God that has brought the curse of suffering and death into the world. But Peter sees God's judgment in the context of hope. In this passage (4:12–19) he is alluding to the prophecy of Malachi:

'See, I will send my messenger, who will prepare the way before me. Then suddenly the Lord you are seeking will come to his temple; the messenger of the covenant, whom you desire, will

[1] Kelly, p. 189.
[2] Kelly presents a strong case for this meaning (pp. 190–191).
[3] So the ASV; the RSV has 'under that name'.

come,' says the Lord Almighty.

But who can endure the day of his coming? Who can stand when he appears? For he will be like a refiner's fire or a launderer's soap. He will sit as a refiner and purifier of silver; he will purify the Levites and refine them like gold and silver.[1]

God's appearing will bring a refining process to purify his people and make their offerings acceptable to him. In contrast, Malachi prophesies that the coming of God will burn as a furnace against the wicked. The fire that purifies the house of God will consume them.[2] Other Old Testament passages also compare God's judgments to the fire that refines silver and gold.[3] Peter seems to have the prophecy of Malachi particularly in view, however, for it combines the thought of God's coming to his temple with the double purpose of his judgment: to purify his worshippers and to consume the wicked.[4]

Peter has already spoken of the refining of our faith through fiery trial (1:17). He has told the Christians he addresses that they are God's house, his spiritual temple (2:4–5). Now he takes from Malachi the image of the purifying of the house of God through fire. *Judgment* must *begin with the* house *of God* (4:17).[5] The fiery trials that Christians experience are the refining fire of the Lord who has come to his temple. But if the very house of God, the people of his own possession, is purged by fire, what will the end be of those who do not obey the gospel of God? Paul answers that question as Malachi does: the end will be destruction from the face of the Lord 'at the revelation of the Lord Jesus from heaven with the angels of his power in flaming fire, rendering vengeance to them that know not God'.[6]

The fire of judgment that will come when Christ comes already burns in the sufferings that Christians endure. Yet

---

[1] Mal. 3:1–3.　　[2] Mal. 4:1.　　[3] Ps. 66:10; Zc. 13:9; *cf.* Pr. 27:21.

[4] See D. E. Johnson, 'Fire in God's House: Imagery from Malachi 3 in Peter's Theology of Suffering (1 Peter 4:12–19)', an unpublished paper. See also Stibbs, p. 163.

[5] As Johnson, *op. cit.*, points out, the NIV translation obscures the allusion to Malachi by translating *family* instead of 'house' (= temple) in 4:17 (the Greek word is the same as that translated 'house' in 2:5) and by changing 'fiery trial' to *painful trial* in 4:12.

[6] 2 Thes. 1:7–8.

how different is the purpose of the fire in God's house from the fire of the last judgment! God's fire in his temple purifies the faith of his spiritual priesthood. By that faith, more precious than refined gold, God will keep them for the glory to come. The flames of persecution, therefore, are a token to Christians of the faithfulness of God who will deliver them from the wrath to come. God has come to his new temple; the Spirit of glory has his resting-place in the new sanctuary of living stones (4:14). Christians should not be surprised by the fiery trials, but should rejoice in the evidence that the Holy One has taken up his dwelling with his people. Fiery trials are not easily endured, but testing does not destroy us, it saves us. Alluding to Proverbs 11:1 in the Septuagint, Peter reminds us of that saving purpose. If even God's saints must endure these judgments, think of the wrath that awaits the unbelievers who now mock and persecute the people of God!

If it is hard for the righteous to be saved . . . Peter is not calling in question the security of that salvation kept for us and 'ready to be revealed in the last time' (1:15). The word for *hard* means 'with difficulty'; 'it does not imply uncertainty of the outcome, but the difficulty of the road that leads to it'.[1] God's purging of his people is not a process that takes place in purgatory after death, nor is it punishment that atones for sin. Rather, his purging is the discipline of suffering and trials by which the faith of his people is purified as gold in the furnace.[2]

Knowing the merciful purpose of their heavenly Father, Christians can commit themselves to him in their suffering. Christ committed himself to the Father, going to the cross; we are called to follow in his steps.[3] He suffered according to the Father's will. Although the Father wills our suffering for a different purpose, it is still for his glory; he is worthy of that total trust that Jesus showed. The word for *commit* (4:19) is used for making a deposit. The Hellenistic world lacked our modern banking system. Someone undertaking a journey might deposit his funds with a neighbour while he was gone. Naturally, he would be concerned about his neighbour's integrity! God's grace appears in his entrusting the

[1] Bénétreau, p. 257.   [2] Stibbs, p. 164.   [3] Lk. 23:46; 1 Pet. 2:21-23

gospel to us; how much more readily may we commit our souls to the *faithful* keeping of our *Creator* (4:19)! 'I know whom I have believed, and am convinced that he is able to guard what I have entrusted to him for that day.'[1]

Only here in the New Testament is God called the *Creator*. Peter reminds us that the Lord whom we trust is the Architect of all things, accomplishing his great design. He feeds the birds and numbers the hairs of our heads; he will watch over us who commit ourselves to his care.[2]

God is our refuge, as the psalmist says. We commit ourselves to him who is our rock and our fortress.[3] But commitment is not simply flight to God from the sufferings that we endure. Commitment is active; we commit ourselves in well-doing. Peter again urges us to *do good* (*cf.* 2:12, 15, 20; 3:13, 16–17). Opposition and suffering open new doors of opportunity to show the love of Christ.

[1] 2 Tim. 1:12.   [2] Mt. 6:26, 31.   [3] Ps. 31:3–5.

5:1–11

10. Living in the suffering church of God

1. The humble rule of Christ's elders (5:1–4)

a. Their fellowship with Christ's sufferings and glory (5:1)

To the elders among you, I appeal as a fellow-elder, a witness of Christ's sufferings and one who will also share in the glory to be revealed...

Peter now moves to the conclusion of his letter, calling his hearers to stand fast in the faith he has again declared to them, and to do so in the midst of the sufferings they must expect. His final charge calls for two attitudes that he has been describing throughout his letter: on the one hand, humility toward others; on the other, bold resistance to evil. These attitudes are fundamental for Christian living in this present world. They are by no means contradictory, as Jesus showed by his example.

Peter begins by calling for humility on the part of those who lead and those who are led. In the fires of trial, the shepherd's leadership gains importance. Peter is Christ's apostle, called to be a shepherd of the flock of the Lord. But his ministry will soon be over. He addresses those, therefore, who must continue to feed and guard the flock. They are not fellow-apostles, chosen, like Peter, to be eye-witnesses of Christ's resurrection.[1] They are, nevertheless, fellow-elders, called by the Lord to exercise oversight in his church. They have received the witness of the apostles, and with them they confess Jesus Christ.

[1] On the office of the apostle see the comments on 1:1.

197

The witness of Peter and the other apostles proclaimed the meaning of Christ's sufferings and glory. Further, the apostles confirmed their preaching in their lives. Peter says that he is *a witness of Christ's sufferings and one who also will share in the glory to be revealed*. Peter witnessed to the *sufferings* of Christ that he had seen in Gethsemane and on Calvary; he witnessed to the *glory* of Christ that he had seen on the mount of transfiguration and after the resurrection. As he witnessed, he tasted of both. He shared in suffering for Christ; he knew the glory of the Spirit of Christ. For Peter, there was much more to come. As he knew from the words of Jesus, final suffering still awaited him; so did final glory.[1] Peter would prepare his fellow-elders to bear their witness by mirroring the gospel in their lives. They, too, share in suffering as they proclaim the suffering Saviour; they, too, taste of glory as they proclaim his return.

Peter's words remind us of Paul's charge to the elders of Ephesus.[2] Paul reminds the elders that he had borne witness to the gospel to Jews and Greeks, enduring trials and plots against his life. He pleads with the elders to remember his example, and to shepherd the flock, the church of the Lord, purchased with his blood. For Paul as for Peter, sharing in ministry means sharing in suffering: suffering now, and glory to come.

As an apostle and eye-witness, Peter was set apart from the elders he addressed, but in the witness of his life he stood beside them.[3] If all Christians partake of Christ's suffering and glory, how much more must the shepherds of his flock do so! With great tact, Peter speaks, not of their participating with him, but of his participating with them. His phrasing shows the humility to which he would summon his fellow-elders.

---

[1] Jn. 21:18–19. [2] Acts 20:18–35.

[3] Bénétreau rightly holds that the distinctiveness of Peter's apostolic witness cannot be eliminated from the passage. He objects to carrying over the *sym-* prefix from 'elder' ('fellow-elder') to 'witness' ('fellow-witness'). Peter's awareness of the special sense in which he is a witness restrains him from calling the elders 'fellow-witnesses' (Bénétreau, pp. 267f., in opposition to Kelly, p. 199). Goppelt calls attention to Paul's use of 'fellow-worker' (Rom. 16:3, 9, 21; Phil. 2:25; 4:3; Phm. 1, 24; Col. 4:11; 2 Cor. 8:23) and 'fellow-servant' (Col. 1:7; 4:12) (p. 322 n. 7).

Peter is concerned for order and government in the church as well as for submission and devotion. He addresses the elders, those who served as leaders, administrators, and judges in the apostolic church. The pattern of eldership in the New Testament church followed that established by the Lord for Israel.[1] Paul ordained elders in the churches he established, and distinguished teaching and ruling gifts.[2] The ministry of teaching elders is emphasized in the New Testament. In this exhortation Peter speaks primarily of the governing function of the elders. He uses, however, the figure of shepherding, a term that includes the feeding of the flock as well as their oversight.

b. Their charge as shepherds of the flock (5:2–4)

Be shepherds of God's flock that is under your care, serving as overseers – not because you must, but because you are willing, as God wants you to be; not greedy for money, but eager to serve; ³not lording it over those entrusted to you, but being examples to the flock. ⁴And when the Chief Shepherd appears, you will receive the crown of glory that will never fade away.

i. The calling of the shepherd

When Peter calls the elders to *be shepherds of* the *flock*, he certainly alludes to his own calling. At an unforgettable breakfast by the Lake of Galilee, the risen Lord Jesus had restored Peter to his apostolic office and charged him to be a shepherd to Christ's little ones.[3] Jesus charged Peter to feed his sheep and to tend them, the two major tasks of the shepherd. In that charge, Jesus was calling Peter to have a part in his own care for his disciples. Jesus is the good Shepherd who gives his life for the sheep. [4]

The Old Testament used the shepherd figure for those charged with the care of the people of God, but especially for God himself and the Messiah. Moses was called from Jethro's flocks to shepherd Israel.[5] Later, King David was

[1] See Appendix C, 'The Office of Elder in the New Testament'.
[2] Acts 14:23; 1 Cor. 12:28; Rom. 12:8; 1 Tim. 5:17.   [3] Jn. 21:15–19.
[4] Jn. 10:14–18.   [5] Is. 63:11.

199

God's royal shepherd.[1] Yet Moses and David were only undershepherds, serving the divine Shepherd.[2] God condemns the false shepherds of his people who behave as wolves, scattering and devouring the sheep. The Lord himself will come to gather and feed his flock; his coming is joined with the coming of the Messiah as the Shepherd.[3]

Jesus, the Messiah and the Lord, comes to be 'the Shepherd and Overseer of your souls' (2:25). He looked with compassion on the scattered sheep of Israel and gathered the remnant flock, calling his own sheep by name. He promised also to gather other sheep; the scattered flock of the Gentiles.[4] They, too, were 'like sheep going astray' but have now been brought back by the Shepherd. For his gathered flock, God promised to raise up faithful shepherds. The elders Peter addresses are themselves the fulfilment of God's promise.[5]

The care of pastors for their flock will be proportional to their care for the Lord. By the Lake of Galilee Jesus had examined Peter about his love for him.[6] Only as he confessed his love for Christ was Peter charged to shepherd the flock of Christ. Love for Christ will kindle compassion for Christ's scattered sheep, the little ones for whom he died.[7] Lucas Cranach's altarpiece painting in Wittenberg shows on the right side Luther preaching, and on the left side the people listening. In the middle Cranach has represented Christ on the cross. The painting was evidently intended to show that worship centres on the preaching of Christ crucified. The people see not the preacher, but Christ. No doubt we should read that picture from the other side as well. The preacher must present Christ; more than that, to know his people, he must know Christ. He must serve the flock in the light of the cross. Their value to the Lord is the price of his blood (1:19).

Love for the Lord will motivate elders to imitate the care of the Good Shepherd. God directed his people as a flock, leading them through the wilderness. So, too, Jesus leads

---

[1] 2 Sa. 5:2; 7:7; Ezk. 34:23; *ANET*, 281 (I, p. 192); *TDNT* VI, p. 486.

[2] Ps. 23:1; 80:1; Gn. 49:24.

[3] Ezk. 34:1–24. See Je. 23:3; 31:10; 50:17–19; Is. 40:11; Mi. 4:6; 7:14. See also Psalms of Solomon 17:45.

[4] Mt. 9:36; Lk. 12:32; Jn. 10:16; see Is. 56:8; 49:8–10.   [5] Je. 3:15; 23:4.

[6] Jn. 21:15–17.   [7] Acts 20:28.

his sheep, going before them.[1] The elder-shepherd is not a cowboy, driving his flock like cattle. He leads them as a shepherd would, walking on ahead.

Central to the work of the shepherd (and of Christ the Shepherd) is the feeding of the flock. False shepherds are condemned for taking from the flock to feed themselves rather than giving of themselves to feed the flock.[2] Again in contrast to the false shepherds, God protects his flock. His rod and staff defend his own; he carries the lambs in his bosom; the sheep with their young are safe with him.[3] Jesus declares that he guards his sheep: none can snatch them from his hand, or from the hand of his Father.[4] Paul presses this duty on the Ephesian elders: they are to guard against the wolves that circle the flock and may appear in the midst of the sheep.[5] The wolves are false teachers who 'distort the truth in order to draw away disciples after them'.

Jesus the Lord came to gather his scattered sheep. He told his disciples that whoever did not gather with him scattered abroad.[6] Faithful shepherds do more than care for the sheep in the fold; like the Saviour, they are seeking shepherds. They witness to the Gentile world in which they are now 'scattered' for the sake of their mission.

To be sure, the work of the Chief Shepherd is as distinctive as is his person. He is the only Lord of the flock; the shepherd's rod in his hand is a rod of iron, for he is the Judge of the nations; he goes before his flock, first to the cross, then to the throne. By his Spirit he gathers the sheep the Father has given him, for he knows them, and they know his voice. At the last, Christ, the Judge of all, will divide the sheep from the goats as no merely human shepherd could do.[7] Yet the Lord of glory calls human beings to serve him as shepherds. By his grace, they too may taste of sufferings and glory, and so have fellowship with him. When Jesus recommissioned Peter he said, 'Follow me!'[8] Jesus, the Chief Shepherd, calls every undershepherd to walk in his steps (2:21).

---

[1] Jn. 10:4; see Mk. 14:28.   [2] Ezk. 34:3.   [3] Is. 40:11.
[4] Jn. 10:27–29.   [5] Acts 20:29–30.   [6] Mt. 12:30; Lk. 11:23.
[7] Mt. 25:31–33.   [8] Jn. 21:19.

ii. The manner of the shepherd

Since the flock is the Lord's and the elder is a servant of
the Lord, shepherding is ministry. Pastoral oversight is not
dictatorial rule (5:3). The dreadful mass suicide in Guyana
of the followers of Jim Jones showed how a cult leader can
compel idolatry. Television viewers watched with horror:
Jones sat enthroned on a wooden platform while his subjects
drank poison and died at his word. The phenomenon is not
limited to bizarre cults like the People's Temple movement.
It begins whenever anyone ascends a religious throne and
starts to draw to himself the obedience that is due to the
Lord.

The elder has authority; he is called to exercise a shepherd's
oversight. Christ the Chief Shepherd (5:4) has called him to
exercise a shepherd's care. But the undershepherd is not a
stand-in for the Lord. He presents the word of the Lord,
not his own decree; he enforces the revealed will of the Lord,
not his own wishes. For that reason, any undermining of the
authority of Scripture turns church government into spiritual
tyranny. If church governors add to or subtract from the
word of God, they make themselves lords over the
consciences of others.[1]

Far from being a lord and master, the elder is to be an
example. That is, he is to lead others in humble obedience
to God by being himself humbly obedient to God. Our one
Lord and Master made himself an example to his disciples
when he wrapped a towel round his waist and washed their
feet.[2] The shepherding elder lives among those he serves
(*God's flock that is* – literally – 'with you', 5:2). They are his
'lot', those whom the Lord has committed to his care ('the
charge allotted to you', 5:3, ASV).[3] No-one is more involved

[1] The Reformers found this tyranny in the additions to scriptural doctrine made
by the Roman Catholic Church in the name of tradition. The same danger emerges
in a different way when Protestant churches release elders from the vows that bind
their authority to the words of Scripture.

[2] Jn. 13:15. See also Paul's example, 2 Thes. 3:9.

[3] The phrase in 5:3 is literally 'not as lording it over the lots'. The term *klēros*,
'lot', is used in the Septuagint to describe the portions of the land of Israel assigned
by lot to tribes and families. What are these 'portions' allotted to elders? The
'portion' may be an office, a specific function (*cf.* 4:10), or it may be a group of
people; a 'house-church', or portion of a congregation assigned to an elder. If Peter
is thinking of the elders of the whole region collectively, the 'portions' may be

with his work than a shepherd. Sheep cannot be managed by telecommunication. The elder addressed by Peter can be an example because he is seen and known by those for whom he cares. His life must support his words, and may be more eloquent by far.

The phrase *serving the overseers* translates a Greek verb from which the word 'episcopate' is derived.[1] Unfortunately, our concept of a bishop (*episkopos*) seems to have lost the flavour that the term had for Peter. He calls Christ 'the Shepherd and Episkopos of your souls' (2:25). There, as here, Peter thinks of oversight in terms of a shepherd's watchful care over his sheep. 'Guardian' may catch the sense better than 'overseer'.[2] The more technical use of 'bishop' to describe an office set over presbyters and deacons does not appear in the New Testament.[3] Rather, Peter here describes the work of the elders as 'episcopal', and Paul, addressing the Ephesian presbyters, tells them to guard themselves and all the flock 'of which the Holy Spirit has made you bishops'.[4] The deeper issue here, however, is not that of the organization of church office, but of its nature. Authority is given to the elders of the church. 'Obey your leaders and submit to their authority. They keep watch over you as men

---

simply the local churches under their care. See Kelly, pp. 202–203; BAGD, p. 435: Goppelt points out that in the context 'portion' is parallel to 'flock' (5:2).

[1] The verb *episkopountes* (5:2) is present in some important ancient manuscripts, missing in others. It may have been added to explain the shepherding or omitted as redundant. Bruce Metzger suggests the possibility of omission because of ecclesiastical conviction, 'namely, that Peter could never have admonished presbyters (ver. 1) to exercise the function of bishops' (*A Textual Commentary on the Greek New Testament*, United Bible Societies, 1971, p. 696).

[2] The verbs *episkeptomai, episkopeō* are used in the Septuagint for God's 'visiting' of his people. The 'visitation' may be of wrath or of mercy (Zc. 10:3). In 1 Peter 2:12 the phrase 'in the day of visitation' is used, probably in the sense of judgment (see Is. 10:3). When the term is linked with the figure of shepherding, however, it describes watchful care. The 'Guardian' (*mᵉbaqqer*) of the Dead Sea community was given a shepherd's charge: 'He shall love them as a father loves his children, and shall carry them in all their distress like a shepherd his sheep' (CD XIII:9, in *DSS*, p. 115). The 'Guardian' examined candidates for membership and monitored their ranking in the community (CD XIII:11, in *DSS*.)

[3] The first description of a bishop as presiding over a council of presbyters is found in the letters of Ignatius to Magnesia (6, 13) and to Tralles (2). Ignatius died about AD 107. Ignatius, however, likens the council of presbyters to the council of the apostles; he does not put a great distance between the bishop and the elders. Clement of Rome speaks of presbyters and bishops as equivalent terms for the ruling office (1 Clement 42, 44, 54, 57).

[4] Acts 20:28; NIV 'overseers'.

who must give an account.'[1] Yet the exercise of such authority is always a service. As Peter reminds us, it is ministerial, not imperial. The despised shepherd guarding his flock in the fields, not a pompous churchman, is the model of pastoral oversight; indeed, the model is the good Shepherd, who gave his life for the sheep.

An American bumper-sticker urges us to 'Question authority' (a sentiment unlikely to endear the operator of the vehicle to a pursuing traffic officer). Is the bumper-sticker in the Protestant tradition? Recalling the challenge of the Reformation to the abuse of ecclesiastical authority, we might think so. Yet the New Testament, and 1 Peter in particular, put the matter differently. Clearly Peter would have us respect God-given authority and submit to it, in the church as in the state. Christian submission to authority, however, is never servile, and Christian exercise of authority is never authoritarian. Our awareness of the Lord gives dignity to our obedience and humility to our rule. In both we serve him. Elders serve in the freedom of the gospel as they watch over the doctrine and life of Christ's flock.

Peter gives another qualification for the way in which the shepherd is to discharge his calling. In addition to humility, there must be eagerness. Just as it is the love of the Lord that yields humble service, so it is love of the Lord that yields diligence. The elder is not reluctant, but *willing as God wants* him *to be*; literally, 'according to God', that is, with a readiness that springs from his grace and runs to his glory. Evidently the choosing and setting apart of an elder to his office was taken seriously in the apostolic church.[2] A man so called might feel obliged to serve even though he would wish to escape the responsibility. The elders who received Peter's letter carried spiritual burdens that weighed heavier as they saw the darkening horizon of impending persecution. In some American and British churches Peter's exhortation would seem strange. Why should any elder serve unwillingly? The responsibility of church office has been trivialized; it is no more than a minor inconvenience that can readily be declined. But in countries where conversion to Christ is illegal and baptism brings a prison sentence, the office of the

[1] Heb. 13:17. [2] See Acts 14:23; Tit. 1:5.

elder carries a different meaning. Quite apart from
persecution, any real shepherd of Christ's flock will soon
feel the weight of pastoral care.

Peter knew, however, that Christ's yoke was easy and his
burden light. The enthusiasm of the elder of the new covenant
springs from the joy of tasting Christ's grace (2:3). The love
of Christ opens the shepherd's heart to share the joys and
griefs of his people. Paul knew the compulsion of his office;
he had no option but to serve Christ. 'I cannot boast, for I
am compelled to preach. Woe to me if I do not preach the
gospel!'[1] Yet Paul was not therefore a reluctant prisoner of
Christ's call; rather, he sought to show his love by going
beyond what was asked of him. He would not only preach
the gospel; he would do it in Corinth free of charge, zealous
to show his grateful love of the Lord.[2]

Paul's surrender of salary as an offering to Christ illustrates
the next contrast in Peter's words. Peter sets eagerness to
serve over against a mercenary interest in church office: the
elder is genuinely willing, *not greedy for money* (5:2). Peter
uses a single word to describe an action motivated by a desire
for 'shameful gain'. The pay that an elder receives is not
shameful. Jesus taught that a workman is worth his wages.[3]
Shame enters when money becomes the motive. This and
similar warnings in Paul's pastoral letters make it clear that
elders were paid in the apostolic church.[4] With the money
came temptation, and sometimes false accusations. Enemies
could say that God's leaders were interested only in the
money, or even that they misappropriated funds. Paul felt
the sting of such false charges.[5] It is hard to better his answer
to the reproach: he became the first 'tent-making' missionary,
labouring at that craft to support not only himself but others
in his missionary team. Paul's strategy may be needed again
today. Enemies of the gospel rejoice when scandal brings to
light the vast sums garnered by television evangelists in the
United States. Even preachers with a recognizable gospel
message discredit their words with constant demands for
money, money that must pass through their hands to build

[1] 1 Cor. 9:16. [2] 1 Cor. 9:18.
[3] Mt. 10:10; 1 Cor. 9:7–12.
[4] 1 Tim. 3:8; 5:17–18; Tit. 1:7, 11.
[5] Acts 20:33; 2 Cor. 12:13–15. See 1 Sa. 12:3–5.

their empires. We may be surprised to see that Cappadocian elders in the apostolic age needed such a warning. Untouched by the pageantry of the medieval church or the hype of television hucksters, they had yet to guard against the lure of the denarius. Poor ministers, too, may be mercenary!

iii. The reward of the shepherd

When the Chief Shepherd appears, you will receive the crown of glory that will never fade away. Peter writes this whole letter as an apostle of Jesus Christ (1:1). From start to finish he speaks for his Lord. He addresses the elders so that they too, may minister as servants of the Lord Jesus. He is concerned with their motives more than with their methods. Peter knows that their relation to Jesus Christ will shape the way they care for his people. To know the Lord is to seek to be like the Lord. Elders will be examples to their flock as they follow the example of *the Chief Shepherd* who gave his life for the sheep.

To speak of the Chief Shepherd is to remind the elders that they are only undershepherds. Their authority is not original: they minister only in Christ's name, and according to his word. He is the Lord, chosen in God's plan before the creation of the world and 'revealed in these last times for your sake' (1:20). Peter had seen his glory; the Father had revealed his Son to Peter.[1] But now Peter looks ahead to the glory to come. *When the Chief Shepherd appears. . . .* Christ who was revealed to Peter in his fishing-boat will be revealed again in the clouds of heaven. (To describe the revelation of Christ's second coming Peter uses the same word that he used in 1:20 to describe his first coming.)[2] Again Peter reflects on God's programme: suffering now and glory to come (1:11, 13, 21; 4:13; 5:1, 10). The Chief Shepherd who will come is the risen Christ, who had gone into heaven, and rules at God's right hand (3:22).

Peter has drawn the elders to remember the good Shepherd, their example; now he draws their eyes forward to the Chief Shepherd, their hope. To be sure, the coming

[1] Mt. 16:17. For the 'manifesting' of Christ in the incarnation, see 1 Tim. 3:16; Heb. 9:26.
[2] See Col. 3:4; 1Jn. 2:28; 3:2.

of the 'great Shepherd of the sheep'[1] must remind every undershepherd of his accountability. Any 'hireling' will fear the appearing of the true Shepherd. For the true shepherd, however, as for every true Christian, the coming of Christ is the source of hope and joy.[2] The night of suffering and labour is over; the dawn of heaven rises with the light of Christ's glory. God's full salvation, ready to be revealed at the last day (1:5), will come with Christ (1:13). The saints will possess the inheritance that is theirs in Christ (1:7; 3:9). What the wicked most dread, and the redeemed most desire, will be revealed: the face of the Lord.[3]

To his faithful shepherds Christ gives a garland of glory. '*Glory*' explains the meaning of the garland; their reward and joy are the glory of their Lord. The Greek word translated *crown* in the NIV can describe any circlet, whether of gold, silver, laurel, or flowers. The word translated *that will never fade away* is *amarantinos;* it is quite possible that the garland is of amaranth, a flower chosen for its 'everlasting' quality (like the helichrysum). The phrase would then be translated 'the amaranthine garland of glory' rather than 'the garland of glory that will never fade away'.[4] Our heavenly inheritance, like the amaranth, is unwithering (1:4).

Jesus Christ desires that those the Father has given him should be with him, should share his victory, his life, his glory.[5] The Dead Sea community, meditating on the Old Testament, anticipated the endless blessing of God's favour:

> And as for the visitation of all who walk in this spirit, it shall be healing, great peace in a long life, and fruitfulness, together with every blessing and eternal joy of life without end, a crown of glory and a garment of majesty in unending light.[6]

Only in Jesus Christ, however, does the promise of the

---

[1] Heb. 13:20.   [2] 2 Tim. 4:8.

[3] Pr. 10:24. Derek Kidner, *Proverbs* (IVP, 1964), p. 89, cites the eloquent words of C. S. Lewis: 'In the end, that Face which is the delight or the terror of the universe must be turned upon each of us either with one expression or the other, either conferring glory inexpressible or inflicting shame that can never be cured or disguised.'

[4] So Bigg, p. 189, supported by Selwyn, p. 232. BAGD suggests 'wreath of amaranths' (p. 42).

[5] Jn. 17:24.   [6] 1QS 4:7, in *DSS.*

Old Testament find realization. The crown of resurrection life is his to give; indeed, he is himself that crown.

> In that day the Lord Almighty
>> will be a glorious crown,
> a beautiful wreath
>> for the remnant of his people.[1]

The faithful elders who receive their crowns of blessing from the Lord will cast their crowns before the throne of him who wore the crown of thorns for them.[2]

2. The humble service of Christ's people (5:5–11)

a. In mutual service (5:5)

Young men, in the same way be submissive to those who are older. All of you, clothe yourselves with humility toward one another, because,

> '*God opposes the proud*
> *but gives grace to the humble.*'

Mutual submission is the key to the pattern of life in Christ's church. Peter keeps returning to this theme. Christians are to find freedom in their submission to God, freedom in which they can submit to others for the Lord's sake. They can honour all people, and submit to lawful civil authority (2:13); Christian slaves are free to submit to their masters (2:18); wives to their husbands (3:1), while husbands show a corresponding respect for wives (3:7). The same principle appears in the relation of Christians to those who ask a reason for their hope (3:15). Because they reverence the Lord, they do not fear people, but can treat them 'with gentleness and respect' (3:15). That same humility before the Lord sustains suffering Christians as they await the return of their glorious Saviour, him to whom all must submit (3:22). When Peter says *in the same way* (5:5), he is continuing his application of this master principle to all the roles and relations of Christ's church.

[1] Is. 28:5; *cf.* 28:16; 62:3; Ps. 21:1–4.   [2] Rev. 4:10.

Young men, in the same way be submissive to those who are older (5:5). The principle of humble submission is clear, but who are the *young* and *older* men of whom Peter speaks? If Peter is thinking only of age difference, the distinction is plain enough, although then, as now, 'young adults' could be an elastic category. But Peter had just been speaking of the authority of the elders, and the verb form he uses indicates an act of putting oneself under fixed authority. His word for *those who are older* is the word translated 'elders' in verse 1.

If the 'elders' in verse 5 are not just older men but church officers, who are the younger men? Some have suggested that they, too, have a fixed status: if not deacons, then the early equivalent of an ushers' association. The young men who carried out Ananias and Sapphira seem to have been a recognized group.[1] The Hellenistic world had its youth associations, and the Dead Sea community was organized in rankings that included a number of classifications for young men.[2] On the other hand, Polycarp, in his Epistle to the *Philippians*, calls upon younger men to submit themselves 'to the presbyters and deacons as to God and Christ'.[3] Since he then addresses the virgins as well, he seems to be speaking of younger men simply as an age group. It is not surprising that young men should be singled out in this call to submission. Our culture did not invent the generation gap!

Peter's call to *humility* is not just for the young. We all are to 'tie on humility' in our relations to one another. The verb suggests the tying on of a servant's apron. Peter remembered the towel that Jesus tied around his waist when he filled a basin and began to wash the feet of his disciples.[4] The humility of those who serve Christ is not merely the absence of pride or the awareness of limitations. Christian humility is realism that recognizes grace. Paul declares: 'For who makes you different from anyone else? What do you have that you did not receive? And if you did receive it, why do you boast as though you did not?'[5]

The Christian knows that he did not make himself or save

---

[1] Acts 5:6,10; *cf.* Lk. 22:26.
[2] Spicq, *Epitres*, pp. 170f., refers to M. Rostovtzeff, *The Social and Economic History of the Hellenistic World* (Oxford, 1941), vol. 2, p. 810, vol. 3, p. 1524, n. 82. See 'The Messianic Rule' (1QSa) in *DSS*.
[3] *Epistle of Polycarp* 5 (*AF*, p. 97).   [4] Jn. 13:4.
[5] 1 Cor. 4:7. *Cf.* Mt. 23:12; Lk. 1:52.

himself. His humility springs from his total dependence on
the grace of God. Added to that is the calling and example
of his Saviour, who had everything to boast of, but 'humbled
himself and became obedient to death – even death on a
cross'.[1]

b. In confident devotion: humble service of God (5:5c–7)

> 'God opposes the proud
> but gives grace to the humble.'

*[6]Humble yourselves, therefore, under God's mighty hand,
that he may lift you up in due time. [7]Cast all your anxiety
on him because he cares for you.*

The humility that serves others is found at the throne of
God's grace. God opposes the proud, as Proverbs 3:34
teaches, not only because pride despises our fellow-creatures,
but because pride rebels against him. The proud person sets
himself against God, and God, in turn, sets himself against
the proud. In contrast, God lifts up those who cast themselves utterly upon his grace.[2]

We find a close parallel to this whole section in James
4:6–10. James quotes the same proverb and contrasts
humility before God with bold resistance to the devil (1 Pet.
5:8–9). Like Peter, James speaks of the care that God shows
to those who humbly cast themselves on his mercy (Jas. 4:8;
1 Pet. 5:7). James then describes the penitent mourning that
forsakes pride to draw near to God (Jas. 4:8–9). Jesus
contrasted the proud prayer of the Pharisee with the tax
collector's humble confession of sin. He concluded, 'For
everyone who exalts himself will be humbled, and he who
humbles himself will be exalted.'[3] The humility of which
Peter speaks is like that of the tax collector; it is not simply
a winsome graciousness, it is the humility of repentance, of
despairing self-distrust that turns to God in saving faith.

[1] Phil. 2:8.
[2] Both Peter and James (4:6) quote this proverb (Pr. 3:34) from the Septuagint.
The reciprocal relation between the proud and God is even more vivid in Hebrew:
'Surely he scoffs at the scoffers.'
[3] Lk. 18:9–14.

Remembering the *mighty hand* of God should surely move us to humility. God's hand had humbled Israel, purging out the rebels and bringing his people to repentance.[1] But Peter speaks of God's hand for another reason. He would remind us of God's power to lift up the humble. At Pentecost Peter declared that Jesus was exalted by and to the right hand of the Father.[2] In God's own time, when the Chief Shepherd appears, humble believers will be lifted up to share his glory.

Peter well knew the power of pride. He had boasted that although all others might deny Christ, he, Peter, would remain true.[3] From the height of that proud boast he fell into the abyss of denial. Was there ever a morning when the crowing of the cock did not remind Peter again of Jesus' word predicting his denials? Yet Peter had been chastened, humbled and restored. His pride had cast him down, but his Lord had lifted him up. The sound of the rooster at dawn brought another memory to Peter. There, in the high priest's house, Jesus stood before his accusers; there, as the cock crowed, Jesus turned to look at Peter.[4] Jesus cared for him! Humbled and restored, Peter now urges, *Cast all your anxiety on him because he cares for you.*

Peter's affirmation is drawn from Psalm 55:22, 'Cast your cares on the Lord and he will sustain you; he will never let the righteous fall.'[5] The psalmist's anxieties arise from the attacks of false friends. The promise is therefore particularly appropriate. Peter is calling for humility in situations of hostility, betrayal, and persecution. Precisely in such situations, Christians are tempted to react in pride, perhaps even to draw the sword as Peter did in the garden of Gethsemane. It is such pride that the promise of the Lord dispels. Christians can trust the *power* of the Lord, for his hand is mighty; they can trust the *faithfulness* of the Lord, for their cares are his concerns.

When the French 'Sun King', Louis XIV, revoked the Edict of Nantes in 1685, a long period of persecution forced Reformed Christians to gather for worship in the fields or mountains. Their pastors were hunted down by the King's

---

[1] Ezk. 20:33–44; *cf.* Ex. 13:3, 9; Dt. 9:26.   [2] Acts 2:33.
[3] Mt. 26:33; Mk. 14:29.   [4] Lk. 22:61.
[5] Peter uses the same words for 'cast' and 'care' found in the Septuagint passage (Ps. 54:22).

dragoons. Yet they preached the message of 1 Peter, urging their flocks not to take arms against the king, but to endure persecution for Christ's sake. So few pastors remained, however, that leadership was taken by self-proclaimed prophets and prophetesses who identified the king of France with the beast of the book of Revelation, and summoned the people to holy war. The result was the Camisard rebellion, an armed revolt that became guilty of its own counter-terrorism.[1] The church took the sword and destroyed its own witness.

The very act of casting our cares upon the Lord often changes them. In the village of Bethany Martha was preparing dinner for Christ and his disciples.[2] She was distracted with the concerns of a hostess, and resented the fact that her sister Mary was listening to Jesus instead of helping her. When she complained, Jesus gently rebuked her. In her anxiety about the many dishes of the dinner, she had forgotten the one 'serving' that counted, the 'serving' that Mary had chosen. Martha's many concerns grew from her pride, pride in many dishes that made her a servant of the dinner. When we cast our cares on the Lord, we often find that they were the concerns of our pride, not the cares of his kingdom.

If the Lord's present care brings an end to anxiety, his future blessing offers a goal of hope. *Humble yourselves . . . under God's mighty hand*, says Peter, endure the testings that he sends, in order that, literally, 'in time he may exalt you'. 'In time' could mean at the appropriate time, but here, as often in the New Testament, the reference is to what Peter calls, 'the last time' (1:5; see 2:12). At the coming of Christ God will vindicate his servants. Glory will take the place of humbling and abasement.[3]

c. In triumphant suffering (5:8–11)

i. The Christian resistance movement (5:8–9)

Be self-controlled and alert. Your enemy the devil prowls

---

[1] Charles Bost, *Histoire des Protestants de France* ('La Cause': Carrières-sous-Poissy, 21924), pp. 169–174.
[2] Lk. 10:38–42.
[3] Mt. 23:12; Lk. 14:11; 18:14.

around like a roaring lion looking for someone to devour.
⁹Resist him, standing firm in the faith, because you know that
your brothers throughout the world are undergoing the same
kind of sufferings.

In a vivid image Peter warns the church of deadly danger.
Our image of *a roaring lion* may come from visits to the
zoo, or from the zoom lens of a television nature series.
Some who received Peter's letter would have a stronger
horror. They had seen human blood dripping from the chops
of lions in the gory spectacles of a Roman amphitheatre. The
time was approaching when Ignatius would anticipate his
death in the Roman Colosseum:

> Let me be given to the wild beasts, for through them I can attain
> unto God. I am God's wheat, and I am ground by the teeth of
> wild beasts that I may be found pure bread . . . Come fire and
> cross and grapplings with wild beasts, wrenching of bones,
> hacking of limbs, crushings of my whole body, come cruel
> tortures of the devil to assail me. Only be it mine to attain unto
> Jesus Christ.[1]

The psalmist ofter pictures his foes as lions, lying in
ambush and waiting to pounce, or roaring in their pride.[2]
Peter's word for *devour* means literally to 'drink down',
picturing the ferocity of a beast of prey. Peter is not speaking
of the threat of martyrdom in an amphitheatre, however.
The danger he sees does not come simply from suspicious
neighbours or from hostile authorities. Lurking behind the
'authorities and powers' (3:22) that dominate pagan life there
moves a more fearful destroyer, the figure of Satan.

A recent reference book describes the blows that Satan has
suffered at the hands of sceptical liberal scholarship. The
devil, we are told, reached his nadir in the 1920s and 1930s,
'but the concept has regained strength (at least as a metaphor)
owing to the horrors of the period since 1939 and to an
increasing sense that the destructive impulses of humanity
may be intractable'.[3] General disbelief in the devil, however,

---

[1] Ignatius to the *Romans*, 4–5 (*AF*, p. 77).
[2] Ps. 7:2; 10:9–10; 17:12; 22:13–21; 35:17; 58:6.
[3] J. B. Russell, 'Devil', in A. Richardson and J. Bowden, eds., *The Westminster Dictionary of Christian Theology* (Westminster, 1983), p. 157.

does not necessarily make a low point in his influence. Presumably Satan, like a lion, may hunt by stealth as well as by terror; he could not ask for better cover than the illusion that he does not exist, or that his comeback is merely metaphorical. Jesus Christ came to expose as well as to destroy the works of the devil.

Peter calls Satan the *enemy* or 'adversary'. The term has a legal connotation; it reflects the Old Testament picture of Satan as the accuser of the saints before the throne of God's justice. In the book of Job, Satan appears in the role of a heavenly prosecutor.[1] In fact, he seems to patrol the earth collecting evidence. Satan's motivation is not zeal for justice, however. Rather, he seeks to discredit God's word and destroy God's works. In Zechariah's vision he stands beside Joshua the high priest as his accuser and is rebuked by the angel of the Lord.[2]

Satan's opposition to the 'offspring of the woman' comes into view when he tempts Jesus.[3] Their encounter resembles a combat, an ordeal in which Satan attacks Jesus with respect to both his calling as Messiah and his identity as the Son of God. Satan's power is seen in his claim to control the kingdoms of the world; his subtlety is evident in the skill with which he quotes Scripture, calling on Jesus to test God's promise.

Jesus repulsed the attack of Satan and defeated him. Later, Jesus said that his casting out of demons showed that he had bound the 'strong man' and could therefore plunder his house, delivering those who were his slaves.[4] With the cross in view, Jesus spoke of his triumph over Satan: 'Now is the time for judgment of this world; now the prince of this world will be driven out. But I, when I am lifted up from the earth, will draw all men to myself.'[5] Jesus saw Satan, a defeated foe, fall as lightning from heaven.[6]

But the fact that Satan has been cast down from heaven and knows that his time is short makes him, in a sense, a more formidable adversary.[7] His fury against the Lord and

---

[1] Jb. 1:6–8; 2:1–6.
[2] Zc. 3:1. Note the request of the psalmist in Psalm 109:6. See vv. 20, 29.
[3] Gn. 3:14–15; Mt. 4:1–11; Mk. 1:12–13; Lk. 4:1–13.
[4] Mt. 12:28–29; Mk. 3:23; Lk. 11:19–22.
[5] Jn. 12:31–32. [6] Lk. 10:18. [7] Rev. 12:12.

his kingdom is the more intense. He may threaten the church from within, masquerading as an angel of light.[1] He may rage from without, using the fire and sword of persecuting tyrants. But the Christian knows that 'The God of peace will soon crush Satan under your feet.'[2] James, in his parallel passage, says, 'Resist the devil, and he will flee from you.'[3] The danger to the Christian is not that he is helpless before the devil. He is equipped with the whole armour of God: the shield of faith will extinguish the flaming darts of the evil one.[4] The danger to the Christian is that he will fail to resist, that he will not watch and pray, that he will not put on the whole armour of God and take the sword of the Spirit. That sword, the word of God, was the weapon Jesus used in his ordeal in the desert; it is ours to use in his name.

Peter calls on us to do what he had failed to do in the garden of Gethsemane: to watch and pray. Roaring Satan is a tethered lion. He cannot tempt us beyond what we can endure, for God will not permit it.[5] No temptation can overtake us that is not common to man; a temptation that has been overcome by others. Peter reminds his hearers, *you know that your brothers throughout the world are undergoing the same kind of sufferings* (5:9). The Lord who prayed for Peter prays for us.[6]

In southern France, overlooking the Mediterranean, stands the Tower of Constance. There, in the eighteenth century, Huguenot women were imprisoned for decades because they refused to surrender their Reformed faith. In the tower room where they were held captive, a stone coping surrounds a round opening in the floor. Inscribed in the stone is the word '*Résistez!*' Marie Durand entered that room in 1729, when she was fifteen years old. Three years later her brother Pierre was hanged at Montpellier. In 1745 she was offered her freedom if she would agree to renounce Protestant worship. She refused all such offers and remained captive for thirty-eight years, resisting the temptations to despair, to suicide, to betrayal. From her imprisonment she began a ministry of encouragement by correspondence. Some of her letters are kept today in the 'Museum of the Wilderness' in the moun-

---

[1] 2 Cor. 11:14; Acts 20:29.   [2] Rom. 16:20.   [3] Jas. 4:7.
[4] Eph. 6:10-18.   [5] 1 Cor. 10:12-13.   [6] Lk. 22:32.

tains of the Cévennes.[1]

If Satan is to be resisted, sober watchfulness is called for. Sobriety includes both alertness and realism. Christian wisdom will recognize the seductions by which Satan would deceive the church as well as the imitations that he would substitute for it in an endless stream of sects and -isms. Peter has already linked our sobriety ('self-control', NIV) to hope and prayer (1:13; 4:7).

Satan can be resisted only in a *firm* and settled *faith*. The word translated *firm* is used in the Septuagint version of Isaiah 50:7. There it describes the fixed endurance of the Messiah in terms of a solid rock:

> I gave my back to the scourges, and my cheeks to blows; and I turned not away my face from the shame of spitting: but the Lord God became my helper; therefore I was not ashamed, but I set my face as a solid rock . . .

As Selwyn observes, the phrase 'solid rock' in this passage would not be lost on the apostle whom Jesus had named Peter, the rock.[2] Jesus, fulfilling the Old Testament passage, had set his face like a flint to go to Jerusalem; we must be rock-solid in our trust in him.[3]

Peter has reminded us that the testings do not destroy our faith, but purify it. Since the peculiar nature of faith is its looking, not to oneself, but to the Lord, it is most strongly grounded when it is most dependent. 'My grace is sufficient for you, for my power is made perfect in weakness.' So the Lord said to Paul, and Paul could therefore say: 'For when I am weak, then I am strong.'[4] In order to resist the devil we draw near to God.[5]

Suffering Christians who look to the Lord also gain comfort by remembering the brotherhood (2:17). Samuel Bénétreau points out four advantages to be gained from knowing that *your brothers throughout the world are undergoing the same kind of sufferings* (5:9). First, there is encouragement in knowing that you are not alone and isolated, suffering in a unique way. Secondly, you are reminded that

[1] Charles Bost, *op. cit.*, pp. 197–198, 200.   [2] Selwyn, p. 238.
[3] See Luke 9:51. The verb is similar to the adjective 'firm' in 1 Pet. 5:9.
[4] 2 Cor. 12:9–10.   [5] Jas. 4:8.

216

the bond that unites you to Jesus Christ also joins you to
the family of God throughout the world. Suffering Christians
have a caring fellowship with those similarly afflicted.
Thirdly, Christians are reminded that suffering is inherent in
the Christian faith. Through suffering they have fellowship
with Christ and their faith is purified. Peter speaks of the
suffering that must be 'accomplished' or 'brought to its end'
by the 'brotherhood'. (The NIV translates *your brothers . . .
are undergoing*.) Suffering has its place in God's plan for a
world destined for justice, peace and glory. Christians know
that the 'brotherhood' does not suffer in vain; their experience of suffering is being brought to the victorious conclusion
that God has designed. Fourthly, knowing of the sufferings
of the brotherhood stimulates hope. The spread of
persecution and trials points to the nearness of the consum-
mation: the promised land is in view.[1]

ii. The assurance of God's saving purpose (5:10–11)[2]

*And the God of all grace, who called you to his eternal glory
in Christ, after you have suffered a little while, will himself
restore you and make you strong, firm and steadfast.* [11]*To him
be the power for ever and ever. Amen.*

Peter closes his letter as he began it, rejoicing in the royal
grace of God in Christ. The hope that will sustain the church
through its fiery trial of suffering is hope in the sovereign
grace of God. It is God who saves, from start to finish.
God's initiative stands at the beginning of salvation. He has
called us by his grace (1:1–2). God's purpose arches over the
end of our salvation. He has called us to his own glory (1:7,
11; 4:13; 5:1, 4). The glory of God, the consuming fire of
his holiness, becomes the transforming light of his love to
those who have been 'chosen according to the foreknowledge
of God the Father' (1:2). God's glory is an inheritance that
can never be devastated, defiled, or turned to dust (1:4). The
glory endures, for it is the blessing of God's eternal presence.
Because the Spirit of glory already rests on the believer, the

[1] Bénétreau, pp. 277–278.
[2] This passage resembles 1 Thes. 5:23–28; 2 Thes. 2:13–17; Heb. 13:21f. See
Selwyn, pp. 239, 369–384.

217

suffering church already tastes of the glory of the Lord (4:14). Paul, too, joins the beginning with the end of salvation: God's electing call and God's final work of glory.[1] 'The one who calls you is faithful and he will do it.'[2]

The glory to which God calls is his glory in Jesus Christ.[3] Peter had experienced the awe of Christ's glory in the cloud that accompanied his Master's transfiguration.[4] Yet after Christ's resurrection he had also joined his glorified Lord on the familiar shore of the Lake of Galilee for a breakfast of broiled fish.[5] Peter's hope of glory was not an indefinable nimbus cloud: it was as definite as the scarred hand of Jesus that passed the breakfast fish. Peter had heard the call of God in the voice of Jesus; he had seen the glory of God in the face of Jesus. He rejoices that God has called others from the nations of the world to share his precious hope. They have not seen Jesus, but, like Peter, they love him.

God's call to the glory of Christ comes through the grace of Christ. God is the God of all grace, grace that can meet every need and prevail in every situation. Peter describes the power of that grace in four verbs: God will complete his work in us, he will establish us, strengthen us and ground us (5:10). Our brief time of suffering will not turn aside his gracious work. With joyful confidence we may cast all our cares on him.

First, God will make us complete (NIV, *restore*). The word means 'to put in order,' 'to make right'. It may describe 'restoring', putting right what was wrong, as a surgeon sets a broken bone. It may also describe 'completing', giving further order by providing what was lacking. Finally, it may mean 'preparing' or 'creating', giving initial order and shape. Peter, of course, had known the restoring power of God's grace after the ordeal of his denial. In this context, however, the thought of God's completing his work in believers is probably foremost. We are not to suppose that these actions of God will take place only after the time of suffering is over.[6] Rather, God's gracious work of completing and perfecting us

[1] Rom. 8:29–30. [2] 1 Thes. 5:24. [3] 2 Thes. 2:14.
[4] 2 Pe. 1:17. [5] Jn. 21: 10–23.
[6] *After you have suffered* is a fair translation of the participial construction, but puts more emphasis on the temporal sequence. For the thought of 'completion' see Heb. 13:21; 2 Cor. 13:9.

begins now, during the brief time of our suffering. Indeed, God uses suffering to perfect us as he leads us to the time when he will complete our transformation in the glory of Christ (1:6–7).

Secondly, God will establish us. 'The Lord is faithful, and he will strengthen and protect you from the evil one.'[1] We are made strong in the sense of being given a firm and fixed position. Jesus, when he predicted Peter's denial, promised also his restoration and said, 'When you have turned back, strengthen your brothers.'[2] Peter, who had fallen away in denial, was made an apostle, a rock of foundation, fixed and solid. He promises to Christ's church the establishing grace he had received.

Thirdly, God will strengthen us. The verb Peter uses is found only here in the New Testament. The noun appears in the Greek version of Job, who speaks of the strength of the lion. C. S. Lewis, in his children's stories, uses the figure of Aslan to represent Christ, the lion of the tribe of Judah. The risen Christ removes our fear of Satan, the roaring lion.

Finally, God will place us on a firm foundation. The psalmist speaks of God's founding and establishing the earth; Peter used the same word to describe his 'founding' of his people.[3] In the same sense Paul speaks of the Colossians as continuing in their faith, 'established and firm, not moved from the hope held out in the gospel'.[4]

All these words describe 'how firm a foundation' is promised to the saints of the Lord. We might understand that Peter, named the 'rock' by Christ, would be particularly attracted to the image of the house of God founded upon a rock. The house of living stone is joined to God's chosen cornerstone (2:6). We are established by the grace of God in the love of God, so that we might know him. Paul describes the richness of God's establishing grace in words to set beside Peter's:

I pray that out of his glorious riches he may strengthen you with power through his Spirit in your inner being, so that Christ may dwell in your hearts through faith. And I pray that you, being rooted and established in love, may have power, together with

[1] 2 Thes. 3:3; see 2 Thes. 2:17. [2] Lk. 22:31.
[3] Ps. 24:2 (23:2, LXX). [4] Col. 1:23; see Eph. 3:17.

all the saints, to grasp how wide and long and high and deep is the love of Christ, and to know this love that surpasses knowledge – that you may be filled to the measure of all the fulness of God.[1]

Overwhelmed by the promise of God's triumphant grace, the apostle Peter can only worship. *To him be the power for ever and ever.* That power of God, the right hand of his grace that raised Christ from the dead, is our hope and assurance. Peter is not wishing, or even praying, that God's power may endure; he is rejoicing in it. The power to accomplish the wonder of his will is for ever his.

[1] Eph. 3:16–19.

11. Final greetings

1. Silas: messenger or editor? (5:12)

With the help of Silas, whom I regard as a faithful brother,
I have written to you briefly . . .

Peter says, 'Through Silas . . . I have written.' The NIV translation *with the help of Silas* takes this to mean that Peter employed Silas in the writing of the letter. The phrase is commonly used, however, to describe not the writer, but the bearer, of a letter.[1] The letter to the church at Antioch from the apostles and elders at Jerusalem was sent 'through the hand of' Silas and Judas Barsabbas.[2] They were 'leaders among the brothers'.[3] Peter's description of Silas as 'the faithful brother, as I account him' supports this understanding. He commends Silas as one worthy to be received. It is evident from the Acts passage that those bearing a letter were not regarded as mere messengers, but as representatives of the sender. Polycarp, in his *Epistle to the Philippians*, says, 'I write these things to you by Crescens, whom I commended to you recently and now commend unto you: for he hath walked blamelessly with us; and I believe also with you in like manner.'[4]

[1] See Polycarp's *Epistle to the Philippians* 14, Ignatius to the *Romans* 10:1. Grudem refers to the notes at the conclusions of the Pauline letters; for example, after Romans, 'written through Phoebe the deacon'. These 'subscripts,' still printed in older editions of the Authorized Version, were in the 'Textus Receptus' manuscripts. While later than the New Testament documents, they do indicate the use of the phrase 'written through' to describe the bearer rather than the writer. Grudem, pp. 23–24.
[2] Acts 15:23, literally.   [3] Acts 15:22.
[4] Par. 14. *AF*, p. 99. Grudem holds that Peter's commendation of Silas fits better

Alternatively, Peter's phrasing could describe the employment of Silas in the composition of the letter. Dionysius, bishop of Corinth in the second century, spoke of the letter they had received from the Roman church as 'written to us through Clement'.[1] This has usually been taken to mean that Clement wrote the letter on behalf of the Roman church (he is not named in the salutation). Since three other men are mentioned at the end of the letter as 'our messengers', it seems that Clement was not a bearer of the letter, but its author.[2]

In any case, Peter's acknowledgment of Silas as a faithful brother would seem to indicate more than that he was a true Christian. Silas, who possessed the prophetic gift, was a brother to the apostle in the work of the ministry.[3] Silas is associated with the apostle Paul in the address of the Thessalonian letters; a Jew but a Roman citizen, he had been a fellow-missionary with the 'apostle to the Gentiles'.[4] Whether he is here described as serving Peter in the preparation of the letter or representing him in its delivery, he is evidently a close associate. As a trusted brother of the apostle, he could interpret his brief letter. 'It is natural that St. Peter should here speak of him as "trusty," one who knew the apostle's mind and could expound it faithfully.'[5]

2. Peter's purpose in writing (5:12)

I have written to you briefly, encouraging you and testifying that this is the true grace of God. Stand fast in it.

---

with the role of a messenger than of a writer. Note also the *Martyrdom of Polycarp* 20, where 'through our brother Marcianus' describes him as the bearer in distinction from Euarestus 'who wrote the letter' (*AF*, pp. 115–116).

[1] Dionysius is cited in Eusebius, IV:23:11. See Bigg, p. 5.

[2] Grudem finds this 'inconclusive', but does not discuss the description of the 'messengers' in Clement, *Corinthians* 65. Kelly feels that the use of 'briefly' in v. 12 so focuses attention on the writing that the phrase cannot refer to the bearing of the letter. Similar phrasing, however, appears regarding Marcianus in the letter of the church of Smyrna to Philomelium (*Martyrdom of Polycarp* 20; *AF*, p. 115).

[3] Bénétreau, p. 280. Silas is identified as a prophet in Acts 15:32.

[4] 'Silvanus' (*cf.* 1 Thes. 1:1, mg; 2 Thes. 1:1, mg) and 'Silas' are two forms of the same name. Silas, after bearing the letter from the 'council' at Jerusalem, became associated with Paul (Acts 15:40, 2 Cor. 1:19). Perhaps it was after Paul's death that he joined Peter.

[5] Bigg, p. 195.

If Silas did write the letter, either as a secretary for Peter or as an inspired collaborator, it is possible that this last section came from Peter's own hand. Paul, who often dictated his letters, might add a PS in his own handwriting.[1] Peter's statement beautifully summarizes the whole letter, and the theology on which it is based. Peter writes to exhort and encourage the scattered people of God. They will be facing fiery trials, but Peter can point them to a sure hope in Christ. Peter's encouragement, however, is grounded in his witness. The verb for *testifying*, or bearing witness, is used in the Greek Old Testament for the testimony of witnesses to the deed of sale for a piece of property.[2] Peter is appointed as an apostle to testify to the facts of the gospel. The gospel is true (1:12), and Peter can attest its truth, for Jesus Christ chose him for that witness. The gospel is the good news of the grace of God, the fact that Christ bore our sins in his body on the tree, and is now on the right hand of God (2:24; 3:22). That grace of God will be brought to us when Jesus Christ comes again (1:13).

Because Peter's witness is true, his encouragement is real. In 2 Peter 2:2 we are warned that 'the way of truth' will be brought into disrepute by false teachers. At the end of this letter, too, Peter is concerned that his readers hold fast to the truth. They have received the gospel of God's *grace*. Let them *stand fast in it*.[3] They cling, not to an impersonal moral code, nor to philosophical abstractions. They cling to the grace of God; not what they have done for God, but what God has done for them in Christ.

3. Salutation and benediction (5:13–14)

She who is in Babylon, chosen together with you, sends you her greetings, and so does my son Mark. Greet one another with a kiss of love.

Peace to all of you who are in Christ.

The ancient city of *Babylon*, doomed by the prophets, had

[1] 2 Thes. 3:17–18; Gal. 6:11–18; *cf.* Rom. 16:22.
[2] Je. 39:25, LXX; see Je. 32:10–12 in NIV.
[3] Other manuscripts read 'in which you stand fast'. This is a smoother expression, but the imperative appears to be the better reading. See Kelly, p. 217.

been reduced to ruins; it was largely abandoned at the time Peter wrote. The Jewish population had left, and there is no evidence of a church there or of any apostolic visit to the place.[1] A small garrison town in the Nile delta also bore this name. It seems clear, however, that Peter is using the name symbolically to refer to Rome. This is also done in the book of Revelation (Rev. 14:8; 16:19; 17:5; 18:2, 10), and in Jewish literature.[2] Peter does not use the name as a code to disguise the place of his writing; that was not necessary. His point is rather the symbolism of the name. Babylon was the great city of world empire to which the people of God were carried captive. Peter writes to the new Diaspora (1:1), the 'captivity' of the people of God living under the empire of Rome, the new Babylon. The name 'Babylon' also suggests the judgment of this world by the coming of the Lord Jesus Christ, a theme that is taken up in the book of Revelation.

Peter's phrase means literally 'the fellow-elect in Babylon'. Since the noun for 'fellow-elect' is feminine, some have thought that Peter was referring to his wife, who had accompanied him on his travels, and who, according to tradition, was also martyred.[3] But for Peter to designate his wife by the phrase 'in Babylon' seems unlikely. From an early time Peter's words have been understood as referring to the church in Rome. That church, like the churches to which Peter writes, is elect, a new people of God, sprinkled with the blood of Christ (1:1–2).

Peter's *greetings* come not only from the church, but also from John *Mark*, whom Peter calls his *son* in the love of Christ. John Mark had been a disciple from the earliest days. After Pentecost, Christians met for prayer in the home of Mark's mother. Peter joined them there when an angel released him from Herod's prison.[4] Many years later, Mark had accompanied Paul and Barnabas on their first missionary journey. He turned back when they entered Asia Minor, and was rejected by Paul as a companion on the next journey. He travelled instead with his relative Barnabas.[5] Still later,

---

[1] Kelly, p. 218, Spicq, *Epîtres*, pp. 180–181. J. Neusner, *A History of the Jews in Babylonia* (Brill, 1964).
[2] *Apocalypse of Baruch* 11:1; 67:7; *Sibylline Oracles* 5:143, 159. See the statement in Eusebius, II:15:2: 'Peter calls Rome "Babylon" metaphorically.'
[3] Bigg. See 1 Cor. 9:5.   [4] Acts 12:12.   [5] Acts 12:25; 13:13; 15:36–39.

however, he was Paul's companion in Rome, and profitable
to him.[1] Papias, who was probably born before Peter's letter
was written, tells us about the writing of Mark's Gospel.
Mark, as Peter's 'interpreter', set down accurately, although
not in order, the teaching of Peter about the words and deeds
of Jesus Christ.[2] Mark was to Peter what Timothy was to
Paul, a 'son' in the sense of the book of Proverbs, but more;
a son in the gospel.[3]

Greet one another with a kiss of love. The gathering of the
church is the setting for this command.[4] The letters of Paul
and Peter were read in the service of worship; the greeting
was given in the service or at its conclusion. Paul uses the
phrase 'holy kiss', but Peter says *kiss of love*: not in contrast,
of course, but to emphasize the bond of fervent love that
must unite brothers and sisters in Christ (1:22; 4:8). The
greeting with a kiss was formalized as the 'kiss of peace' in
the eucharistic liturgy of later ages. It was reduced to a ritual
in which the officiating priest and a deacon put their hands
on each other's shoulders and bowed their heads. This 'kiss'
is then passed on to a sub-deacon and to the clergy in the
choir.[5] The apostles were not programming a ritual; their
desire was for Christians to show outwardly the tender affection that unites them as brothers and sisters in the Lord. The
practice of exchanging greetings in the service of worship or
at its conclusion has been making a belated reappearance in
some churches. Such greetings were not part of gatherings at
the synagogue, but they marked the fellowship and friendship
of the home.[6] In this respect, too, the church is to show that
it is the family of God.

Peace to all of you who are in Christ. Peter concludes his
letter, as he began it, by pronouncing the blessing of peace
in Christ's name (1:2). Peter had himself received this blessing
from the risen Lord, and had been authorized to pronounce
peace upon those who received the gospel.[7] The roar of the
lion or the flames of persecution cannot overthrow the
shalom of Christ's salvation. 'Peace I leave with you; my

[1] Col. 4:10; Phm. 26; 2 Tim. 4:11.   [2] Eusebius, III:39:15 (*AF*, p. 265).
[3] Spicq, *Epîtres*, p. 181.
[4] 1 Thes. 5:26–27; Rom. 16:16; 1 Cor. 16:20; 2 Cor. 13:12. Spicq, *Epîtres*, p. 181.
[5] *ODCC*, pp. 784–785.   [6] Spicq, *Epîtres*, p. 181. Mk. 14:44; Lk. 7:45.
[7] Lk. 24:36; Jn. 20:19, 21, 26; Mt. 10:13; Lk. 10:5.

peace I give you . . . Do not let your hearts be troubled and do not be afraid.'[1]

That blessing of peace is the portion of all who are 'in Christ'. They are God's elect (1:1), chosen in Christ who was foreknown before the creation of the world (1:20). They are sprinkled with the blood of Christ (1:2), who bore their sins in his own body on the tree (2:24). Their union with Christ in his atoning death has ended the reign of sin in their lives (4:1–2). They are believers in the God who raised Christ from the dead and who has given them a share in his resurrection life (1:3–7). In his death and resurrection, Christ represents those who are united to him. By his Spirit he is also joined to them in living fellowship. They have not seen him, but they do love him, and wait with eager hope for his appearing. Peter's apostolic blessing reaches across the centuries and around the globe to all who now share suffering in Christ, and will in a short time share his heavenly glory.

[1] Jn. 14:27.

Appendix A

'Resident aliens' – literal or figurative?

Peter addresses 'the elect transients of the Diaspora' in the regions named (1:1).[1] He also speaks of his addressees as 'alien residents' (1:17; *cf.* 2:11).

J. H. Elliott argues that the literal meaning of these terms must not be lost; he holds that the author is addressing those who are not residents, landowners, or Roman citizens, but are either transients or resident aliens in the communities where they live. Elliott does not deny, however, the religious meaning given to these terms in 1 Peter. Christians are urged, as 'transients and resident aliens', to abstain from the evils of Gentile life (2:11; 4:3–5). They do not belong to their cultural past, but have been bought from it at the price of Christ's blood; they have been alienated from their roots so that they must pass the time of their alien residence in fear (1:17–18). Elliott proposes that both the literal and figurative meaning of these terms be kept. Those addressed are an 'admixture of permanent and temporary strangers and aliens' living in Asia Minor 'under conditions of estrangement and socioreligious alienation'.[2]

Elliott's proposal faces major difficulties, however. Peter is writing to organized Christian communities with elders governing 'God's flock' (5:2–3). Were all the Christian churches of Asia Minor composed of more or less temporary aliens? We may imagine that an American television preacher might address a message to the 'born-again migrants in Orange County, California'. But is Peter singling out indi-

---

[1] *Parepidēmos* ('transient') designates a temporary visitor in distinction from *paroikos*, a resident alien.
[2] Elliott, *Home*, p. 47.

viduals belonging to one social strata within the Christian community? Is he writing only to churches composed of displaced persons? Certainly no letter in the New Testament is more inclusive as it speaks of the 'people of God' (2:10), the 'house' of God (2:5), the 'brotherhood' (2:17; 5:9), the 'holy nation' (2:9).

Further, the figurative meaning that is clearly present offers ample ground for setting aside the literal meaning. Elliott well stresses the time factor in the alienation of Christians.[1] But if, in the figurative meaning, they *became* transients and resident aliens, it is certainly implied that they were not originally such. Rather they were well integrated into their own culture. Their empty manner of life had been handed down from their fathers (1:18). It was the characteristic life of the Gentiles (4:2). Their former associates had accepted them; they became estranged only when conversion produced such a radical change in behaviour.

Indeed, if Peter were thinking of the sociological position of those to whom he wrote, he surely would have used either *both* terms or only *paroikos* in opening words of the letter. Certainly *parepidēmoi*, 'transients', cannot serve as a primarily *sociological* description of all the Christian churches scattered through four provinces.

For Peter to be speaking figuratively rather than literally is not surprising in view of the development of the figure in the Old Testament. The Israelites were 'resident aliens' in Egypt, a situation from which God delivered them. They were also still 'resident aliens' when they received the land of their inheritance: 'The land must not be sold permanently, because the land is mine and you are but aliens and my tenants.'[2] Further, David the king is described as confessing, 'We are aliens and strangers in your sight, as were all our forefathers.'[3] In Psalm 39, attributed to David, the king says the same of himself, addressing the Lord: 'For I dwell with you as an alien, a stranger, as all my fathers were.'[4] Clearly the figurative meaning is not limited to the Platonism of

[1] Elliott, *Home*, p. 44.

[2] Lv. 25:23. (In the LXX, *proselytoi kai paroikoi*.)

[3] 1 Ch. 29:15.

[4] Ps. 39:12 (LXX 38:12, *paroikos . . . kai parepidēmos*) The Septuagint has 'I am a resident alien in the land'. See Spicq, *Vie*, pp. 59–76.

Philo, but is grounded in the Old Testament, as the letter to the Hebrews shows.[1]

---

[1] Heb. 11:9–10, 13–16.

Appendix B

Living rock, living water

In the Old Testament, 'Rock' is a divine name.[1] In the wilderness at Massah-Meribah, Israel accused God of covenant-breaking, of abandoning them to die of thirst. God responded to the charges by standing trial. The elders of the people were summoned to pass before the congregation. Moses took in his hand the rod of judgment. In this formal setting, God stood before Moses upon the rock. As though he were indeed guilty, he received in symbol the blow of Moses' rod. Moses struck the rock on which God stood, the Rock with which God was identified by his name as well as his position. For this reason Paul identifies the Rock with Christ.[2]

From the Rock that Moses struck, water flowed to bring life to Israel. God had presented himself as the source of the water of life as well as of the bread of heaven. That symbol was continued in the Old Testament prophets with the image of the stream of living water flowing from the temple of God's dwelling, founded on the rock.[3] Jesus not only presented himself as the source of living water to the Samaritan woman; he also stood up in the temple during the feast of tabernacles to call people to come and drink from him.[4]

[1] Dt. 32:4, 31; Ps. 89:26; 95:1.
[2] Ex. 17:1–7; 1 Cor. 10:4. The names Massah and Meribah indicate the judicial setting. The root *rib* from which Meribah is derived always describes a controversy in the sense of legal procedures.
[3] Zc. 10:1; 14:8, 16; Ezk. 47; Joel 3:18; Ps. 36:9; 87:7; Je. 2:13.
[4] Jn. 7:37–38; Is. 55:1. See the translation, 'If anyone thirsts, let him come unto me, and let him drink who believes on me. As the Scripture has said, "Out of his heart shall flow rivers of living water" ' (R. E. Brown, *The Gospel according to John*, 1 (Doubleday, 1966), pp. 320–324, 327–328.

John reminds us of the fulfilment of the scriptural image of
the waters flowing from the heart of God. For John the
water that flowed from the spear-thrust on the cross was a
symbol of the water of life from the smitten rock.[1] While we
cannot assume that Peter is suggesting John's theme of living
water when he speaks of Christ as the living rock, we may
at least recognize the richness of the adjective for the apostle.
If the living water from the rock was in view, it might account
for the easy transition that Peter makes from the figure of
drinking and tasting to that of the Rock.

[1] Jn. 19:34; Ps. 78:15f.; *cf.* Rev. 22:1, 17; 1 Jn. 5:6–8.

Appendix C

The office of elder in the New Testament

The eldership in the New Testament church was not a fresh institution. It was carried forward from the Old Testament organization of the people of God. Luke makes frequent mention of the elders of Israel, and introduces, without further description, the elders of the church at Jerusalem to whom relief offerings were brought.[1] Eldership in Israel had for its background the prestige and authority of older men in a patriarchal society. The Old Testament speaks of elders in ancient Egypt and in other nations.[2] We find Abraham's servant described as 'the elder of his house, that ruled over all that he had'.[3]

At the time of the exodus the 'elders of Israel' formed a definite body of men whose authority was recognized.[4] In Egypt the ordinance of the passover was given to Israel through the elders.[5] The institution of elders in Israel was sealed with God's approval. Heeding the advice of Jethro, his father-in-law, Moses structured the government of Israel by appointing judges to govern groups from ten to a thousand, with referral of more important cases.[6] Moses himself, as spokesman for the law of God, served as 'chief justice'. Among the thousands of judges appointed under this system, seventy were singled out as the elders of the nation, to represent all the people, much as the elders of a tribe or city

---

[1] Lk. 22:52; Acts 4:8; 6:12; 11:30. It is possible that the seven chosen to assist the apostles were both elders and deacons in the later sense.

[2] Gn. 50:7; Nu. 22:7.   [3] Gn. 24:2, literally; *cf.* 15:2.

[4] The Septuagint translates 'the elders of Israel' as 'the senate of Israel' (Ex. 3:16–18; 4:29; 12:21).

[5] Ex. 12:3, 6, 21.   [6] Ex. 18:24–26.

would represent their constituency.[1]

Seventy elders were summoned to the feast of God's covenant in Mount Sinai; there, with Moses and the chief priests, they were granted a vision of God.[2] Later they were filled with God's Spirit and prophesied.[3] Prophecy was not a permanent gift, but a sign of God's recognition and approval of their representative office. The elders were not prophets 'like Moses', or teaching priests. Their function was administration and judgment. Yet the possibility of more highly endued elders is suggested in the sign that confirmed their authority: 'I wish that all the Lord's people were prophets and that the Lord would put his Spirit on them!'[4]

The elders often represented the people in political or religious activity. Moses gathered the *elders* and spoke to the *people*.[5] On behalf of the people the elders asked for a king[6] and entered into covenant.[7] Moses and Joshua associated the elders with them in a governing council.[8] We read of elders of the land, of cities, of Judah, and of Israel.[9] In exile, the elders provided continuing order for the community.[10]

Following the exile an aristocratic nobility seems to have continued the functions of a national eldership in Israel.[11] In Ezra and Nehemiah lists of nobles who are 'heads of fathers' houses' are given.[12] The system of local city elders appears to have continued.[13] The roots of the Sanhedrin 'council of elders' reach back into the Persian period. In the Sanhedrin at the time of Christ, lay nobles (in distinction from both the priests and the scribes) had a seat and a voice.[14] Each Jewish community had its council of elders or 'presbytery'.[15] Luke describes the officials who accosted Christ in the temple as 'the chief priests and the scribes with the elders'.[16] Scribes,

---

[1] Nu. 11:24; Ex. 24:1.   [2] Ex. 24:9.
[3] Nu. 11:24–25.   [4] Nu. 11:29.
[5] Ex. 3:16; 4:29. See J. L. McKenzie, 'Elder' in *Dictionary of the Bible* (Bruce, 1965), p. 225.
[6] 1 Sa. 8:4.   [7] 2 Sa. 5:3; Ex. 24:1ff.
[8] Ex. 3:18; Dt. 27:1; Jos. 8:10; see 2 Sa. 17:4, 15; 1 Ki. 20:7ff.
[9] 1 Ki. 20:7–8; Dt. 19:12; Jos. 20:4; 1 Sa. 20:26; Ex. 12:21.
[10] Je. 29:1; Ezk. 8:1; 14:1; 20:1, 3.
[11] Gunther Bornkamm, *'presbys'*, *TDNT* VI, pp. 658f.
[12] Ezr. 8; Ne. 7.   [13] Ezr. 10:7–17.   [14] Bornkamm, *op. cit.*, p. 659.
[15] Lk. 7:3. Massey H. Shepherd, Jr, 'Elder in the NT', *Interpreter's Bible Dictionary*, ed. G. A. Buttrick (Abingdon, 1942), p. 73.
[16] Lk. 20:1, RSV.

as learned in the law, could be distinguished from the elders, or included among them.[1]

Christ's fulfilment of the sacrificial system in his priestly work ended the priestly office among the people of God, but government by elders continued. Jesus' disclosure of the new structure of the church under apostolic authority teaches continuity as well as renewal.[2] It is *his* church, but 'church' is an Old Testament term: the assembly of the people of God. He gives the keys of the kingdom of heaven, but the binding and loosing process is already familiar in the doctrinal and ethical discipline of the eldership in the synagogue. The process of discipline described in Matthew 18:15–20 corresponds closely to synagogue procedure.[3]

Paul distinguishes the gift of rule from the gift of teaching in passages where office is defined in terms of function.[4] Administrators as well as teachers served the church. It would appear that the 'scribes of the kingdom' of whom Jesus spoke were recognized as specially gifted elders whose work was preaching and teaching.[5] At the same time, Paul had to ask the Corinthian church to appoint judges so that financial suits would not be carried before heathen civil courts.[6] Presumably the rich enduement of spiritual gifts at Corinth had so equipped the elders with teaching gifts that none were concerned to adjudicate financial disputes.

By referring to the task of elders as shepherding, Peter emphasizes the ruling aspect of their calling. At the same time, the figure itself suggests the teaching ministry committed to elders of the church.

[1] Acts 6:12; 4:8, 23; 23:14; 25:15.

[2] Mt. 16:18–19; 18:15–20; See 1 Pet. 2:9,10; Eph. 2:12–20.

[3] The 'congregation' before whom a matter was to be tried in Jewish practice was viewed as an assembly of judges.

[4] Rom. 12:8; 1 Cor. 12:28. See 1 Tim. 5:17.

[5] Mt. 23:34; see 7:29; 13:52; 1 Tim. 5:17.   [6] 1 Cor. 6:1–7.

Study guide

The aim of this study guide is to help you get to the heart of what Edmund Clowney has written and to challenge you to apply what you learn to your own life. The questions have been designed for use by individuals or by small groups of Christians meeting, perhaps for an hour or two each week, to study, discuss and pray together.

The guide provides material for each of the sections in the book. When used by a group with limited time, the leader is recommended to decide beforehand which questions are the most appropriate for the group to discuss during the meeting and which should perhaps be left for group members to work through by themselves or in smaller groups during the week.

In order to be able to contribute fully and to learn from the group meetings, each member of the group needs to read through the section or sections under discussion, together with the passages in the letter to which they refer.

It is important not to let these studies become merely academic exercises. Guard against this by making time to think through and discuss how what you discover works out in practice for you. Make sure you begin and end each study by focusing on God in praise and prayer. Ask the Holy Spirit to speak to you through your discussion together.

Introduction

a   What do you understand by the word 'pastoral' (pp. 15ff.)? In what ways is this a 'pastoral letter'?

1. To whom is the letter written?

b   What reasons does Edmund Clowney suggest for Peter's

choice of recipients (p. 16)? What do we know about them?

2. *Who wrote the letter?*

c On what grounds has it been suggested that Peter did not in fact write this letter (pp. 18ff.)? Is this an important issue? Why?

d 'The greatest assurance of the authenticity of 1 Peter comes from . . .' where (p. 20)?

3. *What kind of letter is it?*

e What do you make of the suggestion that 1 Peter is a sermon rather than a letter (p. 22)? Why might this be important?

4. *Where and when was it written?*

f Why does Peter send greetings from 'Babylon' (p. 23)?

5. *What is its message?*

g Read through 1 Peter at one sitting. Now, in your own words, try and summarize the main thrust of what Peter is saying. How does your summary compare with Edmund Clowney's (pp. 23ff.)?

1:1–2
1. *The apostle to the Jews blesses God's true people*

1. *He greets them with blessing*

a What does it mean to greet someone with the words '*grace and peace*' (p. 27)? How does such a greeting become a blessing?

b What significance is there in the way Peter describes himself (pp. 28f.)?

c What lies at the centre of what it is to be an apostle (pp. 29ff.)?

d What makes a church 'apostolic' today (p. 31)? Is yours?

2. He greets them as the true people of God

e How does Peter describe his readers (pp. 31ff.)? Why is this so astonishing?

f How do we know that the inclusion of Gentiles in God's people is not simply a 'divine afterthought' (pp. 32f.)? How does this strengthen Christian assurance?

'The mystery of God's choosing will always offend those who stand before God in pride. Forgetting their rebellion and guilt before God, they are ready to accuse him of favouritism.' (p. 34)

---

g What part does each member of the Trinity play in our salvation (p. 35)?

h What is the significance of the blood of Christ being *sprinkled* (pp. 35f.)? Are these things true for you?

3. He greets them as the people of God in the world

i How does the description of his readers as *scattered* and *strangers* give us 'the key to Peter's whole letter' (pp. 36f.)?

'God's people must be aliens in a world of rebels against God.' (p. 38)

---

j What does it mean to be a 'resident alien' (pp. 39ff.)? What differences does this make to your life?

k 'The theme of Christian pilgrimage stands over against the wandering of an unbelieving world' (p. 41). How does this happen?

1:3–12

2. Bless God for our hope in Christ

1. God establishes our hope in Christ (1:3)

a What is Sartre's image of hell (p. 43)? How does it fall 'far short of the reality'?

b What distinctive ideas are there in Peter's understanding of what hope is (p. 44)? How can he be so sure?

c How does the resurrection of Jesus give us new birth (p. 46)?

2. God maintains our hope: our inheritance (1:4–5)

d What is the difference between *treasure* and an *inheritance* (p. 47)? What does Peter tell us about the latter?

'The wonder of our hope is that the same power *of God that keeps our inheritance also keeps us.' (p. 49)*

---

e Why does Peter say that we are shielded by God's power *through faith* (p. 50)? How does this work out in practice for you?

3. Joy through trials in Christ our hope (1:6–9)

f Peter now gives 'four reasons why we can not only endure trials, but rejoice in hope in the midst of trials' (p. 51). What are these? How do they apply to your life at the moment?

'The whole nature of suffering is changed for the Christian when he realizes that his anguish brings honour to Christ.' (p 53)

---

g 'It is not necessary for us to have been in Galilee with

Jesus' (p. 54). Why not? How can we have the same hope as Peter had without sharing his experience of Jesus?

h What 'apparent paradox forms the warp and woof of New Testament hope' (p. 54)? In what ways do you experience the tension between what we have now and what we will have then?

4. God's promises of hope are fulfilled in Christ (1:10–12)

i Why must glory be preceded by suffering (pp. 55ff.)? What evidence of this sequence have you experienced in your life recently?

j 'Peter is not announcing a general principle that those who look for reward must be prepared to pay in suffering' (p. 58). Why not? What *is* he saying, then?

k How can Peter be so sure that the God of the New Testament is the same as the God of the Old Testament (pp. 58ff.)?

'The least disciple of Christ is in a better position to understand Old Testament revelation than the greatest prophet before Christ came.' (pp. 59f.)

1:13 – 2:3
3. Live obediently in hope

1. Hope is ready (1:13)

a What difference should our Christian hope make to the way we live (pp. 61ff.)? Why?

2. Hope is holy (1:14 – 2:3)

a. The holiness of children of the Father (1:14–17)

b 'The apostolic teaching about God's judgment has been misunderstood' (p. 64). In what ways? How then should we understand it?

c What does it mean for you to live *in reverent fear* (p. 65)?

d What does *holiness* mean (pp. 67f.)? How is it possible for us?
e What difference would a more Jewish understanding of fatherhood make to the way we regard God the Father (pp. 68f.)?

b. The holiness of redeemed believers (1:18–21)

f 'Peter appeals to the two most profound emotions our hearts can know' (p. 69). What are these? What part do they play in your Christian experience?

'God has claimed us as his own, claimed us at a cost that sears our minds with the flame of his love.' (p. 69)

---

g How does the background to the idea of redemption help to deepen our understanding of what Jesus has done for us (pp. 70f.)?
h 'Peter contrasts the traditions that Gentile Christians had received from their fathers with the gospel they have received from the Father' (p. 71). What can you think of in your cultural traditions which might run counter to the truth of the gospel?
i What does Christ's 'divine pre-existence' mean (p. 73)? What evidence for this truth is there in these verses?

c. Holiness through the word of truth (1:22 – 2:3)

j Can you think of any ways in which 'love and truth [are] set at odds in contemporary Christianity' (p. 74)? How can this be put right?
k What characteristics of Christian love does Peter set out here (pp. 74f.)? How can we love like this?

'Because God's love is the source of ours, the message of his love is what kindles ours.' (p. 75)

---

l What pictures are used in these verses to describe the role of God's word (pp. 76ff.)?
m How does your experience of reading the Bible match what Edmund Clowney suggests here (pp. 80f.)?

2:4–10
4. Live as the people of God
I: The life of the spiritual temple

1. The building of the temple in Christ

a What is so striking about the fact that Peter calls Christ the *Stone* (p. 83)? What does he mean?
b What passages elsewhere in the Bible illuminate these verses (pp. 84f.)?
c How does Peter spell out 'the wonder of God's salvation' (p. 87)?
d What truths about the Christian life is the picture of the temple of God intended to convey (pp. 87f.)?

2. The ministry of a priestly people

e What is (a) the *status* and (b) the *ministry* of the church (pp. 88f.)? What further light is shed by the Old Testament allusions in this passage?
f 'The book of Leviticus cannot be amended to admit uncircumcised Gentiles into God's courts' (p. 90). Can you explain, then, how it can be right for non-Jews to be part of God's holy priesthood?
g On what basis does God choose people (pp. 91f.)?
h What is the 'vast difference between the election of Christ and the election of believers in Christ' (p. 93)?
i What are the implications of our being God's *people* (p. 94)?

'There is a spiritual "ethnicity" to the church of Christ; Christians are blood relatives, joined by the blood of Christ.' (p. 94)

---

j As members of God's holy priesthood, what sacrifices do Christians offer to God (pp. 94f.)? How do you go about this?

k What links between worship and evangelism does Peter suggest here (pp. 96f.)? How has this been the case in your experience?

2:11–20
5. Live as the people of God
II: The new lifestyle

1. The new lifestyle's pattern: freedom in bondage (2:11–17)

a What is 'surprising' about Peter's application of the teaching he has just given (pp. 99f.)? In what ways is this 'in direct antithesis to the spirit of the world' (p. 100)?

a. Free in bondage to God: 'Fear God!'

b What is the link between Christian behaviour and the description of us as *pilgrims* (p. 101)?

c In what specific ways do *sinful desires* war against your soul (p. 102)?

d If his readers *live ... good lives among the pagans*, why will they be accused of *doing wrong* (p. 103)? In what ways have you experienced this?

b. Free in submission to others

e What are the differences between the way Christians submit to God and the way they submit to other people (p. 104)?

2. The new lifestyle's practice: submission in role relationships (2:13–14, 18–20)

a. Submission as citizens of worldly kingdoms (2:13–14)

f What is distinctive about 'the Christian pattern of loving service' (p. 106)?

g Why was it difficult for Christians in Peter's day to be law-abiding citizens (pp. 106f.)? Do you face similar problems today?

h 'Peter's description of the function of governments serves indirectly to limit his command to be in subjection to them' (pp. 110f.). What function does Edmund Clowney have in mind? Where would you draw the line in civil disobedience? Why?

b. Submission as servants of worldly masters (2:18–20)

i What 'golden opportunity to show the uniqueness of Christian service' (p. 113) have you had recently? Did you take it? Why – or why not?

'It is the privilege of those who are sons and daughters of the Most High to imitate the magnificence of their Father's mercy.' (p. 113)

2:21 – 3:7
6. Live as the people of God
III: The new lifestyle (continued)

3. The new lifestyle's motivation: Christ's suffering (2:21–25)

a. His saving example: in his steps (2:21–23)

a To what are Christians called in these verses (pp. 116f.)? Why? What does Peter have in mind? In what ways do you experience this?

b Why is it so important to stress both that 'Christ's suffering leaves us an example' and that 'Christ suffered for us' (pp. 117f.)?

c What characterizes the path which Jesus calls every Christian to walk with him (pp. 118f.)? How do you react to

243

this prospect?

'The very torture that Peter wanted Jesus at any cost to escape was the torture that Jesus came to endure.' (p. 119)

---

b. His atoning sacrifice (2:24)

d Can you explain the background to what Peter says here (pp. 120f.)?

e In what ways have we been 'healed' by the wounds of Christ (pp. 122f.)?

c. His saving claim (2:24–25)

f 'Peter makes it clear that Christ has done more in his death than enable us to die to sin' (p. 124). What 'more' does Edmund Clowney mean? How does Peter make this clear?

g What aspects of the image of the shepherd are brought out in these verses (pp. 124ff.)? How do they apply to you?

4. More on the new lifestyle's practice: submission for the Lord's sake in role relationships (3:1–7)

a. Submission of wives to husbands (3:1–6)

h How does Peter signal the 'distinctive behaviour of the Christian wife' (p. 127)? What does this mean in practice?

i In the light of these verses, how would you advise the wife of a non-Christian husband to behave (pp. 129ff.)?

j 'Peter's teaching may be misunderstood' (p. 130). In what ways? How can such misunderstandings be countered?

b. Consideration of wives by husbands (3:7)

k What does it mean for husbands to be *considerate* to their wives (pp. 133f.)?

> *'Marriage ... is the human relationship that God has designed to mirror the love of Christ for the church, and of the church for Christ.' (p. 135)*

3:8–22
7. The blessing of living with Christian suffering

1. Response to suffering in a life of blessing (3:8–12)

a. Called to a life of blessing

a What 'five characteristics of the life that brings blessing' does Peter identify here (p. 137)? What does each mean? Where do they come from?

b. Called to bless in response to cursing

b How should Christians 'get even' (p. 141)? Why? How do you intend to react to opposition?

c. Called to bless as heirs of blessing

c Why does Peter quote from Psalm 34 (pp. 141f.)? How does this help?

2. The blessed witness of suffering for righteousness (3:13–22)

a. The opportunity for witness in word (3:13–15)

d 'Peter is claiming that those who are eager to do good will come to no harm.' How would you answer someone who suggested this (pp. 143f.)?

> *'[Christians] must understand that suffering is not the opposite of blessing.' (p. 144)*

e How does what Peter says here 'prepare the church, not simply to endure persecution, but to find in persecution an opportunity for witness' (p. 145)?

f What experience did Peter have of the fear of men (pp. 145f.)? How did he lose it? How can we?

g How do Christians best 'defend their faith' (p. 149)? How effective are you at doing this?

b. The opportunity for witness in life (3:16–17)

h 'We need a conscience that is both informed and clear' (p. 152). Why is this so important? How can we develop such a conscience?

c. The victory of Christ's suffering (3:18–22)

i Peter has already written about the cross in 2:21–24. What further truths does he bring out here (pp. 154ff.)?

j What suggestions have been made to explain what Peter means by Christ's preaching to *spirits in prison* in verse 19 (pp. 156ff.)? Which do you find most persuasive? Why?

k What symbolic significance is there for us in the story of Noah (pp. 164ff.)?

l What lessons about Christian baptism do these verses have for us (pp. 166f.)? Is this how you see it?

4:1–11
8. The blessing of living as stewards of grace

1. Union with Christ in death to sin (4:1)

a This verse could be understood to mean that 'Christians should not regret suffering, since suffering will advance their sanctification' (p. 169). Why is this unlikely to be the correct interpretation? What *does* Peter mean?

2. The liberty of salvation (4:2–6)

b What characterizes the two ways of life which Peter spells out here (pp. 171ff.)? Can you recall the difference in your approach to the will of God now and before you became a Christian?

c In what ways have you found that your Christian life antagonizes former friends (p. 173)? How do you react to this?

d Why was it that 'the death of Christians created a problem for the church in the time of the apostles' (p. 175)? How does verse 6 help to answer this?

3. Understanding the time of our stewardship (4:7)

e What does Peter mean by *The end of all things is near* (p. 177)? What difference does this make to you and the way you live your life?

f What is the 'one value above others' which being sober and clear-minded gives us (p. 178)? How does this work?

4. Serving in the grace of our stewardship (4:8–11a)

g What does Peter teach about love in these verses (pp. 179ff.)?

h Do you discuss spiritual gifts 'in a way that would surely distress the apostle' (p. 181)? What is Peter's emphasis here?

i Which spiritual gifts have you received (pp. 182f.)? How do you know?

'It is in humble service that we discover the gifts that we have and the greater gifts that we may need.' (p. 182)

---

j What spiritual gifts does Peter mention here (pp. 184ff.)? What instructions does he give about them? Why?

5. The purpose of our stewardship (4:11b)

k In what way can the 'success' of a ministry 'be a graver judgment from God than its failure' (p. 186)? How might this apply to you?

4:12–19

9. The blessing of suffering for Christ's sake

1. The joy of fellowship with Christ in suffering (4:12–16)

a 'If we understand why suffering comes, we will not only accept it, but rejoice in it' (p. 189). How does Edmund Clowney arrive at this conclusion?
b What suffering do you face at the moment (pp. 190ff.)? How do these verses help you to face it?

2. The confidence of commitment to God in suffering (4:17–19)

c How does the idea of judgment fit into Peter's view of suffering (pp. 193ff.)?
d 'Only here in the New Testament is God called the *Creator*' (p. 196). What is the significance of this observation for the way we face suffering?

5:1–11

10. Living in the suffering church of God

1. The humble rule of Christ's elders (5:1–4)

a. Their fellowship with Christ's sufferings and glory (5:1)

a What two attitudes are 'fundamental for Christian living in this present world' (p. 197)? Do you have them?
b What is distinctive about Peter's ministry and what does he have in common with other Christian leaders (pp. 198f.)? Why is this important?

b. Their charge as shepherds of the flock (5:2–4)

i. The calling of the shepherd
c What will 'kindle compassion for Christ's scattered sheep' (p. 200)? How does this apply to you?
d What are shepherds supposed to do (p. 201)? What parallels are there with the role of leaders in the church?

ii. The manner of the shepherd

e What 'turns church government into spiritual tyranny' (p. 202)? How can we guard against this?

f What differences are there between the first- and twentieth-century understandings of the ministry of a bishop (pp. 203f.)?

g Are you easy to lead (pp. 204f.)? Why – or why not?

h Should church leaders be paid (pp. 205f.)? What dangers need to be avoided in this area?

iii. The reward of the shepherd

i What hope does Peter set before us here (pp. 206ff.)? What does this mean to you?

2. The humble service of Christ's people (5:5–11)

a. In mutual service (5:5)

j What does it mean for you to be humble in your relationships with others in the church (pp. 208ff.)?

b. In confident devotion: humble service of God (5:5c–7)

k Why does God oppose the proud (p. 210)? What can we do to avoid the sin of pride?

l What anxieties do you face at the moment (pp. 211f.)? What does it mean for you to cast them on the Lord?

c. In triumphant suffering (5:8–11)

i. The Christian resistance movement (5:8–9)

m To what characteristics of the devil does Peter draw attention here (pp. 212ff.)? How is he to be overcome?

n What advantages are to be gained from knowing that our *brothers throughout the world are undergoing the same kind of sufferings* (verse 9; pp. 216f.)?

ii. The assurance of God's saving purpose (5:10–11)

o Which four verbs does Peter use to describe the power of God's grace (pp. 218ff.)? What do these mean to you?

'Peter's hope of glory was not an indefinable nimbus cloud: it was as definite as the scarred hand of Jesus that passed the breakfast fish.' (p. 218)

5:12–14
11. Final greetings

1. Silas: messenger or editor? (5:12)

a Was Silas Peter's secretary or inspired collaborator (pp. 221f.)? Does it matter?

2. Peter's purpose in writing (5:12)

b Can you explain how this verse 'beautifully summarizes the whole letter, and the theology on which it is based' (p. 223)?

3. Salutation and benediction (5:13–14)

c What does Peter's reference to *Babylon* mean (pp. 223f.)?
d What practical expression do you give to Peter's instruction to *Greet one another with a kiss of love* (verse 14; pp. 225f.)?

'The roar of the lion or the flames of persecution cannot overthrow the *shalom* of Christ's salvation.' (p. 225)